THE
GLASS
CLIFF

About the Author

Sophie Williams is an ex-global leader at Netflix and has held the titles of COO and CFO in London advertising agencies.

She is a TED Speaker ('The Glass Cliff – The Rigged Test of Leadership', 1.5 million+ views) and the voice of Instagram's @ OfficialMillennialBlack. *The Glass Cliff* is her third book.

Also by Sophie Williams:
Anti-Racist Ally (2020)
Millennial Black (2021)

THE GLASS CLIFF

Why Women in Power Are Undermined and How to Fight Back

SOPHIE WILLIAMS

MACMILLAN BUSINESS

First published 2024 by Macmillan Business
an imprint of Pan Macmillan
The Smithson, 6 Briset Street, London EC1M 5NR
EU representative: Macmillan Publishers Ireland Ltd, 1st Floor,
The Liffey Trust Centre, 117–126 Sheriff Street Upper,
Dublin 1, D01 YC43
Associated companies throughout the world
www.panmacmillan.com

ISBN 978-1-0350-3873-2 HB
ISBN 978-1-0350-3872-5 TPB

Text permissions: p. 3, 'In den finsteren Zeiten', from: Bertolt Brecht, *Werke*. Große
kommentierte Berliner und Frankfurter Ausgabe, Band 12, Gedichte 2 © Bertolt-Brecht-
Erben/Suhrkamp Verlag 1988; p. 53, excerpts are used by permission from *Alive at the End
of the World* (Coffee House Press, 2022) © 2022 Saeed Jones.

1 3 5 7 9 8 6 4 2

A CIP catalogue record for this book is available from the British Library.

Typeset in Warnock Pro by Palimpsest Book Production Limited, Falkirk, Stirlingshire
Printed and bound by CPI Group (UK) Ltd, Croydon, CR0 4YY

Visit **www.panmacmillan.com** to read more about all our books
and to buy them. You will also find features, author interviews and
news of any author events, and you can sign up for e-newsletters
so that you're always first to hear about our new releases.

To Best Friends Club.
I want to share an orange with you,
Which is to say: I love you.

Contents

Introduction

In the dark times, will there also be singing?
Yes, there will also be singing. About the dark times.

I remember the first time I realized that we, as women, were in a story of regression, rather than the one of progress I was so used to hearing. It was March of 2023, and I had been selected to be a part of the UK's delegation at the United Nations' Commission on the Status of Women (CSW67) – a week-long series of discussions, debates and planning, hosted in New York. The conference was opened by a speech from António Guterres, the UN's secretary general, who said to us, the assembled delegates:

> We had years and years of incremental progress, [but] women's and girls' rights have stalled now and are going into reverse [. . .] The truth is that half of humanity is largely being left behind; in every region, women are worse off than men, earning less and doing up to ten times more unpaid care work [. . .] Many of the challenges we face today, from conflicts to climate chaos, and the cost-of-living crisis, are the result of a male-dominated world, and a male-dominated culture, taking key decisions that guide our world. And while men still largely make those decisions, women and girls often pay the price.[2]

I was shocked.

Up until that point, I had been so used to the narrative of progress and positive change – the Girl Power of the nineties and my childhood, developing into the 2020s era of the 'girl boss' and 'SheEO'* – that the possibility that we could have stalled hadn't ever crossed my mind. Let alone that we could have fallen into reverse.

The idea that the hard-won rights of women and girls around the world had not only lost momentum, but were actually going backwards, was repeated time and time again during the week of the conference. I heard from researchers, activists, thought leaders and experts from around the world, with a broad range of focuses. From women's bodily autonomy, to digital safety, to access to education and medical care, the message was consistent and strong throughout: we had spent so much time congratulating ourselves on making progress that we'd forgotten to make sure that we were, actually, *still* making the progress we were so proud of.

Being curled up on my sofa, dialling into a conference room at the UN was *already* something I'd never imagined I'd experience, and I'd certainly never imagined that a main theme of our discussions would be that, somewhere between our complacency and the world's misogyny, the rights of women had fallen into reverse.

The secretary general continued:

Women are credited less for their achievements, win far fewer prizes and receive less research funding than men, even when they have the same conditions [. . .] This must change. The male chauvinist domination of new technology is undoing decades of progress on women's rights.

---

* I know, don't worry – I hate those words too – it's not that kind of book. I promise I'm not going to try to talk you into a membership at The Wing (RIP) or tell you that you have as many hours in the day as Beyoncé.

Gender equality is a question of power. For more than a hundred years, that power was gradually becoming more inclusive. Technology is now reversing that trend [. . .] In the face of this patriarchal pushback, we must push forward – not just for women and girls, but for all communities and societies. Without the insights and creativity of half the world, scientific progress will fulfil just half its potential.[3]

We don't have to look far to see that inequity has had a monumental impact on the working lives of women. In fact, we need look no further than the gender pay gap – a gap that we often discuss in terms of progress, and how much it has closed.

According to data from the Office for National Statistics, the gender pay gap for full-time employees in the UK was 8.3 per cent in 2022, an increase on 7.7 per cent in 2021. Among all employees, rather than just those who work full time, the gender pay gap sets working women's finances back 14.9 per cent.[4]

And it gets worse.

In 2023, it was found that, instead of closing, the gender pay gap for higher-educated mothers – meaning those who have a 'post-school education' – had in fact *widened* since the 1970s, with working mothers earning only 69 per cent of working fathers' wages. This means women today are paying a 'motherhood penalty' that is larger than it was forty-five years ago, in 1978, when mothers earned about 72 per cent of the wages of their male parent counterparts.[5]

Speaking about this to *The Guardian*, Dr Amanda Gosling, a senior lecturer in economics at the University of Kent, argued that, rather than being the consequence of societal progress, any closing of the pay gap between men and women since the 1970s 'has largely been driven by economic factors such as the minimum wage and falling wages for less educated men'.

'Barriers to career progression for mothers with some post-school education have hardly shifted,' she said. 'The gap in pay between mothers and fathers looks very similar now as it did in the late 1970s. The story for Gen-Xers is the same for boomers and millennials.'[6]

This is all the more shocking when we consider that, on average, mothers are now better educated than fathers. In 1978, only 10 per cent of fathers and 9 per cent of mothers had any post-school education; by 2019, this had risen to 45 per cent and 48 per cent respectively. 'Arguably, then,' Gosling said, 'the current overall gap between the wages of mothers and fathers is under-stated because it does not control for the fact that mothers are more skilled'.

Sarah Ronan, early education and childcare lead at the Women's Budget Group, told *The Guardian* that the research was 'an indictment of our economy and the structures that underpin it'. She added: 'For decades women have been told to "lean in" while we're actively pushed out. Childcare costs, poor parental leave, and gendered stereotypes about care all conspire to keep women stuck either at home or in low-paid precarious work.'[7]

I'm aware that not every story of womanness is a story of motherhood – I myself am childfree by choice and admit to having something of a blind spot in that area. But this story, which is one of many, and its ability to encapsulate so succinctly an unspoken slide backwards over time, remains something we should be aware of when we think about womanness in a working capacity today.

Over the past few years, I have spent most of my time thinking and speaking, writing and teaching about women's experiences in the workplace – usually with an intersectional look at the roles that race and gender play together. Doing that work, neck-deep in academic papers, trying to find an answer to the question of why there are so few stories of women being successful within high-profile leadership roles, is where I first came across the phenomenon of the Glass Cliff. And now, today, I'm so glad to have the chance to spend some time with you, and for us to explore this strange phenomenon together.

I'm aware it's very likely that, up to this point, you've not heard much, if anything, about the Glass Cliff – even though it impacts all of our experiences. Whether you're in a leadership position yourself, are planning to step into one, or simply work with leaders as part of your professional life, the Glass Cliff has touched all of us in one way or another, often without us realizing it. If you live in the UK, you will have seen it play out in politics, as Theresa May was left to manage the mess that was Brexit after David Cameron's departure.* In the business world, you might have watched Linda Yaccarino step into the role of CEO at Twitter, with a mixture of interest, confusion and morbid curiosity as we wait to see whether she'll become the next high-profile instance of a female leader taking on what looks like a potential poisoned chalice. The spectre of the Glass Cliff is omnipresent; from our workplaces to our political systems and beyond, women are set up to fail.

I have my own personal relationship with both the Glass Cliff and its sister, the Glass Ceiling, firstly as a speaker and educator who is regularly invited into businesses to speak about the former, but also as a woman who has been in several precarious leadership positions throughout my own career.

I first came across the Glass Cliff phenomenon when I was researching for my second book, *Millennial Black*. If I'm honest, after months of writing about the terrible things that happen in Black women's professional lives, I was looking for a win – hoping to unearth a great, and triumphant, as-yet-untold story or piece of research about what happened to the women who beat the odds and finally, firmly, pulled up their seats at the heads of boardroom tables. I wanted something that I could hold up and celebrate – to encourage women, all women, to push through

---

* I'm no fan, but we have to admit that was a tough gig.

adversity and turn the tables in their own favour.* I desperately wanted something to make all of the difficulties and hard work feel worth it, if we could just, *finally*, break through the Glass Ceiling and take our rightful places in the positions where we belong – stepping into spaces where we could not just survive, but thrive. But that wasn't what I found. In fact, what I ended up finding was almost the exact opposite experience. What I discovered was the story of the Glass Cliff, which is at the same time both much more interesting and much sadder than a tale of triumphant leadership and personal success.

This book is an in-depth look at the Glass Cliff. It's designed first and foremost to help you learn what it is, how to spot it, how to avoid it – and what to do if you've already found yourself teetering on its edge. I want you to know that, as scary as the situation may seem, there's always a way to soften the landing, reclaim the narrative and consider your next steps – even when it feels like the ground has fallen out from under your feet.

The Glass Cliff holds women back and limits our careers and prospects as we become more established in our positions and eventually take on the most senior leadership roles. When we recognize the hurdles and barriers that have stood in the way of women's professional success stories up to now, we can begin to understand the very good reasons why some might decide to take on a role, even when they know the chances of success within it are limited.

I want to send you into the world armed with the necessary knowledge to make the choices and to follow the paths that are best for you. I want to show you what the warning signs are, how to spot them, and what you can do to try to protect yourself should you decide to shoot your shot, despite the stacked odds.

---

* Although we know the burden for change shouldn't be placed on the shoulders of those who are suffering most from the impacts of inequity, I did hope to offer some tools, or at least some hope.

I don't want us to accept that limitations to our success are in any way a fact of life or nature – because they're absolutely neither. Instead, I want us all to understand and examine the power that we have, even in areas we might not have recognized before, so we can step forward and examine the role that we can play in breaking the cyclical nature of the cliff, in protecting others from falling foul of its precarious edge, and in refusing to participate in pushing one another over it, regardless of our role or position in the businesses and organizations in which we work.

In order to make meaningful change happen, we need to see and understand that the Glass Cliff plays out in many forums and in many contexts – from governments to charities, from FTSE 100 and Fortune 500 companies to start-ups and sports teams – its threat is ever-present. Though the way in which it plays out can sometimes vary from one setting to another, at its base, the Glass Cliff is a shared experience for many women. Up to now, we haven't had the necessary language to identify it, so we haven't been able to see its prevalence or to push back against it. This is particularly true for individualistic societies like the UK and USA, where we're taught that all of our successes and failures are down to ourselves and ourselves alone – and where the Glass Cliff, left unchecked, thrives the most.

I hope this book will change that and be part of empowering all women to take greater control over the course of their careers.

To understand the Glass Cliff is to understand a story of a structural inequity disguised as personal failure. It's a story of socialized gender norms and expectations forcing women into impossible-to-win positions, as they silently wait for a firm hand in the small of their back to push them off their own personal, professional cliffs, without ever really knowing that, in many cases, factors outside of their control had preordained their fates as inevitable.

But, as I say, it doesn't need to be that way. Don't worry, all is not lost – because, once we understand the phenomenon, we can start to make sense of so many other narratives about women's leadership experiences and potentials that just don't make sense without it.

I truly believe that a key thing that has stopped us from first recognizing and then overcoming the Glass Cliff until now is our current lack of any shared language to explore, explain and identify it.

This lack of a shared vocabulary has denied us the ability to properly frame and understand the experience within our cultural context as a systemic and widespread issue, and has instead pushed us into viewing individual leaders' failures or successes as down to them and them alone. It has reduced working women's experiences to a matter of personal aptitude, rather than rightfully framing them as part of a much wider story.

But, in starting a conversation – in putting down the groundwork to establish some shared language – we can not only better understand and contextualize our own experiences, but also see them playing out on a much larger scale, and we can take back some control. Because words are powerful – and discovering the right words to frame and reframe our own experiences can be transformative.

We need to name the Glass Cliff in order to tame it.

Name it to tame it, as coined by psychologist Dan Siegel, is a psychological tool that encourages people to name and identify difficult and triggering emotions in order to overcome negative thoughts.[8] The theory is that, 'when you experience significant internal tension and anxiety, you can reduce stress by up to 50 per cent by simply noticing and naming your state'. Additionally, 'if we can *see* the emotion, we do not have to *be* the emotion'.[9]

Although we're talking about a cultural rather than psychological phenomenon, our experiences of the Glass Cliff could also be tamed by naming them as such and recognizing that they are most likely not due to our own lack of abilities, but are part of the wider phenomenon.

Once we begin to see things in this way, we can start to recontextualize our own lived experiences and perceived failings. And, once we see that we're not the problem, maybe we can also see the ways that we are, in fact, phenomenal.

There's a chance that you're reading this and wondering how it can be true. Maybe you're even in the midst of a successful and high-flying career, wondering how something so widespread and ubiquitous could have slipped your notice.

Here's the thing about glass: whether it's making up ceilings, cliffs or escalators (we'll come to the escalators soon), it's invisible. We're not supposed to spot it. But once we know it's there, it becomes impossible to unsee.

I know that was the case for me, personally.

In a lot of ways, I came to my own understanding of the phenomenon late – which is to say, too late for it to be most useful to me. I had already worked as a C-suite leader in a London advertising agency before I first heard the term. It was even later still, once I had already joined and left a FAANG* business as a leader with a global remit, that I had the lightbulb moment of realizing the ways in which the Glass Cliff had already touched my own career.

Even once we know the theory behind the phenomenon, learning to recognize the Glass Cliff, and coming to terms with its impact on our career outcomes, often isn't altogether straightforward.

Despite having spent endless hours poring over research into the topic, and even having given the definitive TED Talk on the Glass Cliff in 2021, my understanding of the phenomenon remained very academic, very detached from my own professional life. I knew how it played out, in theory, but hadn't applied that theory to my working life, or the lives of the women I knew.

I don't want this to happen to you, so, to help bridge the gap

---

* Facebook, Apple, Amazon, Netflix, Google – businesses known for high performance and fast-growth stock – where I do not feel I personally faced the Glass Cliff experience.

between the academic theory of the phenomenon and the real ways it impacts on real lives, I have included, at the start of each chapter in this book, a story of a well-known, high-profile instance of the Glass Cliff playing out in the real world. I have done my best to put together what I believe to be accurate retellings of these women's stories using news sources, but, of course, I wasn't there for any of it. I didn't live through it or see these experiences play out from the inside. I also haven't spoken to these women first-hand, so it's also entirely plausible that they may not recognize the phenomenon or accept that they were victim to it – though I believe that all of the examples used offer a good insight into the barriers and obstacles standing in the way of women being successful once they have stepped into leadership roles. It's also worth noting that I have absolutely missed out details in my retellings that cover several months or years of these women's professional lives, but I hope I've captured the important elements. And I hope that seeing these stories, which may already be familiar to you, laid out within the context of the Glass Cliff, sparks recognition that may have been missing before.

For me, the breakthrough in taking my understanding of the Glass Cliff from the academic to the practical didn't happen until I was in a room full of women talking about their own experiences. It was only then, in their company, that I was able to move from the theoretical to the personal, and I began to reframe some of the experiences in my own career that I'd never quite had the words for, up to that point.

I want you to join our fold.

Let this book become a safe space to work through thoughts and to reflect on and possibly reframe your own experiences.

Let the stories of the women shared in these pages become *your* room full of supportive women – allow their experiences to resonate with your own. ·

Allow yourself to find the similarities between their experiences and yours.

Allow it to permeate.

And then – tell the world!

Help other women to recognize their own precarious positions. Use the tips offered in this book to interrogate 'opportunities' before taking them on, and set your own terms and boundaries for success. Strategize together to overcome the hurdles that have been invisible up to now.

Take on the world and win.

Because that's what you deserve, more than anything.

As Emma Lazarus told us, 'Until we are all free, we are none of us free.' So let's get free – and free one another too.

FYI

I want to start our time together by being clear about the language that I'm using, as well as being clear about who, what and where we are talking about, and who, what and where we're not.

As you know, we are going to be talking about, and digging into, the phenomenon of the Glass Cliff – the position that too many women find themselves in once they have managed to break through the Glass Ceiling. But there are some things that it's important to be clear and upfront about from the very beginning in order to set things out on the right foot, and so I'm going to outline those for you now.

Ready?

OK, let's go!

Did you invent the Glass Cliff?
Absolutely not!

The Glass Cliff was first researched and named by academics from the University of Exeter, Michelle Ryan and Alexander Haslam (I've become a big fan – they're like rock stars to me, now!). While their work initially looked only at corporate structure, using a sample group of FTSE 100 companies, further research, mostly led by US-based researchers Alison Cook and Christy Glass (in a lovely bit of nominative determinism), has proven the phenomenon pops up in other areas, particularly politics.

Is the Glass Cliff something that only happens to women?
No, it's not. Although this book focuses on the female experience, the Glass Cliff phenomenon is not limited to women. In fact, research exists that shows racially marginalized men face the same situation when they take on the most senior leadership roles in organizations.[1] This means that the Glass Cliff has the potential to impact the working lives of everyone who doesn't hold the dual identities of *both* whiteness and maleness – which means *all* women and *all* racially marginalized men.

Or, to put it another way, the only people *not* susceptible to the Glass Cliff are white men.

It's also important to note that the research *doesn't* show that every time a woman becomes a leader she faces a Glass Cliff or that there are no examples of white men who find themselves in challenging and precarious leadership positions due to external factors. However, in the instances when the Glass Cliff does play out, those affected by it are *always* women and racially marginalized men.

Do non-marginalized men have their own Glass Cliffs?
When we look at white men's experiences in the workplace, at a group level, we don't see the Glass Cliff phenomenon playing out. In fact, what we see when we look at the research around this group's experiences is a glass metaphor that is the opposite to the Glass Cliff: the Glass Escalator.[2] In this metaphor, the escalator invisibly speeds up men's progress to senior positions, particularly in professions that are female-dominated.

Does intersectionality have a role to play in the Glass Cliff?
Yes, absolutely. As we've just discussed, the Glass Cliff can impact all women and all racially marginalized men. Yet, as we all know,

none of us are one-dimensional beings. None of us are *only* our gender, or *only* our race, because all of us are a whole host of elements and identities that make us *us*, all at once and all of the time.

When it comes to intersectionality and the Glass Cliff, what we tend to see is that, the more intersectionally marginalized identities a person holds, the more likely they are to be susceptible to the phenomenon.

This means that we see the Glass Cliff having an oversized impact on those people who have more than one marginalized element to their identity, or anyone who doesn't fit in with their society's idealized image of a leader. In western society, leaders are traditionally thought of, and expected to be, white males. Racially marginalized women have the double jeopardy of falling outside expectations in terms of *both* race and gender, and so are more susceptible to the phenomenon and face it more strongly than those with only one element that deviates from our expected 'norm'.

How are you defining women?
I am defining women as anyone and everyone who identifies as such.

I'm going to be focusing on women's experiences of the Glass Cliff, and how the phenomenon impacts their professional lives and potential successes in business. But, that being said, I want to acknowledge that gender is a social construct – one that's relatively new and that isn't replicated around the world.

Since gender, and therefore womanness, are social constructs, I also want to acknowledge that the experiences I'm going to be discussing aren't in any way linked to, or a result of, a biological idea of sex. Instead, we need to be able to recognize that the experience and phenomenon of the Glass Cliff are a result of our application of the constructs, constraints and societal expectations we've formed around gender and gender expression in women.

Over time, we have built a shared understanding and expectation of what it is to be a woman, and assigned sets of cultural norms associated with that identity. We have built shared expectations of traits that are soft, nurturing, caregiving and in many ways subservient – expectations that are a result of socialization, rather than chromosomes.

To properly understand and reckon with the experience and phenomenon of the Glass Cliff, we must first recognize that there is nothing in women's bodies or physical make-up that makes them inherently more susceptible to the experience.

Womanness lives in our minds, our socialization and our expectations, rather than in or outside anyone's body.

Is the Glass Cliff something that happens everywhere in the world?

Interestingly, no, it isn't.

The Glass Cliff mostly plays out in countries and cultures where there is an expectation of male dominance, particularly in the workplace. Because the phenomenon is a result of the perimeters we have built, culturally, around performed gender roles, it stands to reason that, in societies where those expectations and roles are expressed differently, gender-based outcomes also vary and so the experience of the Glass Cliff is different, sometimes disappearing altogether.

Researchers in Turkey, for instance, have found that, in their society – which they define as a country where the level of femininity is 'relatively high', while the levels of both individualism and masculinity are 'relatively low' – women are equally likely to step into leadership roles when a company is thriving as they are when it's underperforming.[3]

We also see more instances of the Glass Cliff occurring in countries where individualism is high. In these countries, like the USA and the UK, the idea of a person's professional success is thought of mostly within a vacuum of individual performance. We expect people to succeed or fail on their own, and on their own terms, often without taking into consideration the structural systems and constraints within which they are working. This means that, although the Glass Cliff is more likely to manifest in these societies, it's also much more likely to be overlooked as a group phenomenon and misread as an individual's inaptitude for leadership.

What do you mean by 'under-represented leaders'?
'Under-represented' can mean so many different things in different contexts and for different groups. I am speaking about those people who are most under-represented in senior leadership roles in the UK and the US.

Using data from the Lean In Foundation, we can look at businesses in the US and see that:

- 'Women of colour' represent 19 per cent of the workforce for entry-level positions, a figure that shrinks to just 5 per cent by the time we reach the C-suite.

- White women represent 29 per cent of the entry-level cohort, shrinking to 21 per cent by C-suite level.

- 'Men of colour' also enter the workforce with 19 per cent representation, which shrinks to 13 per cent as they reach C-level jobs.

- White men begin at 33 per cent representation in early entry-level roles, a number that balloons to 61 per cent by the time we look at the C-suite.[4]

It is reasonable to say, then, with white men making up 61 per cent of C-level roles and being the *only* group whose representation *grows* as they become more senior in the workforce, that anyone who does not hold the dual identities of maleness and whiteness is under-represented at the most senior levels of business.

There are points where I need to use terms such as 'minority' or 'women of colour' to be true to the research I'm working with and building on. These are not terms I enjoy or find useful, and so, where I have needed to use them, they are always quoted.

What are the limitations of the work?
As with all work, we are both enriched and limited by the research available to build on. In the case of the Glass Cliff, those limitations include:

- A somewhat narrow definition of gender, only looking at 'male and female' experiences, without the inclusion of non-binary experiences, or reference to trans identities or experiences.*

- A UK and US bias. Most of the research into the Glass Cliff has been carried out by British and North American researchers, and so most of their findings focus on these countries.

- The focus on intersectionality is somewhat lacking. While groups are split by gender, there is no real mention of other intersectional identity elements, such as race, neurodivergence, physical disability, class background etc. Although I do include intersectional data where it's available, it's not available anywhere near as much or as often as I'd hope.

Why look at leaders – people who already seem to be winning – when so many people have a hard time even getting started?[5]
It might seem to be a strange time to be speaking about issues that are faced by those who seem to be at the top of their game – those

---

* To their credit, any stats taken from the Lean In Foundation's Women in the Workplace studies include both cisgender and transgender women – though, as they acknowledge, the transgender groups represent a much smaller sample size.

who have already taken on leadership roles, or those who are about to – when we know there are barriers to career progression from the very beginning of so many under-represented people's working lives. We're not only facing a cost-of-living crisis that is forcing many people to look for additional revenue streams, from Uber-driving to Vinted-dealing, to meet their most basic needs – we're also seeing a record number of labour strikes as workers demand fair payment for their labour. People are struggling to stay afloat.

I get it. It can seem like a real luxury and a privilege to be worrying about whether your (probably) well-paid senior-leadership role has been set up for success or not, when so many are struggling to get off the starting blocks.

But, here's what I think. Being a pioneer, at any point in time, is a difficult and daunting thing to do – it requires courage and tenacity, and we owe it to those people who are doing that work, and taking those risks, to set them up for success as best we can. Or at least to be honest with them about the challenges and potential stumbling blocks they might face.

We know that, in a lot of cases, you need to be able to see it to be it, and so we need to help the people who have taken their first steps towards being it, so they have the best possible chance of success, inspiring the next generation of female leaders to imagine that success as their own and begin building their pathways towards it.

While these women are among the first to step into these highly visible, often precarious roles, I want to ensure they're not the last, and I believe that a part of the way we achieve this is by understanding, reframing and giving context to their legacy and achievements, so we can all benefit and grow from their trailblazing work.

What is leadership?
For the purposes of this book, leadership is stepping into a role with additional responsibilities and visibility, where you are

leading others. In the body of Glass Cliff research, this has usually been limited to C-suite and board-level professionals. But we can see now that the implications of this phenomenon are much more widely applicable than that, as we consider some of the ways modern workplaces have moved from the top-down hierarchical structure to a more modern, flatter structural model.

Why do you call the Glass Cliff a phenomenon, rather than a theory?

In this, I'm taking my lead from the researchers who first named the Glass Cliff. As they explain it, its existence isn't in question – there is strong and robustly proven evidence readily available – although it doesn't exist *everywhere*.[6]

The Glass Cliff phenomenon is nuanced and context-dependent – for example, one business's poor performance may be another's record-breaking year. If the Glass Cliff were a theory, we would be seeking to either prove or disprove it. However, studying and understanding it as a phenomenon allows us to gather confirming and disconfirming evidence and use that to better frame and understand the circumstances where it is likely to materialize, and where it has been avoided.

In other words, we are looking for the conditions that make it more or less likely – rather than proving whether it exists or not.

Is the Glass Cliff political?

Really, it depends on what you mean by 'political'. In the world as we know it, talking about women, the barriers they face and the things that we can do to try to level the playing field is often seen as being political. So, in that sense, yes, I guess it is. But, if we're talking party politics, then the answer is no. The Glass Cliff, as a phenomenon, is entirely apolitical; it is a result of socialization and gendered expectations rather than political preference. The

Glass Cliff doesn't happen more when one particular political party is in power than another, nor does it happen more to people who vote one way or another.

CHAPTER 1

Breaking Through the Glass Ceiling

There is an entire generation of women who are drowning because they were raised with traditional gender roles while being empowered to be independent. These women still take on the majority of house duties while simultaneously killing it in the workplace. They're tired.[1]

In November 2007, Zoe Cruz, co-president of Morgan Stanley, was called to her boss's office and fired[2] – ending her twenty-five-year employment with the business.[3]

'I've lost confidence in you,' the chairman and CEO of the bank, John Mack, told her. 'I want you to resign.' This was a decision that, unbeknown to Cruz, had been approved by the bank's board of directors the previous day.[4]

Cruz, up to that point, had been referred to as one of the most powerful women, and indeed people, in finance – she had been nicknamed 'Cruz Missile' thanks to her ambition, her 'aggressive approach' to risk-taking and her seemingly unstoppable rise through the ranks of the traditionally male industry of banking. In 2005, she was ranked at number sixteen on *Forbes'* list of the one hundred most powerful women in the world.[5] In the write-up for the feature, the magazine said 'she earned a solid reputation as a fixed-income genius after running one of the largest trading desks on Wall Street from 2000 to 2005.'[6] Not only that, but, just three weeks before her sudden dismissal, Mack (who was sixty-three at the time) had signalled that Cruz was his first choice to replace him as the head of Morgan Stanley when he retired.[7]

Mack had earned his own nickname from those who had worked with him over the years: 'Mack the Knife', a label he'd picked up in part due to his 'ruthless focus on clients and on the bank's bottom line'. Speaking to *The Guardian*, Brad Hintz, an analyst at the stockbroker Sanford Bernstein in New York, said, '[Mack] is not a warm and fuzzy person, neither is he particularly forgiving' – as Zoe Cruz had just discovered.[8]

'Of all the recent firings on Wall Street,' *New York* magazine wrote, 'Cruz's is the one that's still vehemently debated. It's not just because a top executive was forced to take the fall for her boss, though that does seem to be the case.'[9]

So what happened to the woman many had thought would become the first female leader of a Wall Street firm?[10]

Twenty-five years prior, when banking was still very much a boys' club, Cruz had joined Morgan Stanley as a twenty-six-year-old. Her almost-all-male colleagues socialized over drinks in strip clubs or playing rounds of golf, and had pictures of pin-up girls in their cubicles. Women were not commonplace as traders on the floor, and Cruz wasn't the most obvious fit.[11]

Indeed, in 2001, a female executive filed a lawsuit against Morgan Stanley, claiming women had been denied opportunities to advance – a suit that was settled in 2004 for $54 million, which was shared between sixty-seven female employees of the business.[12]

Despite the environment, Cruz performed well and, after a series of promotions within the business, she became a managing director in 1990, co-founded the bank's foreign-exchange group in 1993 and eventually became the firm's global head of fixed income, commodities and foreign exchange in 2001.[13]

Speaking to *Fortune*, Cruz said that part of the reason she liked working on the notoriously high-stress trading floor was that she felt it was an area where the performance of men and women could be measured objectively, telling them, 'I like trading because of the unequivocal nature of the report card.'[14]

Cruz was known for her hard work and determination. Balancing her high-profile job with raising a young family, she would regularly work sixteen-hour days – getting up at 4 a.m. to bake biscuits to go into her children's packed lunches.[15] In 1988, when she was actively in labour with one of her three children, she even took a call from the trading desk to discuss positions in a particularly volatile market.[16]

Cruz was well compensated for her work: in 2003, her pay and bonus combined came to a package of $16 million.[17] By 2004, the division that she led had grown revenues to $5.6 billion – representing 14 per cent of Morgan Stanley's total income.[18] By 2006, her compensation from the business had grown to $30 million as Morgan Stanley reported a 51 per cent rise in profits.[19]

Despite her successes, it seems that internal relationships didn't always run smoothly for Cruz. Her tenure and senior role notwithstanding, she repeatedly faced suggestions that she was unqualified for her position.[20] This situation wasn't helped by the support of her peers; on the contrary, there were reports that one particular male senior leader would 'antagonize Cruz in front of the other managing directors, causing her to shake with anger and frustration, wiping tears from her eyes.'[21]

Within the business, Cruz was characterized as a 'ruthless, hard-edged leader who did not do well at smoothing over conflict with her colleagues or subordinates.'[22] This was a reputation that went beyond the confines of the company; an extensive, in-depth article in *New York* magazine about her departure described how, 'From the beginning, she had the uncompromising ferocity that seems to be characteristic of nearly all women who achieve great success.'[23]

The *New York* magazine article also mentioned a particular incident that showed that, as well as difficulties in gaining the respect of male peers at the managing-director level, junior team members were, at least on occasion, equally subordinate and dismissive of her position within the business, and she was 'not taken at all seriously by a number of her male colleagues':

'She'd give these speeches, and the eyes would roll,' says one former executive. The attitude toward attending meetings headed by Cruz was 'take [the] pain and move on,' says a current Morgan Stanley employee. During a year-end management meeting in 2004, one mid-level executive inter-rupted Cruz's speech to ask, 'Are you high? Because I really don't know what you're talking about.'

'High?' Cruz asked. 'You mean stoned?'

'Yeah, exactly,' he said. 'Smoking it.'

Everyone in the room laughed – except Cruz.[24]

Despite these tensions, the divisions of the business Cruz was responsible for not only remained profitable, but grew 110 per cent during 2006, and Mack remained vocal about the intention he had first mentioned back in 2001 – that Zoe Cruz would one day lead Morgan Stanley – saying during a shareholders meeting in April 2007 that the bank's all-time highs in revenues, in income and in earning, were thanks to Cruz, who had revolutionized the institutional-securities group, managing a huge amount of risk in a very smart and disciplined way.[25]

However, like all financial institutions, in 2007, Morgan Stanley found itself on the verge of a catastrophe the likes of which had never been seen as the sub-prime mortgage crisis hit, with the bank on the wrong side of the collapsing value of mort-gage securities. Cruz's division accumulated losses of $3.7 billion,[26] with $6 billion in additional losses across the business being predicted.[27]

Cruz officially 'retired' from her role in December of 2007.[28]

Ultimately, as is the case for the exits of many women in high-profile roles – where both NDAs and speculations run high – there are likely to have been a number of factors involved in the decision to let her go. Instead of being appointed as Mack's successor and eventual CEO of the business, Cruz found herself leaving the company she'd given over two decades of her life to.

She was replaced by two men who jointly took on her respon-sibilities.[29]

◆ ◆ ◆

Like most other people, my understanding of the Glass Cliff began with another glass metaphor – that of the Glass Ceiling.[30] For as long as I can remember, the Glass Ceiling has been a part of mainstream cultural conversation. All of my life, I've seen think pieces, read magazine articles and heard discussions about that invisible, but seemingly impossible-to-break-through, barrier that sits above the heads of women in their working lives, as they try to reach the fullness of their professional potential. The way that it existed in the zeitgeist made it seem like it had been accepted as an inevitability – something that could be acknowledged, discussed and analysed, but never really questioned or challenged. And certainly not overcome.

People were always happy to agree that the Glass Ceiling was there, but they were less keen to suggest anything could be done about it. The Glass Ceiling exists, the world seemed to be saying, and at some point you too will hit your head against it, and that will be how you know you've reached the limit of your professional achievements. Yes, of course, even when you reach that limit, you'll know that there's more you're capable of, and sometimes that next level, taking the next step, will feel so close that you can almost touch it. But *almost* is the key word.

I'm starting this conversation about the Glass Cliff by discussing the Glass Ceiling because, really, the conversation about the Glass Cliff is a conversation about what happens when women break the rules, break through the Glass Ceiling and break out of the roles that have historically been assigned to them in their careers and professional journeys.

When a woman decides that she wants, deserves and has earned more than the limited role she has historically been conditioned to play – and when she has the courage, skills and opportunity to take the next steps towards leadership and the fulfilment of her own professional capabilities – she will often find herself at odds with our society's expectations of her. While this tension begins with trying to break through the Glass Ceiling, all too often it ends with her finding herself in a precarious position, teetering at the edge of the Glass Cliff.

To understand the Glass Ceiling, and then the Glass Cliff, we first need to revisit and understand women's first steps into the paid labour force.

From my perspective, having been born in 1987 and having grown up in the late eighties and early nineties, so much of the conversation around the Glass Ceiling made it feel like a fait accompli – it was there, yes, and while of course it wasn't fair, there was nothing that could be done about it, so why even try?

But, as I got older and took on more senior positions myself, I started to notice that it wasn't always the immovable beast it had been made out to be. Slowly, I became aware that, in small numbers at first, women *were* breaking through their Glass Ceilings and going on to step into positions as the most senior leaders in their businesses. I saw Dame Marjorie Scardino become the first female chief executive of a FTSE 100 company. I saw Deborah Meaden, Karren Brady and Hilary Devey pull up seats in the *Dragons' Den* as powerful (and power-suited) women who were leaders of industry – very much calling the shots. And this shift was reflected in my personal experiences, too, as I worked for businesses that were owned and run by female founders and leaders.

Although women were still deeply under-represented in management and leadership spaces – making up only 2.8 per cent of CEOs and 33 per cent of managers in the European Union, and 4.8 per cent of CEOs and 42.7 per cent of managers in the United States – our visible representation was growing.[31] Between 2001 and 2005, female representation on the boards of FTSE 100 companies increased dramatically. In 2001, 56.6 per cent of boards included female members; this had increased to 74.8 per cent by 2005.[32] And so it seemed to me that, even if the Glass Ceiling was truly there (and I do believe it is), it might be a little more possible to smash through than we had all been led to believe.

Somehow, despite these high-profile wins, our shared cultural narrative wasn't keeping up in real time. Women were stepping into powerful positions in previously unheard of (albeit still statistically tiny) numbers, but the think pieces and magazine articles remained preoccupied with the experience of being trapped beneath the Glass Ceiling – without pushing the conversation onwards. To my mind, the logical question they should have been asking was: What's next? What happens to those women who manage to break through the Glass Ceiling and go on to become leaders in a male-dominated world? Is it amazing?

The answer to that question is the story of the Glass Cliff, which is what this book will be exploring.

But, let's rewind for a moment.

Where did we start?

When we speak about women's roles in the workplace, it's important to remember that women's participation in labour is not at all a new story. In fact, women's labour has absolutely *always* existed. Historically, this work has most often taken the form of unpaid nurturing and caregiving duties within our homes and communities: raising children, caring for the elderly, preparing food, cleaning and creating a safe and stable home environment. Although this work has traditionally been undervalued and overlooked, it has been essential to the formation of both our society and our economy.

What *is* newer, on the other hand, is our formalized and recognized participation in *paid* labour, outside of the home and the family. This is a much more recent development in most western countries, and one that has given us the opportunity to build and define the rules of engagement for ourselves.* Up until recently, we've done a really bad job of this.

Despite the shorter tenure of women's formalized labour participation, as a society, we have quickly and collectively developed a set of norms and expectations around what a woman's role in the workplace 'can' and 'should' be.

Since we were children, we've all been trained to associate different types of jobs with different types, or groups, of people. Think back to childhood picture books, or TV shows, with their depictions of doctors, nurses, firefighters, teachers and so on. If your childhood media was anything like mine, you'll remember that gender roles in the adult world seemed to be firmly, and quietly, set in stone, with very little variation from book to book, story to story. These clear, recurring and distinct roles sent a clear message to us all, as children, about where our place in the adult world was going to be and – perhaps more pertinently – where it was *not*. Rather than being rebutted, this early, quiet socialization was only reinforced as we moved through the educational system. Teachers' gendered biases and expectations

---

* It's important to note that this has usually been in *addition* to, not *instead* of, the domestic and caregiving work still expected of women and girls. Research from Oxfam shows that, up until 2019, women and girls put in 12.5 billion hours of unpaid care work each and every day – an unpaid contribution to the global economy of at least $10.8 trillion a year, more than three times the size of the global tech industry. These figures will only have increased when the Covid-19 pandemic hit the world. Lean In's 2022 Women in the Workplace report shows the extent of domestic labour still being carried out by North American women on top of their out-of-the-home paid work, whereby 58 per cent of women in entry-level roles report being responsible for 'most or all of their family's housework and childcare', compared to just 30 per cent of men at the same level. At the senior-manager level or above, this becomes 13 per cent of men, and 52 per cent of women – showing that, as men advance in their careers, they are often able to take a step back from domestic responsibilities, while women's levels of responsibility 'stay roughly the same'.

around competencies mean they are more likely to encourage male students to pursue more rigorous STEM subjects and (eventually) better paid and more prestigious careers.[33]

Our chances to dream the biggest dreams we can are capped by the imaginations of those who teach us about the world in our earliest years – and so we're set up to be limited, folded into small boxes before we've even begun to make sense of the world for ourselves, on our own terms.

It can hardly be a coincidence that, with all of this early socialization, women are still over-represented in disrespected and poorly paid roles.* According to Oxfam, women represent approximately 70 per cent of the world's health and social care workforce and are deeply over-represented in careers and industries such as teaching, cleaning, retail and tourism – professions that rely on our historically expected and over-exploited 'soft skills'.[34] These are also roles that are suspiciously close to the unpaid, in-home labour that women have traditionally undertaken: cooking, cleaning, caring. And those traditionally female roles, even when formalized into professions, are still some of the least respected and worst compensated roles in our society.†

Again, it didn't need to be this way. None of this is the essential natural order of things. Instead, this is the result of choices that have been made along the line. These inequities exist because of the way we've chosen to structure our world, rather than because of some kind of divine intervention or the nature of human evolution. There is nothing inherently less valuable, challenging

---

* It's very much not a coincidence. It's called Occupational Segregation and it has a huge part to play in gender pay differences and earnings gaps.

† It's worth noting that, while women are over-represented at the public-facing, service-level 'front line' of these industries, they're typically deeply under-represented at an ownership level – taking on the brunt of the physical work, without reaping the rewards of ownership, power or control.

or important about what have become traditional female roles. In fact, these are some of the *most* important roles in a well-functioning society – one that has developed a social infrastructure designed for raising children, caring for the sick and elderly, and building the social bonds of community. We have simply collectively decided not to hold these roles in the same high regard, nor compensate them as well as roles that have traditionally been dominated by men.

◆　　◆　　◆

In 1968, a group of female sewing machinists from Ford's Dagenham plant got their children ready for school, put on their shoes and jackets, and went to the factory where they worked, as usual.[35] Frustrated by a pay structure that they felt blatantly favoured male workers, instead of going inside, the women – who had been on strike for three weeks at that point – boarded a coach to Whitehall with a banner reading *We want sex*.* This was far from the beginning of their battle for equal pay and recognition for their work. Instead, it was the end. After years of fruitless conversations, the machinists, who sewed the upholstery for the Ford cars and vans, had taken the decision to strike – a move that became a national news story, since 'no machinists meant no seats, and no seats meant no cars' – forcing the factory to grind to a halt, with an estimated cost to the company's export orders of £117 million in today's money.

While some of their male colleagues were supportive of the strike, which also forced them to stop working, and therefore earning, during that three-week period, others were less impressed.

_____

* The banner, which hadn't been properly unfurled, read in full: '*We want sex equality*'. 'Men were leaning out of their [taxi] cabs shouting: "We'll be back at 6!"' recalled protester Eileen Pullen, speaking to *The Guardian* at the age of eighty-three, alongside her fellow strikers, forty-five years after the event.

'Some of the men said: "Good for you girl", but others said: "Get back to work, you're only doing it for pin money", recalled Eileen Pullen, one of the strikers. 'A lot of women jeered us. They didn't go to work and their husbands were at Fords and we'd put them out of work'.

'But our wages weren't for pin money,' said eighty-year-old Gwen Davis, in conversation with Pullen. 'They were to help with the cost of living, to pay your mortgage and help pay all your bills. It wasn't pocket money. No woman would go out to work just for pocket money, would she? Not if she's got a family'.[36]

Despite this, the women insist that the financial inequality wasn't the only injustice informing their decision to strike. They also wanted to be recognized for the skills that were essential in their work. Despite their work being classed as B grade – officially unskilled work in Ford's internal banding system – the machinists needed to pass a skills-based test in order to be hired, and so believed their work should be recognized as skilled, putting them into Ford's C grade.

'One of the ladies who worked with me had been a machinist for [Norman] Hartnell,' Davis recalled. 'She'd been a dressmaker making the Queen's clothes. She went for a test at Ford and they turned her down.' The bar, they pointed out, was much too high to be classed as 'unskilled'.

By the time the eight strike leaders wrapped up discussions and headed back to the coach for the trip home, they had agreed a deal to end the strike, and the foundations had been laid for what, two years later, would become the 1970 Equal Pay Act. Yet the story *still* wasn't over for the Dagenham machinists and their efforts for equality.

Although the women did return to work, it was not on the new terms that had been agreed. Prior to the strike, their pay had constituted 85 per cent of the male rate; this subsequently increased, but only to 93 per cent. Furthermore, sixteen years later, the Dagenham women were still waiting to be recognized as skilled, and so were forced to go out on strike once again.

We don't have to look hard to see modern examples of how little has changed. At the time of writing, for instance, 40,000 female employees at the supermarket chain Asda are involved in a long-running equal-pay case against the business.* An email from the lawyer representing the workers involved, which was leaked to ITV, shows that independent experts have found that shop-floor jobs, in which women are over-represented, 'score more highly on average on a range of [crucial] factors, such as knowledge and responsibility, than distribution jobs, [which are] held predominantly by men'. Despite this, retail workers say they are paid £1.50 to £3 less an hour than those in the more male-dominated field.[37]

While it's difficult to compare two different job types, each with its own distinct skills and market expectations, it does seem, much more often than not, to be the women's skill sets that fall into the 'less valuable' category. Time and time again. So often, in fact, that it's become the expectation, rather than an irregularity. As Elizabeth George, a partner at Leigh Day who has acted on workers' rights cases remarkably similar to that at Asda, put it: 'We think we can say, "No, the market forces argument is tainted by sex discrimination. Just because you've always done it, and just because everyone else does it, isn't a material factor."'[38]

---

* Although Asda denied any wrongdoing, with a spokesperson for the business saying: 'It is not a ruling by the Employment Tribunal and is not a decision on the question of equal value. At Asda, male and female colleagues doing the same jobs in stores are paid the same and this is equally true in our distribution centres [. . .] We continue to defend these claims because retail and distribution are very different sectors, with their own distinct skill sets and rates of pay.'

BUT, WHAT ABOUT . . . ?

There is sometimes a (frankly, wild) suggestion from those who want to deny the realities of Occupational Segregation that the underpayment and undervaluing of women's work is a choice that women have made. Maybe you've heard people say that the gender pay gap is a myth, because men and women choose to do different jobs, and the jobs that women choose just so happen to be worse paid than those favoured by men. Silly little ladies just can't seem to get the hang of this money-making game.

This is clearly nonsense.

Traditionally female professions, such as teaching, or nursing, are incredibly demanding, both mentally and physically, requiring an abundance of skills, education and training.

When people are planning their career paths, no one aims to train for years and then work as hard as possible for the least amount of money.[39] But, in a society that values women's work less, those careers that are disproportionately held by women are held in a lower regard, and so they are compensated less attractively, or fairly.

We have accepted women joining the workforce, particularly in times of great need. The war effort saw women rolling up their sleeves and joining formalized work for the first time in previously unprecedented numbers. However, the message has always been clear, and consistent:

Not too much.
Not too well paid.

Not too senior.

And certainly not as leaders.

'We built workplaces for white men [who] had a stay-at-home partner,' observes Reshma Saujani, a lawyer, politician and activist.* 'Whenever you're building anything,' she continued, 'you should always build for the most vulnerable [. . .] Workplaces should be built for single mom[s], [and] women of colour [. . .] If we're building workplaces for [those women], they're going to work for everybody.'[40]

But that's not how we've chosen to build the working world. At all.

Working within the constraints we have inherited – within systems that were not only *not* made to benefit us, but which actively *rely on* an assumption of our unpaid, unrecognized labour – has seen generations of women working the double shift of balancing the demands of work inside and outside the home, toiling beneath Glass Ceilings and never expecting to be able to reach the pinnacle of their own personal capabilities.[41]

But, in recent years, we have all witnessed a shift. Our expectations have begun to change and expand, as women have increasingly begun to demand equality, and more and more have sought to break out of traditional gendered expectations and smash through their Glass Ceilings.

What does the Glass Ceiling look like in the real world?

For all of the cultural conversation about the Glass Ceiling existing, there has been a lack of specificity when discussing *exactly* what we mean, and *exactly* what these invisible barriers that women face in their careers are made up of.

---

* Saujani is also the founder of Marshall Plan for Moms, which invests in women's economic recovery and empowerment.

As we know, we've seen an increasing number of women overcoming the odds and taking their rightful places in leadership and decision-making roles, heading up various businesses. But, in order to properly appreciate their achievements, we need to recognize some of the major barriers they faced along the way.

The Broken Rung

Before a woman, or anyone, has the opportunity to begin thinking about their path towards leadership, they need to take their first step and get their first break. This is, sadly, where the problems of progression that plague so many women during their careers often first come to life.

The Broken Rung refers to the challenges that female employees face in getting their first management opportunity and taking the initial step on the ladder towards leadership. From this very first step, this very first rung, there is a gender imbalance at play – one that only becomes more pronounced as we look further up the ladder.

Even when we look at the very beginning of the pipeline, we can see a gap. Despite women in the USA making up 57 per cent of college-level graduates, fewer women than men are hired into entry-level roles.[42]

The next stage of the journey is the first promotion, and the story there is no better. In fact, for every hundred men promoted from the entry level to a first management position, only eighty-seven women are promoted* – reinforcing the existing gender disparity created by hiring.[43] This means that, from the first step into the most junior levels of management, men already significantly outnumber women. Research has shown that, 'if entry-level women were promoted at the same rate as men at the same level, the number of women at the most senior positions of SVP [senior vice president] and C-suite levels would more than double.'[44]

---

* And only eighty-two 'women of colour'.

This is a problem that only becomes more heightened when promotions are made to mid- and senior-level management and leadership roles – since, as men are over-represented at the lower-management tiers, there are simply more of them to choose from when making ongoing, upward appointments. And so, of course, men are more likely to be selected to take the next steps of advancement up their career ladders, creating and reinforcing a gap that goes some way to explaining why, when we look at C-level roles in corporate America, men represent 74 per cent, and women only 26 per cent.

Being overlooked for promotions and advancement

At the end of 2022, only one in four C-suite leaders was a woman, and only one in twenty was a 'woman of colour'.[45] Historically, there have been arguments put forward – by those who want to deny or minimize the reality of structural workplace inequities – that this is due to women lacking the education or ambition to take on those roles. But, in reality, we know that's not the case. In fact, as we've already seen, women in the US make up the majority of college graduates, and 78 per cent of both male and female leaders say they want to be promoted to the next level in their careers, but the opportunities to take on those roles do not seem to be granted equally.[46]

Recognizing this, women are increasingly opting to take on the burden of managing their progression themselves – leaving jobs and switching companies to build and navigate their own pathways to success and progression. In 2022, research carried out by the Lean In Foundation and McKinsey found that 48 per cent of women in leadership roles who had changed jobs in the previous two years said they did so 'because they wanted more opportunity to advance'.[47] It's interesting to note that, while almost all companies track gender representation of employees overall, 'only 65 per cent track for gender differences in promotion rates', leaving themselves open to continued invisible disparity.[48]

Workplaces have also not usually been structured to put women's advancement front and centre. In fact, women overall are 24 per cent less likely than men to be offered advice from a senior leader – advice which, had it been offered, may have helped them to plan, navigate and negotiate the next steps of their career.[49] But it goes far beyond that. Research from MIT[50] shows that, even when women received higher performance ratings than their male colleagues, they were likely to receive a lower score for their 'potential', leaving them, on average, 14 per cent less likely to be promoted than their male counterparts.[51] When we look at and understand factors like these, we can really begin to understand how, even after progressing beyond the Broken Rung, women's leadership potential has still been hampered by factors outside of our own aptitude or control.

A perception that there are 'already enough'

For a long time, many businesses have viewed gender inclusion as a tick-the-box exercise, being more than comfortable with doing the bare minimum when it comes to gender representation at all but the most junior, entry-level, lowest-paying roles. This is reflected by the shocking stat that 'almost 50 per cent of men think women are well represented in leadership in companies where only one in ten senior leaders are women' – the most begrudging nod to inclusion.[52]

If most senior leaders are men, and if those men are satisfied that female advancement is well taken care of with only 10 per cent representation at senior level, then it's no shock that they – as the people with the power to influence and drive hiring, promotion, progression and retention initiatives – have not brought this lens to their recruitment strategies up to now.

Being perceived as a risky investment

Since most senior leaders are both white and male,* it's likely that most women will be led or managed by someone who holds those dual identities – which can create both real and perceived power imbalances, further to the imbalances inherent to any hierarchical working relationship – even in 'flat' organizations.[53] Even when managers take the time and effort to establish mentoring, collaborative relationships with their teams, there are hurdles that need to be overcome. Because, as a lot of research has shown, while women are *over*-mentored in the workplace, they often lack sponsorship – which is what really makes a difference in actual career progression and promotions.[54]

So what are the barriers to building those connections that are deeper and more meaningful than mentorships?

Firstly, a successful relationship of this kind requires non-marginalized leaders to be able to understand and empathize with the challenges that their marginalized team members face in their progression journeys.[55] This is often difficult, because those challenges are likely to be misaligned with the over-represented manager's own lived experiences – and so the leader's advice and guidance is often misguided, failing to take into account intersectional differences.

Secondly, there has been an element of risk or perceived risk, as a result of institutional prejudice, that needs to be acknowledged and overcome.

It has been noted by researchers that managers might be more cautious in putting forward for a new role, or sponsoring, a 'minority' person from their team† because they may feel that

---

* At senior manager/director level, white men make up 47 per cent; this rises to 61 per cent in the C-suite, even in 2022.
† In the context of this research, 'minority' is used to refer to group power rather than numerical representation – though it is true that women are outnumbered at all levels within the workplace.

under-represented protégés are scrutinized more closely and so have less chance of being successfully appointed to a new position.[56]

This feeling of increased scrutiny is not limited to the experience, or the perception, of the managers; indeed, 'minority' employees often realize that they represent bigger risks to their bosses, or potential sponsors, because they are aware of the assumptions and prejudices that people hold about them at a group level. This, understandably, has an impact on their behaviours, making them become tentative or overly cautious in making decisions, as they attempt to mitigate against any discomfort that their boss or sponsor may feel in supporting them.[57] Because both employees and managers are aware of these feelings of risk, even bosses and mentors who feel socially comfortable and have developed good personal relationships with their 'minority' team members may hesitate to push them forwards for quick promotions or high-risk assignments that could put them on the fast track – since avoiding this type of risk avoids not only potential failure for the protégés, but also potential damage to the sponsor's own reputation and credibility, should the wider team not endorse and take on their recommendations.

Even when someone *is* put forward for a new role or opportunity, the same research shows that their chances of being accepted and appointed are *indeed* limited because often these decisions have been made not by individuals, but by groups, committees, board members or investors – all of whom need to be individually and personally convinced and assured of the candidate's ability to perform as required in the role. Those managers who did push for the advancement of their team members or protégés noted that creating the same opportunity for an under-represented employee took more work than for a comparably talented or experienced over-represented protégé. They believed this was because of the perceived risk that others felt they would be exposing themselves to if they were seen to be taking responsibility for – or backing – a 'minority' manager, and so they needed to invest additional time, effort and political manoeuvring into convincing their colleagues that their protégé would not be a huge risk.[58]

Everyday discrimination

Most people are aware of microaggressions – the regular slights and demeaning comments or (inter)actions that people with marginalized identities routinely face, whether intentional or not. Christina Friedlaender defined microaggressions as 'the subtle yet harmful forms of discriminatory behaviour experienced by members of oppressed groups', which I think sums them up perfectly.[59]

Women, on the whole, face microaggressions in the workplace more often than their male colleagues – with two thirds of women reporting that they 'experience sexist behaviour at least sometimes in their current workplaces',[60] and 73 per cent of women reporting facing 'day-to-day inequities, discrimination and bias'[61] at work.*

Gender-based microaggressions in the workplace can manifest in all kinds of ways, but these are some of the most common:

- **Women's voices are diminished.** While it's true that conversations move quickly and everyone gets cut off, interrupted or overlooked from time to time, studies have shown that women are interrupted at a much higher frequency than men in the workplace,[62] by both men and other women.[63] Twenty per cent of women report being interrupted or spoken over in meetings 'frequently',[64] and a study at George Washington University found that, when men were talking with women at work, they interrupted 33 per cent more often than when they were talking with other

---

* The likelihood of experiencing demeaning microaggressions is even more common for both disabled and LGBTQ+ women, with research finding that, compared to women overall, both groups are more likely to have colleagues comment on their appearance or tell them that they 'look mad' or 'should smile more'.

men.[65] Research also shows that those women who do perse-vere in an attempt to make their voices heard often find themselves to be penalized or punished for choosing to speak up or to assert themselves within the conversation[66] – with female executives who spoke more than their peers receiving 14 per cent lower ratings for 'perceived compe-tence' from both their male and female colleagues.[67] On the other hand, when men take the same action, speaking more than their peers, it is not only more likely to be accepted, but praised – resulting in them receiving 10 per cent *higher* ratings in competence from their peers, being more closely associated with power, and their managers reporting that they believed them to be more helpful than if they had not dominated the conversation.[68]

- **Women's ideas and contributions are overlooked.** Not only are women more likely to be interrupted or spoken over in work conversations, they are also much more likely to have their ideas, thoughts or contributions incorrectly attributed to a louder or more dominant male colleague. Even at a leadership level, 37 per cent of women report experiencing a co-worker taking or being given credit for their idea, compared to just 27 per cent of their male counterparts.[69] UK-based research found that 62 per cent of female employees said that they are 'less likely to get their ideas endorsed or taken up in a working environment than men',[70] which perhaps isn't surprising when we take into consideration research from the University of Delaware, which found that 'men are given more credit than women [when speaking at work] even when saying the exact same thing'.[71]

- **Women are forced to repeatedly prove competency in their area of expertise.** There is conventional wisdom among good leaders of people, which is, essentially: hire good people, and try not to get in their way. If we hire experts in their fields and trust them to do good work, then we have no need to micromanage them, and everyone's job becomes much easier. Unless, of course, they're women – in which case, it's much more likely that, even when we hire experts, they will regularly encounter scenarios that force them to re-prove and reassert their expertise, rather than being able to get on with the roles we hired them for. Thirty-nine per cent of female leaders overall* report having been in scenarios in which they have had their judgement questioned in their area of expertise, compared to 28 per cent† of male leaders.[72] One way this undermining questioning manifests is having someone imply that you're not qualified for your role, and so being called on to provide 'evidence' of your competency‡ – a situation that only 16 per cent of men overall, and just 6 per cent at a leadership level, reported having found themselves in at work, compared to a staggering 31 per cent of women§ who have endured the experience.[73] This could be explained by the fact that, even at a leadership level, women are twice as likely¶ as male leaders to be mistaken for someone more junior.[74]

---

* And 55 per cent of Black women leaders.

† The numbers are very similar to those at more junior levels in their careers.

‡ Or, like Cruz, having a junior team member asking if you're high, which I think is beyond unbelievable.

§ This is a figure that raises to almost half of Black women, at 42 per cent.

¶ Again, it has been found that women with a larger number of marginalized intersectional identities face more instances of microaggressions than others. Black women are more than twice as likely as white women to hear someone in their workplace express surprise at their language skills or other abilities. Lesbian women are twice as likely as women overall to feel like they can't talk about their lives outside of work. And women with disabilities are more than one and a half times as likely as women overall to *regularly* hear demeaning remarks about themselves or others like them.

Microaggressions and their impacts are often overlooked, down-played or dismissed in our day-to-day lives and in our experiences in the workplace. They don't feel big enough to take to HR or to make a formal complaint about, but they still leave us feeling unsettled and with the nagging sense that *something* isn't quite right and we don't belong as well as we'd hope to. When I speak to people about this quickness to dismiss the experience of facing microaggressions, the reasoning seems to be, well, the word *micro* is built into the term – so how damaging or noteworthy can these experiences really be? Especially since comments and slip-ups that are unintentional can fall into the category.

I would argue that this does a great disservice to the experiences of marginalized and under-represented people as they move through the world, overlooking the huge cognitive load that comes with dealing with daily slights and unfounded challenges, while placing an unnecessary and unhelpful emphasis on the *intention* of the person who has been hurtful, or harmful, over the *impact* of their words or actions on the person who is on the receiving end.

It also overlooks the fact that, while individual microaggressions may seem small, those who face them usually face them frequently – and facing a lot of aggressions, even if they're 'only' micro, adds up quickly. Like a thousand paper cuts, or a barrage of mosquito bites, what could be seen as small inconveniences to people who experience them rarely can quickly become a much bigger problem, resulting in burnout for many.[75]

Knowing that you are likely to face microaggressions in the workplace, preparing and steeling yourself against them, and dealing with their impact on your confidence and sense of belonging – all while you persevere with working and trying to progress within an environment that feels hostile to your presence – is a big cognitive and emotional burden that we ask women and other marginalized groups to carry, usually invisibly and in isola-tion. Those people who experience these affronts are rarely able to avoid that burden, and the time, energy and attention it takes up cannot then be focused into their work, relationships and developing their future prospects.

Sometimes microaggressions make us feel, implicitly, that we don't belong in a space, and at other times the message is much more explicit. Edward Enninful, the outgoing editor-in-chief of British *Vogue*, has spoken about returning to the Condé Nast office, Vogue House, for the first time since the lockdown closures – and being stopped by a white security guard, who shouted to inform him, 'Deliveries go through the loading bay.'[76] Another high-profile example is that of barrister Alexandra Wilson, a criminal and family lawyer who, on a single day in court, was mistaken for a defendant on four separate occasions and ordered to wait outside the courtroom for her case to begin – an experience that she described as leaving her 'absolutely exhausted' and 'nearly in tears', later telling the BBC, 'This really isn't OK . . . I don't expect to have to constantly justify my existence at work.'[77]

Rather than having the mental resources available to invest into planning their next steps up the career ladder, women who face microaggressions are burning out, feel that their workplaces are less fair environments, and are three times more likely to think regularly about leaving their jobs.[78]

No one should have to prepare themselves for systemic inequity and face their working lives with the knowledge that, despite their aptitude and abilities, every day will be an uphill struggle – but that has been the experience for generations of women as they have struggled and come to hit their heads against the invisible, limiting barrier of the Glass Ceiling.

But what happens to those women who *do* manage to break through?

TL;DR: *Too Long; Didn't Read*

- The Glass Cliff is related to, and for many women follows on from, the experience of the Glass Ceiling.

- From childhood we are socialized to associate professions with genders. School teachers have been shown to encourage boys over girls in STEM areas such as maths, even when they show the same interest in, and aptitude for, the subject.

- Women's traditional working roles are linked to our socialization and our expectations that women are caregiving and nurturing.

- The Broken Rung means that women don't get equal access to their first workplace promotions.

- Facing slower promotions and less access to advancement means that 48 per cent of women leaders have felt forced to move companies to manage their own progression.

- In America, 74 per cent of C-level roles are held by men.

- Under-represented employees are perceived as a greater risk, and so face more difficulties in securing sponsorship and access to leadership opportunities while at work.

- Women face an abundance of microaggressions in the workplace, from being interrupted, spoken over and having their ideas stolen or misattributed, to having to repeatedly prove their competence and expertise. Where women are penalized for being outspoken, men are praised.

CHAPTER 2

The Glass Cliff

The End of the World was a nightclub.
Drag queens with machetes and rhinestoned
machine guns guarded the red and impassable
door on Friday nights. Just a look at the crowd,
all dressed up and swaying outside, made people
want to yell the truth about themselves to anyone
who'd listen, but no one heard.

SAEED JONES[1]

In July 2012, *Forbes* ran an article about Marissa Mayer which began: 'Did Marissa Mayer just receive the job offer of a lifetime or did she just ascend to the pinnacle of the Glass Cliff? That's the question that will be answered over the next several months as Mayer takes over as CEO of Yahoo.'[2]

Five years later, when, after a tumultuous period as the struggling internet giant's leader, Mayer stepped down from her role – amid widespread reports that she had been left 'tarnished' – it seemed that the question had been answered.[3]

But how did her story begin?

After joining Google as their twentieth employee and staying in the business for thirteen years, Marissa Mayer accepted a role as the incoming CEO of Yahoo, a choice which she said was 'reasonably easy' to make. When she had first joined Google, the business would carry out surveys, and 'people didn't understand the difference between Yahoo and the Internet.' Yahoo was, according to Mayer, 'one of the best brands on the Internet.'[4]

Announcing her appointment to the role, *The New York Times* said, 'Marissa Mayer, one of the top executives at Google, will be the next chief of Yahoo, making her one of the most prominent women in Silicon Valley and corporate America.'[5]

However, despite being a household name, Yahoo had not had an easy ride for the previous few years.

In its article announcing Mayer's appointment, *Forbes* ran a piece saying that 'Yahoo, to put it politely, is something of a troubled concern. The company's been an Internet has-been for years, with a stock price to match that assertion.'[6]

Business Insider pointed out that Yahoo's apps for Android and iPhone were 'embarrassing', adding that, 'while competitors took months or just weeks' to update and refresh their products, Yahoo took 'years'.[7]

Forbes and Business Insider weren't alone in their poor characterization of the business; although *The New York Times* acknowledged that Yahoo had once been 'a pioneering Internet company that helped shape the industry in the 1990s', it conceded that, by the time Mayer stepped in, the business was struggling to remain relevant.[8] Facebook and Google had established themselves as 'web giants', while Yahoo had 'struggled to create a distinct strategy, even though its audience remains among the largest on the Internet.' As a result, Yahoo was facing the prospect of laying off thousands of employees in a bid to stymie financial losses. 'The big question', the article said, 'is whether Ms. Mayer – or anyone – can help Yahoo regain its former stature.'[9]

From the start, it was clear that Mayer would have her work cut out turning the fortunes of the business around.

Yahoo's period of difficulty, and its struggle to find stability and market fit, was reflected in a period of tumultuous leadership successions. If we include interim CEOs, Mayer was the fifth person to hold the position in a period of less than twelve months,[10] with her predecessor spending less than four months in the job before being ousted[11] after concerns were raised that his resume may have been 'less than accurate'[12] (which he has since referred to as an 'inadvertent error').

Despite the clear challenges from the outset, Mayer took on the role, and Yahoo rolled out the (literal) purple carpet for her arrival and decorated the office with posters of her face and the word *HOPE*.[13]

While the risk was clear from the start, some believed stepping into the CEO role was a strategic move for Mayer, and one worth making. As *Forbes* put it: 'Mayer certainly has reason to take the risk [. . .] Many observers believed that, while publicly prominent, Mayer had gone as far as she was going to go for the foreseeable future at Google. Moreover, Yahoo is considered such a mess by so many people, it's unlikely Mayer will accrue much – if any – blame if she fails to turn things around. Conversely, if she can pull a turnaround off, Mayer will be a superstar.'[14]

Unfortunately, this wasn't quite the way things played out.

During her time as the leader of Yahoo, Mayer was able to make some positive changes. 'Within months,' Businesses Insider wrote, 'Yahoo was launching products at a pace it hadn't hit in more than a decade. Within a year, Yahoo was winning awards and praise from the press for its product design. By the summer of 2013, tens of thousands of people were applying for Yahoo jobs every quarter. Yahoo finally had a team of hundreds working on apps for smartphones.'[15]

She rebooted various products, sunset others, and acquired a huge forty-one start-ups.[16]

But the role was not smooth sailing for Mayer. She faced endless scrutiny and criticism during her time as the CEO of the internet giant. Like Karren Brady, she was criticized for the length of her maternity leave (both leaders were criticized for how short, rather than how long their breaks were. Brady took three days after the birth of her daughter;[17] Mayer reportedly returned to work after two weeks of maternity leave[18]). She was also criticized for 'refusing to dwell' on sexism in the workplace,[19] for 'trying to be Steve Jobs'[20] and for being overly didactic, with employees reportedly being told they needed to do things 'because Marissa said so'.[21] The criticisms were endless.

And some of them were well deserved.

In 2013, under Mayer's leadership, Yahoo suffered a huge data breach in which customers' passwords, private messages and personal information were stolen.[22] At the time, the breach was thought to have impacted a billion Yahoo customers' accounts, but, in 2017, Verizon (who had become the owner of the Yahoo business) confirmed that the breach had impacted all three billion of Yahoo's users' accounts.[23]

This wasn't the only difficulty under Mayer's watch as CEO. While at Yahoo, Mayer made bets on several acquisitions that failed to provide the hoped-for boost to the business.[24] 'During her tenure, she bought 53 companies for more than $2.3 billion, the vast majority of which have had their personnel absorbed into Yahoo while their products have been killed,' said analyst Dan Olds.[25]

The question of staffing had been in discussion before Mayer arrived and was only exacerbated by the influx of staff absorbed by the business after mergers. In the early days of Mayer being in role, the board had made it clear that not only were they in favour of making significant staffing cuts, but they believed it to be necessary and essential to dramatically cut roles, slashing head-count in the business by between 35 and 50 per cent.[26]

Mayer disagreed.

Despite this, early in her tenure she discovered that, prior to her arrival, plans had begun to be put in place to build partner-ships with external brands in order to outsource work, thus reducing internal headcount.

Not only that, she also quickly discovered that another of her predecessors, who had only remained in the role for four months, had put in place a project that would, according to Business Insider, see Yahoo 'reduce its number of data centres from 31 to six and its workforce of 15,000 employees and 3,000 contractors by as much as a third.' This plan had not been kept confidential from team members. In fact, 'hundreds of Yahoo employees were told that eventually they were going to be fired, but not just yet.'[27]

Despite the fact that reducing the firm's headcount by thou-sands was very much what was expected from Mayer as a leader, it was a change she refused to make.[28] Instead, she reportedly told the board that 'layoffs of any kind, let alone 35 per cent to 50 per cent cuts, would be too damaging for employee morale' and that 'Yahoo was going to need all the talent it could find to turn around, and she didn't want to risk putting good people on the street.'[29]

Understandably – both because of the poor public perception of the business and the looming threat of mass layoffs – when Mayer joined Yahoo, morale was low, with reports indicating that the business's offices were empty for the weekend by 4.30 p.m. on most Thursday afternoons. Mayer battled this dwindling morale by putting in place a weekly meeting with all staff on Friday afternoons, called FYI, which was intended to bring 'radical transparency' to the struggling business and its demotivated employees by encouraging them to ask challenging questions of the businesses leadership – even about confidential topics – and have them answered in a live weekly forum by either Mayer herself or one of her senior leadership team members. The meeting was, in part, a response to a long-held complaint by Yahoo's employees, who felt their leadership lacked communication and transparency, meaning staff were forced to learn about what management was planning by 'reading the press.'[30]

Unsurprisingly, a lot of the questions raised during FYI sessions related to job security. Mayer tried to soothe concerns at a meeting in 2012, by saying, 'As of right now, we're not looking at layoffs. We're looking at stabilizing the organization. I can't make a promise that there won't be a change in that in the future, but as of right now, there's no active planning or conversations going on.'[31]

FYI sessions seemed to be adding value to the business, providing a much-needed bridge between senior management and the employees who had felt left in the dark up to that time.

Going against the expectations of Yahoo's board was a risky decision, one that led to increased scrutiny on Mayer. Rather than slashing headcount as expected – which would have seen whole teams being exited from the business regardless of individual members' performances – Mayer instead chose to focus on improving employee performance, introducing quarterly performance reviews (or QPRs).*

One week, in late 2013, an employee asked if they could submit questions anonymously for an upcoming FYI session, a request that Mayer agreed to. According to Business Insider, 'When the questions came in, they were so brutal that Mayer decided not to wait until a Friday to address them.'[32] The most up-voted anonymous questions were all about the QPRs – which were heavily criticized by some for introducing unnecessary competition between employees in the business and discouraging top performers from working together.

Although Mayer tried to explain the logic behind the QPRs system, tensions with the staff remained high.

In 2014, Mayer announced Yahoo's 'lowest quarterly earnings figures for a decade.'[33] This led to one analyst suggesting that Yahoo no longer made sense as a stand-alone, independent business, arguing that, instead, one of tech's 'Big Four' (Apple, Amazon, Facebook or Google) should acquire it. This suggestion wasn't made as a result of a single poor performance report. It was noted that, although Yahoo had a market value of $33 billion at that point, it also had a stake in the Chinese business Alibaba worth $37 billion, meaning that, 'if you subtracted that position, the entirety of Yahoo's core business, all its web products and content sites, actually had a market valuation of negative $4 billion.'[34] In this 'sum-of the-parts valuation', the business which Mayer had once believed the general public couldn't differentiate from the internet itself could be said to be worth 'less than nothing.'[35]

It might be the best solution, the analyst suggested, to find a

---

* Mayer had learned the OKRs (objectives and key results) system for employee management and performance measurement at Google, rebranding them for Yahoo as quarterly performance reviews (or QPRs), a performance management system still recognizable in one form or another in most big tech businesses to this day. In this system, managers ranked their team's performance by quartiles against a bell curve of their colleagues' scores.

buyer for Yahoo who would 'sell off its Asian assets and absorb its business units', an approach that would 'make a lot of money for Yahoo's shareholders . . . even if it meant gutting the company and losing Mayer as CEO after only two years'.[36] It was an approach favoured by the board, one of whom wrote in a letter to Mayer that, should she decide to retain the business's stake in Alibaba and pursue 'large acquisitions and/or a cash-rich split, both of which have been speculated', such actions 'would be a clear indication to us that significant leadership change is required at Yahoo'.[37]

Once again, Mayer would take a risk and go against the expectations of the board. Even though Yahoo had already sold half its shares in Alibaba back to the parent company prior to Mayer's arrival, in a deal where the shares were valued at $13 a piece, Mayer didn't succumb to board pressure to sell the business's remaining stake. As it happened, two years later, Alibaba had a record-breaking IPO, with the value of shares quickly reaching $68 at the end of day-one trading, before rocketing up to $181[38] – earning Yahoo back its initial investment several times over.[39]

Regardless of the success or failure of her decision-making, Mayer had to contend with constant press scrutiny and ongoing challenges from 'activist investors' on the board throughout her time as the leader of Yahoo. She regularly battled calls for her resignation as 'Yahoo's core business failed to pick up', members of the senior leadership team left and the business continued to make expensive acquisitions that failed to provide a return (including the billion-dollar buyout of social-media giant Tumblr).[40]

Mayer would also come under fire for business expenses, 'including $108 million a year for free food for employees and a $7 million end-of-year bash to ring in 2016'. This criticism was particularly stinging since, despite her reluctance to lose staff, 'more than 2,000 job cuts came in 2015 and 2016'.[41]

In 2015, telecommunications giant Verizon launched a multi-billion-dollar takeover of Yahoo. A year later, soon after the merger was complete, Mayer stepped down from her role as Yahoo's CEO and from the business's board.[42]

Speaking about her tenure within the business, one analyst commented: 'She was poorly matched to the job from day one [. . .] It wasn't that she didn't work hard. She just lacked the needed skills to execute a turnaround, and the Yahoo board was no apparent help, either.'[43]

◆　　◆　　◆

Taking on a new role in a business is an exciting moment. Stepping into a new position, particularly one in leadership, is usually the culmination of years of work, expertise and experience – and the cause of much-deserved celebration. In most cases, we enter new roles full of excitement and passion – ready to make our mark and establish ourselves in the next step of our professional journey. The world, at this point, is our oyster. Or at least that's how it should feel.

It might be for this reason that so much of our cultural discussion about female career advancement has been satisfied with stopping at the Glass Ceiling – if we acknowledge the existence of that barrier, we are then able to build our own imagined narratives about those pioneering women who do manage to break through it. Not filling in the details beyond that point allows us to picture a new leader flourishing in an environment where her upward trajectory knows no bounds, and the sky is the limit.

But, unfortunately, that is very often not the case. All too frequently, the reality of what happens next is the story of the precarious position of the Glass Cliff, where female leaders are set up to fail, through no fault of their own, before they've even begun.

I don't want to sound like the bearer of bad news. I had such high hopes about the next stage of female career advancement to begin with. In fact, *I* first discovered the existence of the Glass

Cliff when I was looking for examples of success – shining little jewels that I could hold up and glint in the sun as proof that, with enough willpower, determination – and maybe a bit of luck – women in the workplace could ascend and be successful in the most senior seats of power, proving our prowess and opening up the doors for future generations of under-represented leaders to walk through more easily.

My approach and expectations were flawed for two reasons.

Firstly, the burden for change should never be laid at the feet of those who are facing the greatest marginalization. Just as we know better than to expect Black and Global Majority people to 'solve' racism, while simultaneously suffering from its systemic, often life-threatening impacts, framing female progression within the expectation of increased 'willpower or determination' is never going to be the solution to overcoming systemic bias, prejudice and sexism. As we'll come to see, that mistake is essentially how we've got into this position in the first place – because, in individualistic societies like the UK and the US, the perception that all of our successes and failures are ours and ours alone has played a big part in limiting our ability to recognize, tackle or build a shared language around the experience of the Glass Cliff for too long.*

The second reason my initial thinking was flawed was because,

---

* Individualistic cultures are those in which the needs and desires of individuals are given a greater worth and emphasis than those of the group. Those of us who live in such cultures are more likely to report that independence, competition, personal freedom, individual choice and personal achievement are highly valued, and so the needs of individuals shape social behaviour to a greater degree than the needs of larger groups.

We are more likely to believe in ideas such as being 'self-made' and see individual successes or failures as ours and ours alone, rather than within a context of wider societal factors.

Research suggests that the most individualistic cultures are the US, Australia, Great Britain, Canada and the Netherlands, in that order. Whereas the most collectivist cultures are said to be Venezuela, Colombia, Pakistan, Peru and Taiwan.

although some stories of stratospheric success do exist, they are few and far between – much more so than I had hoped or realized. What I found instead, time after time, was a story of an *almost* success. Or a *temporary* success. Or, worst of all, a crashing fall from an impossible position on an invisible cliff, as female leaders repeatedly found themselves being put into leadership positions that they were destined to fail in before they even began, despite their best efforts.

Wreaking Havoc

In 2003, *The Times* in the UK ran an article on the front page of their business section with the headline 'Women on board: a help or a hindrance?', written by journalist Elizabeth Judge.[44] In her article, Judge put forward evidence which she claimed showed that those FTSE 100 companies in the UK that had appointed women to positions on their boards had since suffered from 'poor stock-market performance', losing both money and value. Judge particularly noted that those businesses which performed best in the Female FTSE Index* performed *especially* poorly on the stock market.

The tone of the reporting is strange and seems to relish the opportunity to debunk the 'myth' that women can be successful leaders or board members.

The article begins:

> SO MUCH for smashing the Glass Ceiling and using their unique skills to enhance the performance of Britain's biggest companies. The march of women into the country's boardrooms is not always triumphant – at least in terms of share price performance.
>
> Analysis of FTSE 100 shares shows that companies that decline to embrace political correctness by installing women

---

* The FFI, which ranks FTSE 100 companies in terms of the number of women on their boards.

on the board perform better than those that actively promote sexual equality at the very top.

Judge's article, which has since been truncated and all but removed from the *Times*' website, asserts that the presence of women in the boardroom has 'wreaked havoc on companies' performance and share prices', before concluding that women are in fact bad for business and that 'corporate Britain might well be better off without women on board'.[45]

It's a weird tone to want to take.

Nonetheless, it's an interesting assertion and, if it's true, it's absolutely worth both researching and reporting on.

However, in every important way, Judge's reporting of the findings misses the mark, something that researchers Michelle Ryan and Alex Haslam – who would later go on to coin the term the Glass Cliff – would find. Galvanized by having seen and doubted the validity of Judge's piece, they started to dig into the data in order to find, and tell, the *real* story of women's journeys to leadership positions and the impact they have on businesses once in place.

The main difficulty with Judge's telling of the story of women 'wreaking havoc' in boardrooms across the land is simply that the *beginning* of the story is missing – a very important omission. Without the context that the start of the story gives us, the reporting very much sounds as though we women have stomped our little stilettoed heels up to board tables, taken a seat, looked around and whispered to ourselves, 'Oh, god – I actually have no idea what I'm doing here.'

But that's absolutely not the case, as we can see when we take the time to examine what's happening in those businesses *just before* the arrival of women into these roles – something Judge had failed to consider in her piece for *The Times*. In this context, a much clearer and more interesting story begins to open up before us, which is both startling and essential to our understanding of the situation.

And that's what we're here to discuss.

What we see when we take that slightly more zoomed-out view, when we pull back the curtain just enough to peep at what's actually going on behind the scenes, is just how poorly these businesses were performing *before* the appointment of their new female leaders and board members – and just what circumstances are likely to be at play *before* women are given the opportunity to show their professional leadership capabilities.

What we can see is that, all too often, women have found themselves isolated, unsupported, hyper-visible and left in charge of failing.

The sky's the limit?

We need to talk about that hyper-visibility, because much of the rhetoric around the appointment of women to leadership roles is triggered by the fact that they're visibly different. A major reason why female leaders may feel hyper-visible when they break through the Glass Ceiling and take on senior roles is because the chances of them becoming an 'only' in the space increases.*

I'm sure this is a familiar experience for many of us who have stepped outside our comfort zones and challenged preconceived gendered expectations of the limits of our capabilities. Those women who have found themselves in this position will recognize the feeling of coming to realize that, while you know you're just you, others might see you as something much bigger and more visible than that. They may perceive you as a proxy for everyone like you, and so see your personal successes, or failures, as indicative of the abilities of the whole group you've come to represent in their minds.

---

* The first or only person like themselves – in terms of a characteristic such as gender, race, sexuality etc. – to occupy a space or to currently be in a similar position within the organization.

Suddenly, these women have, or feel they have, the future success and prospects of *all* potential female leaders resting on their shoulders – a huge pressure, and one which can quickly make new under-represented leaders feel as though there's a lot more at stake than they bargained for.

We already know that senior leadership roles tend to skew heavily towards both whiteness and maleness in demographic representation, so there is a strong chance that a woman taking on a role at that level may find herself to be the first and the only female to operate in that space. As Dr Jen Welter, a former professional football player and gold medallist, who became the first female coach in NFL history, noted at a panel event in 2023: 'When you're a "first", that inherently means "only" [. . .] I wanted to ensure that, as the first, I was not the last.' For her, this choice 'means being visible, it means being vocal and it means sticking your foot in a door to make sure other people get there.'[46]

Looking around, realizing we're breaking new ground, we often feel the need to perform as well as possible, not just for ourselves and our personal reputation, or sense of success, but to make sure we're not responsible for the door slamming behind us before anyone else has had the opportunity to break through alongside us.

Which is a huge weight to carry.

But it's one that trailblazing female leaders have taken on, for the benefit of us all, despite what some might have us believe.

BUT, WHAT ABOUT . . . ?

For many of us, growing up in an era with films like *The Devil Wears Prada* or *Mean Girls*, we've been taught to see female competition, particularly in the world of work, not only as something that's unavoidable, but as something that can be desirable – pushing and motivating women to be the best of the best, no matter the cost. And so, if your personal individualism is high, this might all seem a bit ... *meh*, to you. Of course, being an only can be difficult for some people, but maybe you feel like, if you were able to be in that position, you'd absolutely smash it out of the park. And who knows? Maybe you're right. But I do want to spend a moment to take a closer look at onlys and the reality of their experiences.

- Twenty per cent of women say they are often the only woman or one of the only women in the room at work: in other words, they are onlys. This is twice as common for senior-level women, where around 40 per cent are onlys.

- Women who are onlys are more likely to stand out in the spaces they find themselves in, and to be seen by others as a proxy for all women. They report feeling 'heavily scrutinized, held to a higher standard, on guard and left out' – all of which has a negative impact on their mental health.

- Those women who are onlys at work report suffering from a greater number of workplace microaggressions: more than 80 per cent of onlys face microaggressions at work vs 64 per cent of women as a whole.

- Women who are onlys are twice as likely as other women 'to be asked to prove their competence', are 100 per cent more likely to be mistaken for someone more junior and are about twice as likely to be subjected to degrading remarks at work.

- Women who are onlys are twice as likely to be subject to sexual harassment in their careers.

- Women who are onlys are 150 per cent more likely to think about leaving their jobs.

This is all increased for Black and Global Majority women, physically disabled women, and gay and bisexual women.[47]

Women are put in charge of failing

When businesses are looking to appoint a new leader, those that opt to appoint a woman are likely to be in the midst of a very different set of circumstances than those that appoint a male leader – a difference which shows us that, while talent, aptitude and ability are genderless, access to opportunity seems to be less so.*

When Michelle Ryan and Alex Haslam investigated and analysed the performance of businesses in the time immediately prior to appointing a female leader, what they found was shocking.[48]

They found that, in times of general financial downturn, the companies that appointed female senior leaders had already 'experienced consistently poor performance in the months preceding the appointment.' This meant that 'women were more likely than men to be placed in positions already associated with poor company performance.'[49]

Or, to put it a different way, they found that women were more likely to achieve leadership positions in businesses that were *already* known to be in a period of difficulty – when there was a greater degree of risk – making their chances of success less likely and more difficult to achieve, and associating them with a perception of failure before they'd even begun.

---

* Two important things to know about the Glass Cliff phenomenon:
1. It's important to be clear that the Glass Cliff is a phenomenon that has expanded since its initial discovery, and we can now clearly recognize that the experience isn't only applicable to gender, as we can see the same outcomes playing out for racially marginalized men who are under-represented in leadership spaces.
2. The phenomenon has also been shown not to be limited to corporate settings; in fact, the same experience has been shown to play out for coaches of sports teams, where coaches who are racially marginalized are more likely than white coaches to be 'promoted' to losing teams, and in the world of politics. However, for this book, our focus will primarily be on the gendered experience of the Glass Cliff in corporate workplace settings.

This means that the relatively poor performances of those companies that Judge mentioned, which she claimed were the result of 'political correctness' in board-level appointments and a demonstration of women's inherent lack of leadership qualities, were actually very likely to be, at least in part, the result of the businesses' pre-existing performance.

This finding meant it wasn't that women were responsible for financial downturns of businesses when they became leaders, but rather that periods of financial downturn within businesses were often responsible for the appointment of women leaders.*

And so the Glass Cliff was defined.

What exactly is the Glass Cliff?

The Glass Cliff is the phenomenon that shows us that female leaders are much more likely to be given the opportunity to step into leadership roles within businesses or organizations that are *already* in a *prolonged* period of poor performance.

Although a dip in valuation or stock performance has been the measure of a badly performing company that we've used up to now, it's important to know that a 'poor performance' period could be a whole number of things, such as a high-profile scandal or a reputational risk where the tarnish is likely to be passed on to the new leader.[50] Whatever the difficulty is, we see those businesses that are *already* experiencing prolonged periods of difficulty being suddenly much more likely to appoint a female leader to their most senior leadership roles.

This means that 'women are selected for leadership positions

---

* In a piece of much later research, in which Ryan and Haslam looked back at a decade of research into the phenomenon, they noted, 'This [tendency for women to be appointed in moments of crisis or difficulty], indeed, may be one reason why – in the wake of the 2007–2008 Global Financial Crisis – more women have secured more top positions', which is an interesting suggestion.

ahead of similarly qualified men when (*and only when*) there is a high risk of organizational failure'.[51]

Although Ryan and Haslam's original research came from the University of Exeter, I want to be clear that this issue isn't limited to the experiences of women in the UK. Researchers from the University of Utah subsequently conducted a similar study in which they looked at CEO changes in Fortune 500 companies in the USA over a fifteen-year period – so a huge data set – and what they found showed exactly the same.[52] Those companies that appointed under-represented leaders were more likely to be in a prolonged period of some form of crisis than those who appointed white men to the role of CEO.

And so it's reasonable to say that, when women take on roles within businesses that are at risk of organizational failure, their chances of being successful in making meaningful change are limited, and their chances of being seen to fail, and either falling or being pushed off that cliff, are heightened through no fault of their own.

When we add to this the fact that women are usually given less time in their new leadership roles to succeed or fail,[53] and that they are also less likely to be given the tools or support needed to turn failing businesses into well-performing ones,[54] we can begin to see some of the difficulties that we're up against, and why we have so few success stories of women not only taking on the most senior leadership roles, but thriving once in place.

Now, of course, the Glass Cliff doesn't happen in the event of every appointment of a female leader. Not every woman is appointed to lead when a business is already in some kind of trouble beyond her causing – some women step into fantastic roles at well-per-forming businesses where they are supported to make a great success. It's also the case that some men in leadership roles have jobs that are risky assignments. The assertion of the discussion is not contradicting these facts at all. What the Glass Cliff phenom-enon does show us, though, is the *likelihood* of different groups finding themselves stepping into these high-risk positions in struggling organizations – something that research shows us is almost twice as likely to happen to female, rather than male, leaders.[55]

BUT, WHAT ABOUT . . . ?

Before we get into talking deeply about the Glass Cliff itself, I want to be really clear – because there will be some people who point to the fact that, although in small numbers, women *are* represented at a senior leadership level, and so surmise that the Glass Cliff phenomenon is unfounded or untrue. These are the same type of people who said that racism must not exist, because Barack Obama was able to become president of the United States.

To put it clearly and simply – that's just not how it works.

To become a Glass Cliff situation, not only is the context of a role appointment important, but there also needs to be a lot of different and seemingly disconnected elements at play, simultaneously (which we'll discuss in the next chapter). That is to say, there is nothing psychological or biological, and nothing that makes up an essential part of business life, that means the Glass Cliff is the inevitable end to a woman's experience when she steps into even the most senior roles. Not unless the conditions have already been set in motion (which they disproportionately have been for the appointments of women and racially marginalized people).

Researchers into this topic draw a parallel with global warming: noting that a cold winter shouldn't lead us to dismiss global warming or believe it to be untrue. In the same way, the fact that there are women who have avoided the precarious position of the Glass Cliff doesn't mean it doesn't exist – it just means the context and determining factors in that instance led to a more secure appointment.

The aim of those researchers (both those investigating the Glass Cliff, and global warming), as well as the aim of this book, is not to prove that the phenomenon is real, but to look at the contexts and instances within which it occurs, and what can be done to mitigate both its likelihood, and its impact.

Understanding the phenomenon

The Glass Cliff, as a phenomenon, exists in practice when women and other under-represented leaders are appointed into leadership roles. Many long-term studies have looked at and recognized its existence in high-profile businesses, in multiple countries around the world. And yet, because women remain so under-represented in these professional positions, even studies like the piece from the University of Utah, which looked at a fifteen-year data set, can be somewhat limited in their sample sizes. And so we can learn a lot about the Glass Cliff, and our own bias towards it, by looking at hypothetical situations and thought experiments, three of which we'll discuss now.

Experiment 1:

In 2007, Ryan and Haslam teamed with a third researcher, Tom Postmes, to conduct an experiment.[56] Participants were given the details of a hypothetical leadership job vacancy in a business that was said to be either performing well or poorly. They were also given descriptions of three candidates for the leadership role (the roles being recruited for in the study included a financial director in a struggling company, a defence lawyer for a 'highly criticized case', and a political candidate for a hard-to-win seat): 'a male and a female candidate who were equally well-qualified, and a third male candidate who was clearly not suitable for the job.' Just as the real-world research had shown, the study's participants felt that the female candidate was 'more appointable when organizational performance was said to be declining, than when it was improving.'

Experiment 2:

Harvard Business Review also conducted their own hypothetical research into the Glass Cliff phenomenon.[57] In one of their studies, 119 college students were asked to read two newspaper articles about an organic food company, whose CEO would soon retire. For one set of the students, the outgoing CEO was said to be a man, and for the other, she was portrayed as a woman. Also, in the articles that half of the students were asked to read, the performance of the company was listed as poor (shops closing, team members being let go), while the other half read about the business being successful and growing. After reading the articles, the students were asked to pick between two equally qualified candidates for the role – one male and one female. Of the students who had read the scenario about a successful flourishing company with an existing male CEO, 62 per cent chose a male to take on the new position. However, of those who had read that the business was struggling, only 31 per cent opted for the male candidate, with 69 per cent choosing to bring in a new female leader in that instance. For those who had read about a business with an existing female CEO, that percentage remained the same. As *HBR* put it: 'The Glass Cliff disappeared'.

Experiment 3:

Our final experiment also comes from the *Harvard Business Review*.[58] In this experiment, 122 students read an article about a supermarket which, again, was either struggling or performing well, and where, again, the CEO was about to be replaced. The students then read descriptions of a male and a female candidate, before being asked to make their selection of who would make the best new CEO. They found that those who believed the business was struggling were more likely to appoint a new leader with traditionally female traits, while those who thought they were discussing a well-performing business were more likely to pick a male successor. This meant that the majority (67 per cent) of participants selected a man to head the successful company, while most (63 per cent) thought the woman should take over the company in crisis.

Of course, as well as theories and experiments, there are also plenty of real-world, lived-experience examples of the Glass Cliff playing out in real time, as you'll find at the start of each chapter in this book. Sadly, Zoe Cruz and Marissa Mayer are far from alone in their experiences.

Going into this chapter, I said I didn't want to be the bearer of bad news, so you might wonder why I'm telling you all of this. It certainly doesn't seem like good news! But I really believe that it's important to start this conversation because, once we know what we're up against, we can begin to make the necessary changes. Or at least we can begin to see our own experiences in a better, and less personal, light.

So, now we've had a look at some of what's going on, let's spend a little while talking about *why* that might be.

BUT, WHAT ABOUT . . . ?

There might be some people who can be sympathetic to women stepping into new leadership roles under difficult circumstances, but feel that, despite the odds being stacked against them, a leader's role is to change the fortunes of a company. And so, they might argue, anything that happens before a leader joins is irrelevant to the opportunities for, and expectations of, success once in-role.

It's unreasonable to expect someone taking over the leadership of a poorly performing company to be just as successful as someone who is stepping into the equivalent role in a well-performing company – the ground that needs to be made up, and the morale that needs to be rebuilt, are tall orders to ask of even the most experienced leader.

That being said, initial research into the Glass Cliff did find that, despite the businesses taken over by women being much more likely to already be in a period of poor performance, 'in a time of a general financial downturn, companies that appointed a woman actually experienced a marked *increase* in share price after the appointment.'[59] This finding is backed up by further evidence showing that, 'during a period of stock-market decline, companies which appointed women to their boards were more likely to have experienced consistently poor month-on-month stock-market performance in the period preceding the appointment than companies which appointed men. However, in the three-month period after appointments had been made, this difference was attenuated and the stock returns for companies which had appointed women were no different from those which had appointed men.'[60]

It's also interesting to learn that, even when businesses do perform well by objective measures such as accountancy once a woman has been appointed to their board, research shows that they are *still* perceived to be underperforming by subjective measures such as stock performance, which relies on human interactions and perceptions.[61] In fact, more research shows us that 'companies with male-only boards enjoyed a valuation premium of 37 per cent relative to firms with a woman on their board', which can lead to the company's devaluation by investors.[62] (Companies with at least one woman on their board were valued by investors at 121 per cent of the book value of their assets, while those with all-male boards were valued at 166 per cent of their book value.) The fact is that these perceptions don't accurately portray the reality of the business's performance.

So things are actually either fine or great, depending on which study you look at, even though we might not see them as being that way. Which, with the odds being stacked as they were, is pretty amazingly good going, if you ask me.

Why does the Glass Cliff happen?

It's very tempting to want to point fingers, now that we've discovered this new and often unspoken barrier in the pathway of women in leadership. Once we know there's a problem, it's natural to want someone to blame as a way to focus our efforts and energies in order to make change. But one thing about this phenomenon that makes it unusual is that it seems to be largely subconscious – not really associated with explicit bad intent from anyone perpetuating it, but much more linked to our culturally held understandings and expectations of gender roles. This is why it's important to remember that, when we see the Glass Cliff playing out, it's not as a result of any idea of biological sex, but of culturally curated gender norms and stereotypes, as we saw with the students in the second *Harvard Business Review* experiment above, since they were assessing suitability based on gendered traits rather than identities. Let's dig into some reasons that might explain the existence of the Glass Cliff, and why we're too often setting women up to fail.

Think manager, think male; think crisis, think female

The 'think manager, think male' phenomenon is robust and well researched.[63] It simply means that, when the majority of us are asked to imagine a leader or a manager, we quickly conjure up in our minds the image of a man. And, really, that's unsurprising, since, all through our lives, the pages of our children's books, history books and business papers have been stuffed full of the names and faces of men who have taken up space in leadership positions. We often talk about people being under-represented, but we talk a lot less about the inverse; it's important to remember that, for one group to be under-represented, another has to be over-represented. And, in business settings, men in leadership positions have been *so* over-represented that they have become our shared mental shorthand for those who are 'best suited' to hold those roles. The trope is so firmly established in our minds that we have come to associate those qualities we think of as stereotypically male with those that we think of as making a traditionally 'good leader' – qualities such as dominance, confidence, independence and competitiveness.[64]

That is, of course, unless there's a crisis. Because newer research seems to suggest that, while 'think manager, think male' still holds true in most instances, in times of crisis, we might see it being replaced by 'think crisis, think female'.[65] But, why would that be?

Expectations of soft skills

It might be that, when a business is in a moment of difficulty, navigating a period of poor performance, most likely with a less-than-excited-and-enthusiastic general workforce (it's hard to stay motivated when things are going badly and your job feels under threat), our perceptions of what the business needs, and so in turn the qualities of leadership that we look for in someone stepping into the role, undergo a shift. This shift in our thinking means that what have traditionally been seen as lower-value and more feminine qualities, such as 'emotional sensitivity, strong interpersonal skills, morale-building capabilities and a collaborative leadership style', suddenly take on a premium, where they have otherwise been dismissed or even been seen as a liability (think of the old-fashioned misogynistic stereotype of an erratic female leader – overly emotional and unable to regulate herself professionally, womb running wild around her body).[66]

This is backed up by the finding that, when women do break through the Glass Ceiling and take up the most senior leadership positions in businesses, they are likely to be appointed to lead in roles that involve a greater deal of working closely with others, e.g. in areas of personnel and human-resource management, rather than with production. In these roles, with their greater reliance on human interactions – as well as the additional emotional labour and potential for interpersonal conflict associated with them – an emotionally intelligent and collaborative skill set is essential.

Using Covid-19 as an example of a time in which even strong businesses found themselves struggling to navigate an uncertain future, we can see that senior women were consistently ranked and rated as better leaders by those they worked with – with their interpersonal skills of collaboration, communication and relationship-building making their teams feel understood and listened to, which in turn inspired trust and confidence in their leadership plans.[67]

Women make good scapegoats

Although women have been shown to make better leaders during times of crisis,[68] there is a caveat to that finding which becomes clear when we dig more deeply into 'think crisis, think female'. Follow-on research from Ryan and Haslam revealed that the stereotypically feminine traits that might lead to women being appointed to lead during times of business difficulty were especially well received 'when the manager was required to simply stay in the background and endure the crisis, or become a scapegoat for poor company performance', with the researchers noting that 'these findings are consistent with suggestions that women who are selected for Glass Cliff positions may be getting set up to fail'.[69]

I'd like to dig into that study for a moment.

Ryan and Haslam, in their roles as Glass Cliff researchers, wanted to learn more about the phenomenon in relation to the 'think crisis, think female' idea. They carried out an experiment in which participants were not only given details of a company in crisis, but were also given descriptions of what would be expected of the leader of the company during that crisis. The options were:

(a) to stay in the background and endure the crisis;
(b) to take responsibility for the inevitable failure (i.e., to act as a scapegoat);
(c) to manage people and personnel issues through the crisis;
(d) to be a spokesperson providing damage control;
(e) to take control and improve company performance.[70]

Participants in the study were then asked to rate stereotypically male and female characteristics in terms of their desirability in each of the contexts. What they found in this study was that, when leaders were expected to act as a spokesperson (d) or take control of the company to improve its performance (e), there was no bias towards bringing women or traditionally feminine characteristics into the leadership role.

However, when the leader was expected to quietly endure the crisis (a), act as a scapegoat and take personal responsibility (b), and particularly when the leader was expected to successfully manage people (c), the bias towards 'think crisis, think female' returned, and women were favoured for the opportunity, if you can call it that.

In summarizing this finding, the researchers said that this shows 'women are appointed to Glass Cliff positions not simply because they are thought to be able to turn things around, but rather because they are perceived to make good scapegoats or, more charitably, because they are perceived to have the appropriate skills to handle staffing issues that are likely to arise in times of crisis.'

This willingness to put women into positions where they are likely to be attributed unfair blame – not unlike what happened to Marissa Meyer – echoes the thoughts of Kristin J. Anderson, psychology professor at the University of Houston, who wrote that 'one possible reason for putting women in positions with greater risk of failure is that women may be seen as more expendable and better scapegoats.'[71]

In times of poor performance, then, like those in which we see the Glass Cliff playing out, it's very possible that women might be the preferred choice not because there's an expectation that we'll change the fortunes of a business, but because we are seen as being good people managers, who are also able to take the blame for organizational failures beyond our control,[72] and even those that happened before our arrival.[73]

Signalling a new direction for a struggling business

It might be that, when a business is in an extended period of difficulty and its fortunes don't seem to be changing, people who are responsible for the success of that business look for ways to signal that they are making a big change and moving in a bold new direction.[74]

This can be achieved quickly and efficiently by bringing in an under-represented leader, if the business hasn't been led by one before, which might go some way towards explaining why racially marginalized men also suffer from the Glass Cliff and why the phenomenon's impact seems to be negated when the business has historically already been headed up by a non-traditional leader (as in Experiment 2, above). Thekla Morgenroth, a researcher at Purdue University who looked into the phenomenon in 2020, explained to the BBC that 'the actual stereotypes or the attributes that you assume these groups have don't really matter. It's really just about, "Oh, they're different." It doesn't really matter how they're different as long as they're visibly different.'[75]

Women make good stopgaps

Another train of thought is that, when a business is struggling, appointing someone – even if you don't really believe in and aren't willing to support them – is better than doing nothing. And so women may be brought in during times of difficulty, without the expectation of being able to make transformational change, even if she does have the necessary skill sets, as something of a holding pattern. 'You just put them there until you have a better solution,' Clara Kulich, a researcher from the University of Geneva, said in an interview with the BBC, 'but you don't really believe in what they can actually do.'[76] This takes us back to the discussion of not being given the tools or time necessary to make real change – nor the investment, which companies are unlikely to make in leaders who they merely see as tiding them over until the right man for the job comes along.[77]

Making a win/win scenario

Speaking cynically – it's very possible that, if your business is in a prolonged period of poor performance, the most prudent thing you could do, and be seen to be doing, is to bring in an underrepresented leader. Someone unlike anyone you've tried in the position up to now. It could be that canny businesses know this, and the Glass Cliff is, at least in some ways, a result of them hedging their bets.

Think of it this way: if the business is in trouble, how it's been run, or who has been running it up to now, has not been working. And so, if you bring in someone completely different, a fresh set of eyes and a new perspective, you're likely to get one of two outcomes. Either their new way of thinking and working is successful and transforms the business, so long as you allow them the time and support to implement their changes (which is sadly often not the reality[78]) – in which case, great. Or – they don't. In which case, the new leader can be blamed for all of the problems and exited from the business – pushed off her Glass Cliff. The business is then able to return to the direction of an over-represented leader,[79] while still benefiting from the glow of having given a woman a go, like the inclusive and progressive* business they are.[80]

But, why does it matter?

Since learning about the Glass Cliff, I've made it my mission to tell as many people about it as I can, from doing the TED Talk on the topic to going into businesses, charities and even governmental bodies and departments to raise awareness and discuss solutions. And, while most of the time people are both intrigued and shocked to hear about the phenomenon, there have been occasional instances of dismissal.

That's not to say that people have challenged the idea that the phenomenon exists, or that it particularly impacts under-represented leaders – their responses don't tend to question the data so much as the idea that it matters. It's less a bold 'That can't be true' and more a disinterested 'Well . . . so what?'

When I dig into these people's responses more deeply, their question can usually be paraphrased as something like, 'I'm sure

---

* (The most bombastic side-eye possible. ☉☉)

it's very bad, but . . . really, why does it matter? We were meant to diversify, we were meant to give more people opportunities. That's what people said they wanted, and we've done it. So, as long as that's happening, why does any of the rest of this matter? Good leaders will be good no matter what, and, if not everyone is meant to be a leader, well, that's not really my problem.'

And that's where they're wrong. Because the Glass Cliff impacts all of us, not only the people who are bearing the brunt of its impact in their jobs.

It's natural for people to use the past to inform our expectations about the future – we all do it, and, while it's not foolproof at all, it's usually the best proxy we have for making informed decisions and guesses about how things will play out. And so, in a culture like ours, where we see so few female leaders being appointed, if an oversized proportion of those who we *do* see successfully rising in the ranks are battling conditions that mean they're being set up to fail before they even begin, we're creating an association between female leadership and failure, which will only make it harder and harder for women going forwards.

And so it matters, a lot, to *all* of us, if we ever want to really even out the playing field and build a working world that is the meritocracy we were sold.

Here are some of the reasons I think it matters the most.

Undermining the leadership potential of individual women

Of course, the people most directly impacted by the Glass Cliff are those who experience it directly – those people who have worked hard, broken through the Glass Ceiling and have both the ability and the opportunity to take on what should be the role of their dreams. Only for it to become the stuff of nightmares.

Research shows that, although women are more likely than men to take on leadership positions in high-risk environments, they are less likely to be given the support or the actual authority to make those positions successful,[81] and so they have on average a shorter time in these high-profile, high-risk leadership roles, with 38 per cent of female CEOs being fired from their positions versus 27 per cent of male CEOs.[82] Time and support in a role are essential for success, and, since women are pushed out at higher rates than men, they're not often given the necessary time to turn what could be a rocky start into a bright future, unlike their male counterparts.

Even though leaders in Glass Cliff situations have usually inherited the problems they are tasked with correcting, if they are not able to successfully and quickly resolve them and put a struggling business back onto its feet, research shows that, instead of remembering the position the business was in before she joined, people will hold the female leader fully responsible for the bad state of affairs. This means that she herself becomes 'synonymous with failure', which impacts her ongoing career opportunities.[83]

Research also shows us that, once a role becomes untenable and the female leader either chooses to leave or is pushed out, the explanations for the company's poor performance are more likely to focus on the perception of the 'individual traits and abilities of the leaders involved than on the situational and contextual factors' surrounding it. This means that, because women are disproportionately over-represented in precarious positions, they are also disproportionately the subject of unfair criticism and blame for negative outcomes, compared to their male counterparts, even when they are not the cause of the issue.[84]

This is something that we see evidence of when we look at who gets future opportunities to lead, and how often.

It might be reasonable to think that, if someone has a high-profile misadventure in business, it would be prudent to give them some time and space before reappointing them to a similar role in a new business, but we see that even this rate of reappointment looks different for men and women who have 'failed' in leadership. As Alison Cook, a Glass Cliff researcher, noted in an interview, 'They get these opportunities, and they're amazingly talented and extraordinary women, and if something goes wrong, I'm not seeing them get pulled back into another company.'[85]

BUT, WHAT ABOUT . . . ?

Some people, when they hear about female leaders having a higher likelihood of being pushed out of their roles, try to frame it as no bad thing. They reason that, 'Well, if the company has brought in a woman before, they'll probably do it again. After all, they've shown that they're open-minded, haven't they?' Unfortunately, this is very rarely the case. When we look at Fortune 500 companies as an example, we can see that, in reality, of 608 CEO transitions, an outgoing female CEO was only replaced by another woman in four instances.[86]

FOUR.

Rather than opening the door for another woman, the outcome of the Glass Cliff experience is usually a safe return to the 'norm' of traditional white male leadership. This is known as the Saviour Effect.[87]

The Saviour Effect is the phenomenon that means, when an under-represented CEO or leader leaves, they are more often than not replaced by a white male leader.[88] This signals to everyone, from investors to colleagues, shareholders to the media, that the business is back on track – and, importantly, back in a safe pair of hands.

Undermining the leadership potential of all women

As we've discussed, when people are onlys in spaces, particularly working spaces, they often find themselves to be significantly more visible and face the pressure of being expected to represent the entirety of their group. While this is an unfair, unrealistic and huge emotional burden to carry, it is still very much the case, and is a part of why the Glass Cliff does a disservice not only to the women experiencing the professional precariousness, but to all those who might be (lazily) lumped in with her.

When the examples we have of female leadership are disproportionately seen to be failures, without the understanding of the harsher context in which that female leader was brought in, the story that is then told about women's 'natural abilities' to lead only becomes worse and worse.

When two relatively rare things happen at the same time, such as a woman being appointed to lead a business and a business performing badly for a long period of time, research shows that, rather than viewing them as unconnected, separate things, we perceive them as being 'meaningfully related'.[89] Which means that instead of having two boxes in our heads . . .

1. This business is run by a woman
2. This business is performing badly

. . . we lump both unusual occurrences into a single box . . .

3. this female-led business is performing badly

. . . thereby creating a causation effect in our minds, rather than a correlation. This means that women who do take on these leadership positions may be in even greater danger of being blamed for negative outcomes that were initiated well before they started their new roles. And so those who make the selections for the next generation of leadership candidates will be unlikely to opt for a female, particularly in a business not already experiencing crisis.[90]

See it to be it

As well as making businesses unlikely to opt for female candidates once they have (incorrectly) established in their minds a causal link between female leadership and failure, the prevalence of the Glass Cliff also has an impact on the expectations and desires of those who would become the next generation of female leaders.

We all know the old adage that you have to see it to be it, and in recent years I've heard a lot of discussions about role models and how inspiring it is for young women to see these leaders taking on their rightful positions in leadership. I would argue, though, that seeing a stream of women struggle and then be branded as 'failures' isn't the kind of inspiration that the next generation is looking for.

Unfortunately, having an under-represented leader isn't always the boost we might imagine for those who share their identities at more junior levels of the business. Instead, it can cause some unexpected issues.

White men are mentally checking out for under-represented leaders

While I can't claim to *like* anything related to the Glass Cliff phenomenon and how it impacts and limits women's careers, there is one piece of research that I hate most of all. Which is not in any way to say it's bad research. It's good research. It's important research. But what it shows us is so important in continuing the story of the impact of the Glass Cliff, I sometimes wish I didn't know it.

Let me tell you what research shows happens to white male 'top managers' when they find themselves being led by a CEO who is anything other than *both* white and male like themselves. I first came across this while researching for my TED Talk on the Glass Cliff, and since then it has been the thing that's played on my mind most, and the thing I'm most frequently asked about in discussions of the phenomenon. As always, I'd gone in looking for a good story, a success story. Again, I was looking for a glimmer of hope, wanting to see teams rally round and support under-represented leaders, keeping them away from their Glass Cliff edges.

But that's not what I found.

This is what I found instead.

Rather than looking into what the experience of stepping into a CEO role is like for an under-represented leader, a piece of research from the University of Michigan looked at what the experience of having an under-represented leader (either by race or gender) stepping into the highest leadership role in a business was like for the white male managers who found themselves with a new boss.[91]

From the Lean In Foundation data that we've looked at, we can see that white males are the only group whose representation grows as the level of business gets more senior. This is to say, while every other group is more represented at lower-status levels of employment, with their representation shrinking as they become more senior, white men are the only group of whom there is a *higher* percentage in the most senior levels of business. And so their feelings, and the ways in which they interact with both one another and with a new leader when one steps into the role, are likely to play a huge part in the successes or failures of that leader. Especially since, as research notes, 'The lack of prior consideration of the reactions of top managers to the appointment of a minority-status CEO is especially noteworthy given that the direct reports of minority-status CEOs are likely to be disproportionately white males, with such demographic differences liable to significantly influence white managers' intrapsychic and behavioural responses.'[92]

The first thing the research found was that, when a non-traditional CEO is appointed – in the case of this research, either a Black and Global Majority person, or a woman – the white men who make up the majority of the senior management team are likely to view this new CEO as substantially different from themselves, as an out-group rather than an in-group member, since both race and gender play a large role in not only our own self-identities, but the immediate identities we associate with people when we meet them for the first time.[93] Building on existing research that shows we view 'out-group' people less positively and as comparatively less capable and effective than people who are more overtly similar to ourselves, these white male leaders are likely to use their own internal biases to make less-than-favourable judgements about their new leader's strategic leadership capabilities, potential effectiveness in their new role, and their performance. The researchers note that 'in addition to the "generic" intergroup biases just described, white male executives also tend to manifest negative biases specific to racial minorities and women and their leadership abilities. There is evidence that white males tend to look upon racial minorities and women as less qualified for and less effective in leadership positions, including executive leadership positions.'[94]

Now, if that were all, it would be unfortunate, but probably not the end of the world. Under-represented leaders would have an uphill battle, but maybe over time they would be able to turn the tide and 'prove themselves' to be worthy of their position. However, this is very much only the beginning of the story, and the impact of the mistrust and lack of support from these white male senior leaders is where the story gets really sticky.

So, aside from feeling cautious of their new leader, how else does this group behave when a non-traditional CEO steps into the role?

One of the biggest and most important things that happens in this scenario is that these white male leaders report feeling less able to 'personally identify' with the business they work for when the leader doesn't mirror back their identities of race or gender. Added to that, they also report feeling less 'personally invested' in the business, so they create distance, which means that their work performance and output begin to suffer as a result.

One reason for this could be an assumption that the new leader is the beneficiary of some kind of affirmative action, rather than being qualified to take on the role on their own terms, as a result of their proven merit. As the research notes:

> Intergroup bias also regularly manifests as a tendency to discount the achievements and career accomplishments of out-group members, with people tending to overstate the degree to which out-group members' successes are due to special treatment [. . .] Whites tend to believe that successful African Americans have succeeded in part due to preferential selection processes such as affirmative action; men tend to hold similar beliefs regarding the career successes of women. These predominantly subconscious assumptions will contribute further to the tendency for white males to underestimate the capabilities of a racial minority or female CEO.[95]

While they feel that leaders who are like themselves must have earned their roles, they are less likely to believe the same of those who differ from themselves in terms of either race or gender.

What also happens is that, once the new CEO is in place, white male managers are then found to have less favourable views of important aspects of their firm and its future prospects – because negative assessments of out-group members don't end at the personal. Instead, they routinely extend to judgements around the CEO's ideas, proposals and initiatives, meaning that this group of senior leaders is less 'bought in' to supporting and making successful the overall strategy that the new CEO is working to implement and deliver, negatively impacting their willingness to personally identify with the business they work for.[96]

Since there is an assumption that something other than merit has been instrumental in securing the most senior roles for women, it could be that female CEOs are seen as a risk by white male senior managers, and no one wants to be pulled over the edge of someone else's cliff. This is a self-preservation tactic from these managers, who may believe, consciously or subconsciously, that creating and maintaining distance between themselves and a leader who they perceive as being risky is the best tactic for their long-term career.

When we keep in mind what we have already seen about the businesses that appoint under-represented leaders – that they are much likelier than average to already be in a persistent period of some kind of crisis or poor performance – the impact of this is huge. Even the best leader isn't going to be able to turn the tide of a poorly performing business single-handedly. She needs her team, particularly her most senior team members, to be active advocates for both the business and her vision for it. And if her very presence, as a woman or racially marginalized person, prevents this buy-in from the start, her chances of being pushed off the Glass Cliff are raised before she's even had the chance to begin in earnest.

And, again, that would be a bad enough story if that were the end of it. But, again, sadly, it's not. Because there are other, equally unexpected consequences for businesses once an under-represented leader steps into a role, this time regarding how that impacts those who would become our next generation of non-traditional leaders.

I had expected to find evidence of a trickle-down effect for the more junior team members when an under-represented leader stepped into the business, not least because we know that the Glass Cliff can be mitigated by a business having a history of female leadership. If that's the case for leaders who follow under-represented CEOs, I thought, there must be some benefits for the more junior team members who are there at the same time as them. Unfortunately, that's not what the research shows us – at all.

What the research *does* show us is that, instead of being uplifted by having a CEO that mirrors their own identity, female or racially marginalized employees can actually suffer a negative impact, not because of that CEO's behaviours or aptitudes, but because of how having an under-represented CEO impacts on white male leaders' willingness to help others within the business.

The research shows us that the reduction in personal investment and identification with the business that white male senior managers experience when they have a non-traditional leader means that they become less likely to offer help – including, importantly, both task-related help and career assistance – to their colleagues and junior team members. This is of course an absolutely essential part of any manager's job.[97] Worse still, they don't stop offering this help to white male employees. It was found that their lower personal investment in the business and their reduced willingness to offer help and support to colleagues had particularly negative effects on fellow executives who were 'racial minorities' or women.

Could it really be true that, instead of having an uplifting, inspiring impact, out-group biases mean it actually disadvantages exactly those we'd hoped to see benefitting?

When I read this section of their paper, my heart sank:

Classic sociological work on status suggests that, when an individual member of a particular social group acquires a high-status position, the benefits can 'trickle down' to other members of the group who occupy lower-status positions. This study provides evidence for a kind of reverse . . . effect in which the appointment of an individual to a prominent high-status position can actually disadvantage other category members (i.e., fellow racial minority and female executives) who occupy lower status positions in the hierarchy, due to the biased responses of white male top managers [. . .] This tendency for white males to provide less help to their minority-status colleagues following the appointment of a female or a racial minority CEO is particularly unfortunate, given evidence that minority-status leaders already tend to be disadvantaged in receiving help from their peers.[98]

The Glass Cliff bites twice

I find this research to be absolutely heartbreaking, not least because these findings only go to show how biases mean the Glass Cliff bites twice. In distrusting a CEO who doesn't mirror them in terms of both whiteness and maleness, these top white male managers disengage from their companies and their working responsibilities within them, meaning the newly appointed non-traditional leader is going to have even more difficulty gaining the necessary support, buy-in and hard work from her team to turn a struggling company into a successful one – which pushes her ever closer to the edge of the cliff.*

And even that's not all, because not only does the professional output of these white male managers decline, they stop doing an essential element of any manager's duties – managing and developing their teams. But, as we've seen, they don't do that equally; instead, they are most likely to stop offering support and guidance to anyone in their team who is part of an under-represented group. Or, to put it a different way, anyone who isn't *both* white *and* male. Withholding time, attention, support and guidance from any group, but particularly groups that already struggle to gain sponsorship, can only disadvantage those individuals, who

---

* I'm sure you've heard of 'twice as hard for half as much'.

could have, with the proper (read: equal) provision of care and attention, risen through the ranks to take up positions as the next generation of leaders in their own right.

If there's one hopeful thing, it is this: just like everything else, this isn't a fact of nature. This is a fact of biases, social conditioning and expectations. And, don't get me wrong, those aren't easy things to undo. But it's also not impossible. Even small changes, such as making sure businesses avoid having an over-representation of white male managers (or any single homogeneous group) at the most senior levels, can mitigate the impact of this potential disengagement.

Since most C-level leaders are currently white men, it would be reasonable to presume that people from other racial and gender groups must be more used to working in businesses with leaders whose identities don't mirror their own in both, or even either, of those regards. And so their expectation of having their own identities mirrored back to them from the highest levels must be reduced.

In order to lessen the risk of disinvestment, which is not only bad for under-represented leaders, but bad for business overall, we must diversify not only the C-suite, but also senior management layers. Since we know that the senior management layer of a business is likely to be over-saturated with white males, the results of this study are particularly unsettling because appointing an under-represented CEO is likely to cause a hostile reaction in that group. Yet the problem becomes much less acute if we are able to diversify this layer of leadership. If we can ensure that the management layer is made up of a group of people with a wide range of racial and gender identities, the risk of them not being able to relate to an under-represented leader would be greatly reduced.

TL;DR: *Too Long; Didn't Read*

- The phenomenon of the Glass Cliff was first identified and written about by researchers Michelle Ryan and Alex Haslam, after *The Times* published a piece titled: 'Women on board: a help or a hindrance?'

- Rather than *causing* the downfall of businesses, women are often brought into leadership roles at already failing businesses – making their chances of success limited from the start and effectively leaving them in charge of failing.

- 'Think manager, think male' recognizes that, as a society, we've come to associate leadership with maleness. However, when there's a problem, this default is replaced by a new stereotype: 'think crisis, think woman'.

- Once they break through the Glass Ceiling, under-represented leaders often find themselves as 'onlys' – the first or only person like themselves (regarding gender, race or sexuality) to occupy a space within the organization, which leads to greater pressure and visibility.

- Some reasons that the Glass Cliff exists may be because of our cultural expectations of women, including:

  - Women are stereotypically perceived as being more nurturing and caregiving, a skill set that's not usually valued in leadership, but becomes essential during times of crisis.

  - Women make good scapegoats. If a female leader is brought into a business and isn't able to immediately solve all of the issues the business is facing, she's easily blamed for those issues and removed from the company.

- An under-represented leader signals a new start, or a change of direction. When a business is in a moment of difficulty, a good way to signal a fresh start and a bold new direction is to bring in a leader who is different from any leader the business has seen before.

- Women make good stopgaps. Because women's professional lives are treated less seriously than men's, women are more likely to be brought in while the search for 'the right man for the job' continues.

- Businesses claim cultural kudos for being progressive when they bring in a female leader. Even if that female leader subsequently has a short tenure in the business, the company receives kudos in the eyes of the public for being daring and inclusive.

• Not having the language to understand and frame the Glass Cliff as a cultural phenomenon has led us to believe the blame for professional 'failures' lies solely with individuals, undermining our perception of women's leadership potential overall.

• Rather than being supportive, white males have been shown to mentally check out of businesses and roles where the leader doesn't mirror both their whiteness and maleness – creating even greater obstacles for female leaders to overcome. This checking out also manifests as withdrawing their support from the more junior team members who they are managing – though not equally. They mostly withdraw their support from under-represented team members – reducing their potential to go on to take, and be successful in, their own leadership positions later in their careers.

CHAPTER 3

Worth the Risk?

The loneliest moment in someone's life is when they are watching their whole world fall apart and all they can do is stare blankly.

F. SCOTT FITZGERALD [1]

In 2016, Theresa May, a low-profile member of David Cameron's cabinet, regarded as a professional and reliable, albeit unexciting, member of the Conservative Party, became the UK's second ever female prime minister.[2]

May stepped into the role without a general election after her predecessor, David Cameron, resigned – immediately after leading the British people to a referendum in which they voted, against Cameron's advice, to end their forty-year relationship with the European Union.

Up until that point, May had had a quietly successful career in politics. She was described as being 'single-minded, unshowy and diligent', having joined the Conservative Party in the late 1970s, a time at which the party 'favoured men from more privileged backgrounds than her own.'[3] Despite this, she served as the MP for Maidenhead from 1997 and worked as the home secretary for six years before stepping into the role as prime minister; she understood both politics and the nuances of the party she had been involved with her entire life.

When, following the Brexit referendum, David Cameron resigned as the leader of the Conservative Party, May took on the role as his successor relatively unchallenged by rivals, portraying herself as a 'steady pair of hands' to lead the country through what was likely to be a difficult and messy period of Brexit negotiations and deals.

The Washington Post described the political landscape at the time: 'Britain has voted to leave the European Union. Cameron has resigned. The man considered the front-runner in the race to replace him decided not to run. The leader of the party that championed Britain's exit from the E.U. has quit.'[4]

Theresa May had become an unelected prime minister with one clear and all-encompassing task: lead Britain through Brexit and out of the European Union. She stepped into a role in which she was asked to deliver on the results of a referendum that she hadn't called, which had resulted in an outcome that she had been opposed to – all while being under intense public scrutiny.

This is not the first time a woman in the UK's Conservative Party has been a part of the Glass Cliff conversation, though it *may* be the first time at the prime ministerial level. In wondering why women in the party had won 'significantly fewer seats' than their male counterparts, researchers looked at the UK's 2005 general election. They found that 'this discrepancy in performance was completely explained by the fact that female candidates contested seats that were significantly more difficult to win.'[5] Which is to say, women in the party won less often because 'men were selected to contest seats that were easier to win, while women were selected to contest seats that were unwinnable.'[6]

Could the same thing have happened in this scenario? Were men in the party unwilling to step into what many knew would be an impossible-to-win scenario? It seems very likely.

Writing in *The Times*, Ryan and Haslam noted:

[May] finds herself in the unenviable position of being left to sort out a crisis that was not of her own making. Mirroring effects seen in a range of other contexts, what we see in her case is that the men who created the problems seem unwilling to step up to the leadership plate. Happy to bide their time, they wait in the wings for the dust to settle.

It may be difficult to feel sympathy for the prime minister because she undoubtedly knew the exact nature of the mess she was getting herself into. However, we should also recognize that she, like many other women who seek leadership positions, may have been unlikely to secure such a position had all been rosy. For would-be female leaders the choice is often between the poisoned chalice or nothing at all.[7]

Ryan elaborated further in a separate piece, in which she said, 'what you see is all the men going "why would we want to stick around for that?" We see Cameron walking away. We see Johnson walking away [. . .] It's not that they want women to fail. It's that they themselves don't want to fail.' She went on to note that, since opportunities for leadership roles can be so few and far between for women, 'If they want to have opportunities, they often have to take them when there's some leadership vacuum.'[8]

Despite having been opposed to the proposition of Britain's exit from the EU, once in office, May adopted the mantra 'Brexit means Brexit' and delivered a 'harder-than-expected' vision for Brexit in January 2017 – just three months later triggering Article 50 of the Lisbon Treaty, starting the formal two-year process to take Britain out of the European Union.[9]

Later that year, in a bid to legitimize herself as the nation's leader, May called a snap election. She had a strong lead over Labour in opinion polls, and said that the country needed 'certainty, stability and strong leadership' following the EU referendum. However, despite winning the largest share of the vote that the Conservative Party had seen since Margaret Thatcher's 1983 post-Falklands election victory, Labour also saw the biggest percentage increase in their vote since 1945, successfully drawing in and consolidating millions of anti-Tory voters from smaller parties.[10] May had done well, but not well enough. Not as well as expected. Not well enough to establish herself as a prime minister with a public mandate to lead. Instead of establishing herself as an elected leader, May hadn't performed as well as advance opinion polling had led the party to anticipate – and she had further issues coming up, even within her own party, as she tried to bring the 'will of the people' to life following Cameron's referendum.

'Whatever one's feelings on Brexit,' Ryan said in an interview with Vox, 'the situation is a difficult one to navigate, and her leadership popularity is suffering as a result.'[11]

In December 2018, MPs launched a vote of no confidence against May in a formal attempt to remove her from power. She survived by 200 votes to 117, and parliamentary rules prevented the launching of another vote of the same kind for twelve months – but internal support for May's leadership was increasingly difficult to come by. As the BBC put it, 'it was just the beginning of a seemingly never-ending cycle of political torture she would go on to suffer at the hands of her mutinous MPs.'[12]

May continued to struggle to get support for the deals she put forward. Her proposed Brexit deal would eventually be rejected three times by Parliament. The first time, the deal was rejected by 230 votes, which represented the biggest defeat for a government in parliamentary history. A total of 118 Tory MPs defied orders and voted against the deal.[13]

By the time she reintroduced a 'slightly tweaked' deal for the third and final time, there were open calls, from within the Conservative Party, for May to resign as prime minister. May agreed to resign if the deal was accepted. The deal was, once again, rejected. Power continued to slip further away from May, as her cabinet openly discussed alternatives to her deal and junior ministers resigned with such regularity that they barely made the news.[14]

In May of 2019, in an 'emotional statement' outside of Downing Street, May announced that she was resigning as the prime minister: 'It will always remain a matter of deep regret for me that I have not been able to deliver Brexit,' she said, adding, 'It is now clear to me that it is in the best interest of the UK for a new PM to lead that effort.'[15]

Even though May didn't propose the Brexit referendum and was not on the side of Leave before becoming the prime minister, she was left to manage the consequences, often without the support of her party. 'It's quite possible, even though Cameron called the referendum which created the current turmoil, that May will be remembered for it', Marianne Cooper, a sociologist at Stanford University, told *The Washington Post* at the time. 'Years from now, will it be Cameron or May who we most associate with Brexit? Whose reputation is going to be permanently tied in the country's collective memory? He's exiting off stage pretty quickly. He may have caused it, but she has to fix it.'[16]

On Christmas Eve of 2020, Boris Johnson, who stepped into the role of prime minister following May's departure, was able to reach a trade deal with the European Union. While May said that she would vote in favour of the agreement, she told MPs she had offered them a 'better deal' in 2019.[17]

•   •   •

After everything that we've seen and spoken about up until now, maybe you're feeling like it's all a bit pointless. Maybe you expect me to say that, knowing what we know, women should recognize that, however hard we work, however successful we are, however much potential we have, it's all for nothing – because, even when it seems like things are finally working out for us, when we've smashed through the Glass Ceiling and overcome bias and prejudice, the odds remain against us.

I want you to know that's not how I feel, and I hope you don't either. But I can understand if you do – for now, at least.

My intention in spending this time explaining the Glass Cliff isn't to stop women in their tracks, or to say that its mere existence means we're doomed and we should all give up this silly idea of progress. Not at all. Instead, my intention is to shed a light on the experience and to give us the opportunity to be better prepared to recognize and avoid it in our next ventures, should we want to.

But, it's also important to recognize that, even when we know about the Glass Cliff, and even when we suspect that we might be stepping into a situation where we're likely to fall into its trap, sometimes that's still the best next step for us.

Or, at least, the one we still want to take.

So, in instances like that, how do you assess if it's worth the risk?

Is the juice worth the squeeze?

In one business I worked for, a common question my team would ask before committing to a new project or initiative was: 'Is the juice worth the squeeze?' Is the time, effort and resources needed to make this project a success worth the reward we believe we can get at the end? If the juice was worth the squeeze, off we'd go, but if not – back to the drawing board, until next time.

When we're talking about our careers and next steps, it can sometimes be hard to estimate the potential juice at the end of the squeeze. None of us really know how things will work out, long term, and what can seem like a great opportunity to me, might feel a lot less appealing to you, and vice versa.* The risk of taking on a new role where you're susceptible to the Glass Cliff might feel totally acceptable or absolutely unthinkable to you, and it probably depends on a number of factors in your own life and

---

* I've also learned that things can feel like absolute professional disasters at the time, but often, in hindsight, take on a different shape. For instance, the first time I was fired was from an admin role in my early twenties, and I was devastated, but I now see that, without it, I never would have learned what a bad working environment looked like, nor how to check a contract with a fine-tooth comb – something that's been invaluable to me in every job I've taken on since. I can also now see that, without the payout that accompanied my termination, I never would have started to build up savings rather than living pay cheque to pay cheque.

career up to this point. Either way, it's your choice to make. But that doesn't mean we can't go into things with our eyes as firmly open as possible.

Identifying you're in a situation where the Glass Cliff is likely

It's not that every role in every business where a woman is hired is a potential Glass Cliff situation, but, for those that are, it isn't always obvious from the beginning.

As we've seen, for the Glass Cliff to play out, there needs to be a certain set of factors already in motion. The phenomenon is not a universal truth, and it absolutely does not exist in a vacuum or in isolation – instead, it relies on particular circumstances and expectations working together. As Michelle Ryan noted, 'Our research suggests that the Glass Cliff is multiply determined', making it impossible to point to a single factor that shows us, without question, that we're walking towards danger.[18] But there are some combinations of factors that we can be alert to. So here is a recap and a quick checklist of the factors to look out for that make a new opportunity more likely to be a potentially precarious position.

Current performance

As we've seen, those businesses and organizations that have been in a persistent period of poor performance (valuations, stock price, reputational scandal etc.) are more likely to break from the norm and hire an under-represented leader to turn the tide of their fortunes.

For publicly listed companies, it is easy enough to look at their share price over the past five months, and you can have a quick Google for any public issues or controversies you might not have been aware of.

History of leadership

In businesses that have been historically run by women, the risk of the Glass Cliff almost disappears for new leaders, because women in leadership no longer represent a break from the norm and can't be perceived externally as a new risk factor.

Have a look at the make-up of the business and its leaders – not only at a board and C-suite level, but also at senior management tiers. Do they do a good job at gender equity, or do we see women disproportionately huddled at more junior levels? While you're there, have a look at their pay-gap data, which all businesses in the UK with over 250 employees are required to share annually (Covid-19 notwithstanding). This serves two purposes. Firstly, why would you want to work in a business that doesn't value women? And, secondly, if it's difficult to get an idea of gender representation at different levels in a business, the pay-gap data can be a useful way to get a peep: a big gender pay gap in a business often means that women are clustered in lower-paying, more junior roles, while men, and their larger salaries, have floated to the top. (Or been carried there by an invisible Glass Escalator, which we'll discuss soon.)

Unclear aims or objectives

As we've seen, one risk for women in Glass Cliff scenarios is being appointed as a temporary stopgap until the business can find, and bring in, the right *man* for the job. No one wants to unknowingly be a placeholder for someone else's success. If aims and objectives in the role are unclear or seem to be mostly focused on re-engaging or re-motivating a waning team, you might find, on taking the role, that you're on the edge of a Glass Cliff.

Unclear support systems

One contributing factor to women being unsuccessful in Glass Cliff situations is a lack of internal support systems, which are necessary to establish wider team buy-in to their visions. Without these support systems, women are not able to establish the authority needed to make their leadership a success. Does this role have other senior leaders around it, and do you feel they are likely to be supportive advocates within the business?

Hiring new, over promoting internally

Interestingly, research shows us that CEOs who come in as external hires are more likely to find themselves in precarious positions than those promoted internally, and that women are more likely to be in that position than men.* It's a more difficult transition to make as an external hire, because, as well as already being outside of most people's expectations of a leader, these women also find themselves as outsiders within the business itself. As Ryan and Haslam put it, 'it's a tougher job [because] they don't have as many connections in the company to understand how things work'.[19] This means that, as well as leading the company and establishing themselves in their authority, they are simultaneously trying to learn the ropes of a new environment, which goes some way to explaining why CEOs who are brought in as external hires are 6.7 times more likely to be quickly dismissed than those who have been promoted internally.[20]

Trapped between a ceiling and a cliff edge

If you're in discussions about or have already taken on a role which fits some of the criteria above, there is an increased chance of

---

* Thirty-five per cent of women, versus just 22 per cent of men.

being susceptible to the Glass Cliff. But that doesn't necessarily mean taking on the challenge is out of the question.

You might feel that, although you're aware you could be stepping into circumstances that make success more difficult or less likely, you're ready to take that risk, grab the bull and your career opportunities by the horns and take your next steps with your eyes wide open. And there are lots of very, very valid reasons why this might be the case.

A lack of other opportunities

Returning to our example of Theresa May in the 2016 election, it's very likely that she knew the situation she was stepping into was deeply precarious, even as she spent her first night in Downing Street. Of course, she *may* have been blind to any of the potential difficulties she would face. But it's much more likely that she simply believed this opportunity to take on the most powerful role in the country wasn't one that would come twice. 'It is likely that a Prime Ministership during Brexit was the best that she could hope for,' wrote Michelle Ryan of May's decision. '[S]he wasn't in a position to wait around until a better opportunity came about, as Boris Johnson did.'[21]

She may have believed that her soft skills* were what was needed to shepherd the country towards stability as it wrangled with the result of a Brexit referendum that she had been against. Or she may have believed that this was likely to be her only shot at the highest leadership position, and so decided to go for it despite the odds.

While we know that talent isn't gendered, it is still sadly the case that, in many businesses, the pathways to progression are. When opportunities feel few and far between, we might be more

---

* Though, as it has been noted by many, softer skills aren't necessarily May's forte.

inclined, when one does come our way, to shoot our shot – even if it's a long shot – because it could be a long time before we get another chance. We might even worry that this one opportunity, despite the odds being stacked against success, is our *only* chance.

In Chapter 2, we saw that many leaders, mentors and sponsors are reluctant to put forward 'minority' protégés for promotions or new opportunities, as they feel (correctly) that they may be subject to increased scrutiny and are worried that it will be more difficult to convince senior stakeholders to share in their belief of their potential. We've also spoken about the Broken Rung, which sees many women being overlooked in favour of their male counterparts for what would be their first big break – the first step on the ladder towards management roles. Women, even when they're ready for their next step, are passed over for progression time and time again throughout their careers, as managers and leaders fail to see and correctly recognize the potential they hold.

Although women are 7.3 per cent more likely than men to receive high performance ratings, their potential remains underestimated by their employers – as they are, on average, ranked 5.8 per cent lower by their managers for their perceived potential.[22] Unfortunately, this bias against seeing the potential in female employees is only strengthened as women progress in seniority. Researchers have found that 'women receive progressively lower potential scores relative to their actual future performance as we rise up the corporate ladder'.[23] Looking at male and female employees with the same performance and potential ratings, they showed that women go on not only to outperform men in future evaluations, but that they are also less likely to leave the firm, even though they've had their potential underestimated. Despite this, these underestimations in ratings of potential do not appear to self-correct: even though the women in question outperform their potential ratings, they continue to receive lower potential evaluations in the future. These persistently low potential ratings apply regardless of whether women continue in their current role or are promoted and perform well in their new role.[24]

Women are used to feeling invisible

Even when women work hard, go above and beyond, and take on tasks outside of their own job roles to help the company run as smoothly as it can, their work and efforts are all too often overlooked or not taken into account in conversations around progression and promotions.

This is in part because women are much more likely than men to take on 'non-promotable' tasks within businesses – such as organizing events, taking notes, sitting on committees or ERGs, or taking on the unglamorous but essential admin tasks that, in many workplaces, don't form an explicit part of anyone's job description.[25] This is known as office housework. These tasks are usually time-consuming, but are not directly linked to revenue-driving or profile-building activities and so are not taken into consideration when it comes to discussions about pay rises or promotions.[26]

Men, on the other hand, while not being kept occupied with this poorly valued and overlooked type of work, tend to find themselves with more capacity to take on the opposite of office housework – which is known as glamour work. Glamour work is high-profile tasks and projects that *are* usually linked to generating profit for the business, and often give people the opportunity to work and build relationships with senior team members who can later become sponsors or advocates for their success.

Women have become used to their contributions being overlooked and undervalued – almost as though they're invisible. It could be that, when we finally *do* receive the recognition we deserve and are rewarded by being offered a promotion or a new opportunity – a chance to step out of the shadows and reap the rewards of our work – we jump at the chance, even if the circumstances of the new role are somewhat less than ideal.

Being promoted later and more slowly

Research has shown that women are 14 per cent less likely than men to be promoted within a company each year, with managers who control progression placing a high value on qualities that are not only highly subjective, but also more traditionally associated with male behaviours, such as 'assertiveness, execution skills, charisma, leadership, ambition'.[27]

Women overall are also less likely to have a lot of face time with senior leaders in their businesses, and perhaps because of that are also less likely to receive advice from managers or senior leaders about career progression and advancement. Despite research showing that those employees who *do* receive such advice are much more likely to be promoted. Again, it could be that women are so used to being overlooked that, when someone does finally recognize our abilities and leadership potential, we feel the need to seize the opportunity quickly, even when it's not ideal, for fear of losing out on what could be our only chance.

Negotiating against a blank wall

Over the past few years, I have noticed a trend when speaking about women's lack of progression and promotion within businesses – and that is a quickness to blame women for the obstacles in their paths. 'Women would get promoted more,' the most common rebuttal seems to be, 'if they *leaned in* more. If they spoke up, advocated for themselves and acted more like leaders, they would get the promotions they're looking for.'

If only it were that simple. In reality, women and men ask for promotions at very similar rates, and, at senior levels, women ask for promotions more often than their male counterparts.[28] Despite this, women are still promoted more slowly and less often than men.

Women who lobby for a promotion are more than twice as likely to receive one as those who don't.[29] However, in response to asking for promotions, 30 per cent of women were characterized as being 'bossy', 'aggressive' or 'intimidating', compared to 23 per cent of men.[30]

Although, for everyone, negotiating is shown to lead to better outcomes than simply accepting offers on face value, many men report not needing to negotiate as often as women to get what they're looking for; indeed, 'men are more likely to say they have not asked for a raise because they are already well compensated or a promotion because they are already in the right role.'[31]

Using your voice is one thing, but to get the end results we're looking for, it requires someone to listen.

The impact of Covid-19

Oxfam estimates that Covid-19 cost women, globally, over $800 billion in lost income in a single twelve-month period.[32] That's an amount which is equivalent to the combined GDP of ninety-eight countries, and which doesn't account for losses for those working in 'informal industries', such as garment workers or domestic workers – groups in which women are, once again, over-represented.

According to a study from the McKinsey Global Institute, women make up 39 per cent of the global 'formal' workforce – but have accounted for 54 per cent of all job losses due to Covid[33] – a figure that Oxfam[34] believes represents more than 64 million jobs.*

During my time at the United Nations summit, António Guterres gave a speech in which he shared some sobering statistics. He told the assembled crowd from around the world that, pre-pandemic, the UN estimated we were collectively 100 years away from achieving gender equality. Reassessing that number in 2023, taking into account the impact of Covid-19, it had risen dramatically – now standing at 300 years overall, with the UK estimated to be 120 years away from gender equality.

---

* Or 5 per cent of all women's formal work, compared to a 3.9 per cent overall loss for men.

Instead of making the progress we had hoped for in terms of women's equality and their professional and financial security, we are losing ground.

Covid has hit women hard.

So often, women are left to bear the brunt of global societal factors that are beyond our control, and expected to clean up the mess we didn't create. And so, when everything, everywhere, feels to be a somewhat risky proposition – why not take on some risk on our own terms? Why wouldn't women – senior, smart, professional women – say, 'Fine. I understand there's a potential for this to go wrong, but at least I will have given it a go'?

I think that's exactly what we're doing when we make the choice to step into precarious positions and try to achieve the most senior professional successes.

A calculated risk

Patricia Peter, who is the head of corporate governance at the British Institute of Directors, has argued, 'I know of women who don't want to sit on a board that isn't a challenge, and who feel that if they go to a company that's doing quite well, they might not be noticed.'[35]

I'm not sure how on board with this sentiment I am.* Personally, I think it would be far better and easier for everyone if, instead of putting women in disproportionately risky situations, we created the conditions for them to be successful *and* to get noticed in organizations set up for success.

But maybe my thinking on this is wrong. Maybe it's limited. And maybe it's underestimating women's appetite for risk, as they take on new ventures.

Women who choose to face the Glass Cliff head-on are not stupid. Of course they're not – they're super-smart professionals at the top of their game. They're not naive or under-informed;

---

* I'm *fully* not on board with this sentiment.

instead, they are people, ready for leadership, who have assessed a situation and feel like there's a chance that they can turn someone else's mess into their own success. As Alison Cook, a professor of management at Utah State University and a long-term researcher into the Glass Cliff, put it: 'It's not that it's just happening to them, they're making this happen.'[36]

These people are trailblazers and risk takers, and have been throughout their careers.

An increased appetite for risk

When looking at people who decided to take on Glass Cliff positions, Cook interviewed thirty-three women and 'people of colour' in senior leadership roles across a range of industries,[37] and found that they had something very interesting in common: nearly all of them had chosen to lean into uncertainty, and had taken on *multiple* risky, make-or-break assignments during the course of their careers.[38] Not through chance, circumstance or bad luck, but by design, as a deliberate strategy to prove themselves and build their careers.

Cook told the BBC, 'So many of them have had this agency throughout, and they've set themselves up to prove their leadership worth early on. They have these situations throughout their entire career. They are known as "turnaround artists" [. . .] They're good in these really tough situations, because they've had to be over and over and over.'[39]

This sentiment is shared by Jane Stevenson, who heads CEO succession at search and consulting firm Korn Ferry. She told Vox, 'Women are much more willing to take on a low-success-probability situation because they felt maybe they were uniquely equipped to make a difference.'[40]

It might be that, when faced with a moment of difficulty or a mess to clean up, men and women view the situation somewhat differently. 'Women feel a great sense of purpose and a great level of commitment to the communities they're involved in perhaps in a different way than they think about their own career trajectory,' Stevenson said. Evelyn Orr, vice president of the firm's research arm, added, 'There's a certain profile of person who is less concerned with what a challenge might mean for them personally if they were to fail.'[41]

Shooting your (potentially long) shot

Taking on a risky role is, by its very nature, not risk-free. As we've seen, women who fall from the Glass Cliff are less likely to be given a second chance, and the need to constantly clean up a mess and re-prove yourself time and time again is exhausting.

Despite the set of leaders we've just discussed who have made a habit of seeking out and taking on career-defining, challenging career moves, there is experimental research which shows that women may view risky leadership opportunities as less attractive than men do, overall.[42] Women are less likely to say they would accept roles perceived as being higher risk, yet they remain over-represented in these spaces. The lack of low-risk roles on offer might go some way to explaining why we see women so willing to take on these challenges – or, to borrow some words from the original researchers, 'it remains possible that these perceptions of desirability are tempered by availability', such that risky opportunities become more attractive to women as it becomes clear to them that those are the *only* real opportunities being offered.[43]

I think we now have all we need to be able to assess situations and opportunities, and to decide what's best for us – whether that's saying, 'No, thanks, I hate it', or, 'Yes, please, I feel ready and willing to give this a go.' What's right for one person may well not be what's right for the next, but, when we do decide to take the plunge, there are some tools that we can use from the outset to make our chances of success higher, and keep us further from the edge of the cliff.

TL;DR: *Too Long; Didn't Read*

- The Glass Cliff is 'multiply determined', which means several, sometimes seemingly unconnected, elements need to come together in order for the phenomenon to occur. These include:
  - Current performance: is the business doing less well than it has historically?

  - History of leadership: has the business only had white male leadership up until this point?

  - Unclear aims and objectives: is there a clear and agreed picture of what success looks like, and the timeframe for it?

  - Unclear or missing support systems: can you rely on your colleagues for support and buy-in?

- There are some instances in which, even when we're aware of the Glass Cliff and the risks it poses, we might still choose to take on what we know to be a potentially precarious position. These include:

  - A lack of other opportunities to progress: women are 14 per cent less likely than men to be promoted within a company each year. Women also receive worse rankings for their potential on average, even when they score more highly for their performance.

  - Being used to feeling invisible: women are disproportionately expected to take on the small, often invisible tasks that are required to keep a business running, but which are not usually taken into account in decisions around progression. Doing this kind of work means women are often seen as being too busy to take on glamour work – high-profile assignments linked to progression and contact with senior team members.

– Having an appetite for risk and a track record of being a change maker: many people who take on roles which are likely to face the Glass Cliff have a track record of taking on challenges that others may shy away from, although this may be due in large part to a lack of other opportunities available to them.

• Covid-19 has disproportionately impacted the experiences and working lives of women: women represent 54 per cent of all job losses due to Covid – a figure that adds up to more than 64 million jobs.

• Pre-Covid, the United Nations estimated that we were one hundred years away from achieving gender equality. In 2023, that rose to 300 years overall, with the UK estimated to be 120 years away from gender equality.

CHAPTER 4

Setting the Conditions for Success

I cannot make you understand.
I cannot make anyone understand
what is happening inside me.
I cannot even explain it to myself.

FRANZ KAFKA[1]

In December of 2013, General Motors made headlines by announcing Mary Barra as their new CEO – making her the first woman ever to lead a global automotive company.[2] And, unusually for businesses where women are brought into leadership roles, the business seemed to be doing well.[3] The US government had just sold its remaining shares of the company – which it had bought as an investment when the business faced bankruptcy during the 2008 financial crash – and, by all accounts, it was back on its feet.[4] The recovery had been so strong, in fact, that *Elle* magazine ran a piece about it when Barra's appointment was announced, pointing out the tendency for women to be brought in to lead companies in some kind of moment of crisis. They noted that, 'by hiring Mary Barra to lead a company that's on the upswing, her colleagues are saying: We trust you to keep this good thing going, rather than, We're going to give you this piece of garbage and trash you when you can't turn it into gold. And at least so far, we haven't heard endless talk about her child care arrangements or her work life balance policies, like we did with Marissa Mayer. That, to me, feels like real progress.'[5]

Barra had spent her entire career in General Motors, having already worked within the business for thirty-three years before stepping into the top role. She knew the business well and understood its slow-moving and at times unnecessarily complicated nature. When she became head of HR in 2009, for example, Barra inherited a ten-page dress code, which she reduced to just two words – 'dress appropriately' – allowing managers on a team-by-team basis to interpret the message for themselves.[6]

It seemed that, as a new leader of a business that had already overcome the challenges of the 2008 financial crash, she was set to build on her pre-existing internal knowledge, simplify messy or unnecessary internal operational processes, and take the company from strength to strength.

But this optimism was sadly short-lived.

Just two weeks into Barra's term as CEO of GM, disaster struck in the worst way imaginable.

It was revealed that faulty ignition switches in GM cars had led to twelve deaths, which meant that 1.6 million vehicles needed to be recalled. Over the next two months, a total of over 3.1 million GM-made cars would be recalled for faults with ignition switches, brake parts, air bags or other components.[7] At the time, there was speculation that the figure for those who had lost their lives may be even higher than the twelve to thirteen initially reported.[8] By 2018, Business Insider reported 124 people had died and a further 275 had been injured as a result of the manufacturer's faulty components.[9]

As would be expected when a crisis of this magnitude hits a business, all eyes turned to the company's CEO to offer an explanation for the tragedy and to outline the steps being taken to ensure a disaster of this scale would never happen again.

As attention on the case continued, and more and more recalls were announced, the pressure only grew as it became clear that information about the faults wasn't news to the company. It was reported that General Motors had known about them for over ten years, but had failed to take any action.

Although Barra had only been in her role for two weeks when these problems arose, and an investigation cleared her and other senior executives of any direct involvement in the recall delay, she was still in the spotlight as the leader of GM – expected to offer an explanation for the fatal shortcomings and for why the business had failed to act sooner.[10]

'I cannot tell you why it took years for a safety defect to be announced . . . but I can tell you that we will find out,' Barra testified before a US House of Representatives panel:

> As soon as I learned about the problem, we acted without hesitation. We told the world we had a problem that needed to be fixed [. . .] We did so because whatever mistakes were made in the past, we will not shirk from our responsibilities now and in the future. Today's GM will do the right thing. That begins with my sincere apologies to everyone who has been affected by this recall, especially to the families and friends of those who lost their lives or were injured.[11]

The messages that Barra sent internally seem to have been just as sincere and unshirking as those made publicly. After commissioning a report into the incident, Barra fired fifteen people from the business and 'disciplined' a further five for the decade-long delay between the safety issues first being reported and the business's move to recall the affected car models.[12] 'Something went wrong with our process in this instance,' she told employees in an online video message, 'and terrible things happened.'[13]

Despite these actions, and her lack of involvement in the circumstances leading to the issues with the vehicles, several newspapers criticized Barra for 'dodging the question of responsibility' for the flaws.[14]

Others, however, praised her open and forthright response to the issues, and her willingness to accept personal blame, despite not holding personal fault in the situation: 'Mary Barra understands the value of taking full responsibility for G.M.'s latest, high profile challenges, especially if she wants to send the message that this is a new G.M.,' said Karl Brauer, an analyst with the auto-research firm Kelley Blue Book.[15]

In a statement released at the time, Barra said the report into the faulty elements had uncovered that:

Repeatedly, individuals failed to disclose critical pieces of information that could have fundamentally changed the lives of those impacted by a faulty ignition switch. If this information had been disclosed, I believe in my heart the company would have dealt with this matter appropriately.

I hate sharing this with you as much as you hate hearing it. But I want you to hear it. In fact, I never want you to forget it. This is not just another business crisis for GM. We aren't simply going to fix this and move on. We are going to fix the failures in our system – that I promise. In fact, many are already fixed. And we are going to do the right thing for the affected parties.[16]

This was an unusually forthright and personal statement from a CEO going through the biggest crisis of her career – a crisis that cost the lives of so many innocent people. By all accounts, Barra rode the challenges of her new role well, identifying a 'pattern of incompetence and neglect' within GM that led to the fatal issues within their vehicles, making the necessary changes and introducing processes to prevent an incident of the same kind happening again in the future.[17]

Barra was taking the fall for a situation not of her making, as is the case for so many female leaders, but hers was an unusually immediate and lethal example of the Glass Cliff phenomenon.[18]

Another thing that made Barra's experience of the Glass Cliff unusual was that she survived it. Perhaps the reason is because the timeline evidently showed that the issues impacting the business were inherited rather than caused by her, a correlation-versus-causation sequence that is rarely so clear for all to see in instances of businesses appointing women to lead during a crisis.

In 2014, in a town-hall meeting, Barra said to the staff at GM, 'I never want to put this behind us. I want to put this painful experience permanently in our collective memories.'[19]

As a response to dealing with this crisis, Barra put in place a number of internal processes designed to militate against the chance of something similar ever happening again within the business, including making it as easy as possible for GM employees to report safety concerns by launching an internal 'Speak Up For Safety' hotline, noting that 'the best time to solve a problem is the minute you know about it [. . .] Most problems don't get smaller with time.'[20]

In 2018, GM was one of only two global businesses to have no gender pay gap.

In 2022, Barra ranked number four in *Forbes*' list of Power Women.[21]

•　　•　　•

It's not difficult to imagine a scenario in which a woman has gathered all of the necessary information and recognized that an opportunity open to her is likely to be susceptible to the Glass Cliff – and yet decides to take the risk and to go for it anyway. In a scenario like this, it's important to understand that her choice doesn't mean that she's dooming herself to unmitigated failure. Not at all. In fact, the choice to go in with eyes wide open allows us to be alert and mindful of setting up conditions for success, on our own terms, before we've even begun.

One way of setting ourselves up for success is to be deliberate and vocal about exactly who we are, what we're willing to give to a role or a business, and what success looks like both for ourselves and our new employer, right from the very start.

Before taking on a role

As we've already seen, things become a lot less scary when we can simply name them. Even this smallest act of taking control can be all we need to feel equipped and powerful enough to face challenges and trials as they come to us.

Up until now, the Glass Cliff has been an invisible and over-looked phenomenon for many. It's not hard to see why – it speaks to the difficulty that we all have in identifying systemic barriers while we're experiencing them. The fact that glass is used in so many analogies about the workplace isn't a coincidence. In 'The Transformation of Silence into Language and Action', Audre Lorde asks us to consider, 'What are the words you do not yet have? What do you need to say? What are the tyrannies you swallow day by day and attempt to make your own, until you will sicken and die of them, still in silence?'[22] Without having had the words to understand the Glass Cliff, people's chances of even recognizing it, not to mention overcoming it, have been almost non-existent. Like fighting an invisible opponent – the odds are very much not in your favour if you can't actually see or name what you're up against, let alone describe it to other people.

But, now, we *do* have the words, and that means we have taken back a little bit of power. We can use that newly found power to start these very necessary, although potentially difficult, conver-sations, to set ourselves up for the best success possible, as early as we can. And who knows? Maybe we can even come out on top.

So where do we begin?

Start by identifying the risk

Realizing that a position has a high likelihood of falling foul of the Glass Cliff, but deciding to go for it anyway, can be a scary moment. It can feel like you're really taking on a huge risk, single-handedly, and your chances of falling or being pushed off the cliff can feel overwhelming.

The first step in preparing to take on a role which has a high chance of being susceptible to the Glass Cliff is acknowledging it, out loud. Bring your concerns and hesitations to light as early as possible in conversations and negotiations.

Acknowledge both the circumstances and your feelings around

them. Socialize the idea that the role you're stepping into may be riskier than usual. Remove any mystery or ambiguity. Take the opportunity to frame it on your own terms. After all, you're about to take on a big challenge – one that's likely to be a lot easier if you're able to go into it with knowledge and control over your own narrative.

From initial discussions around a new job to going through the interview process and fact-finding about the role, and even when you've stepped into the position – make the Glass Cliff a topic of conversation.

That said, I'm aware it's not easy.

All of this talk about knowledge and power isn't to say that it's not scary to have these conversations. It is. Job negotiations are hard at the best of times, let alone in a context like this, where I'm asking you to point out to your potential employers that the way they've run things up until now means your chances of being successful are already limited.

But, as I hope we can all agree, having these chats is nowhere near as scary as not having them. Nowhere near as scary as going silently into a risky position without any protections, swallowing tyrannies day by day.

So *do* ask questions. Lots of them.

Ask about the history of the business, how it's performing, what its biggest challenges have been up to now. Ask about its history of leadership and what the biggest perceived challenges are expected to be. Find out what exactly success looks like in this role, and whether they are mindfully, deliberately setting up the conditions to allow you to achieve that. Ask what the time-frames for key indicators of success look like. And, finally, ask if they have heard of the Glass Cliff, and if they are aware that the role they're hiring for has a high chance of falling into the phenomenon's trap.

Share your concerns with them, transparently and openly. Bring the Glass Cliff into the light.

You can also use this time, before you've actually stepped into a precarious role, to identify factors that they might not be aware of, but which might lead to you having a more challenging time once in place. For instance, if the business has only had over-represented leadership, ask them about it. Don't be afraid to be direct. We now know that, when a business appoints a woman during a time of crisis, the likelihood of the Glass Cliff emerging relies on a history of male leadership prior to that appointment. If the business has had a more egalitarian and inclusive set of leaders, the Glass Cliff all but disappears. Once we ask the right questions, we can get closer to finding out the information that will help us to make the choices that are best for us.[23]

Having open conversations about your concerns around a role before you've even signed a contract can feel really intimidating, and we might worry that, if we ask too many questions, make too many points or seem too annoying, the opportunity will be snatched away from us. But, in the same way that we wouldn't expect someone to accept a senior (or hopefully any) job offer without asking about and trying to negotiate a salary and benefits package, we shouldn't be accepting roles in businesses that aren't prepared to take the time to set us up for success. It's also worth noting that, just like those businesses who are reluctant to discuss remuneration, those who are cagey or unwilling to engage in discussions about the potential risk of the Glass Cliff are very unlikely to have your long-term best interests at heart. A company that is unwilling to recognize the risks that its employees will probably encounter, and to work with you in advance to identify the things that can be done to maximize your chances of success in the role, is unlikely to become a company in which you can beat the odds and overcome the Glass Cliff. Especially as we know that, in order to avoid falling victim to the phenomenon, support, time and buy-in are essential.

The importance of a support network

It's important to understand that, even if the business is in a moment of poor performance or crisis, not all crisis situations are equally risky. Research shows us that the availability of support within the company can significantly change how precarious a position is.[24] Participants in a study by Ryan and Haslam, which reviewed a decade of evidence, explanations and impacts of the Glass Cliff, were given a scenario that showed a business that was in crisis, and they were asked to assess the suitability of male and female leadership candidates to lead the business through that period of difficulty. The participants in *this* study were told that the leaders either could or could not rely on the 'support and confidence of relevant stakeholders and the larger organizational network'. And *that's* what proved to be the major difference in their decision-making approaches. In instances in which support and resources were available, the participants opted most often for the male candidate to take on the role. However, when those elements of support were said to be unavailable – or, to put it another way, when the conditions for the Glass Cliff were created – the female became the participant's leader of choice. The research went on to say that, 'Additional data indicated that the woman was selected for the leadership role under these circumstances because participants expected that she would be better at gaining acceptance within the organization. However, where social resources were available to the leader, participants reverted to the more traditionally gendered assumption that a leader who was male would be more effective than one who was female.'[25]

Interestingly, in that same study, the researchers found that the participants only recognized that a role was precarious when social resources or a support network were missing. This suggests that leading during a crisis is seen as being *less* risky when a strong supportive network is in place to help a leader navigate challenges and manage risk – something that those women who face the Glass Cliff are so often lacking from the businesses they're within.

This means it's essential to determine (or at least try to determine) the level of support available inside a role or organization if we're going to stand a chance of making new roles into success stories. But, of course, that's not the only area of support that we can use should things get tough.

It's also important to remember, and to lean on, your *external* social networks – the people who have already seen you take on and overcome challenges, who are likely to be in your corner, should you need them, if things start to feel tricky in your working life.

Be open with your personal network. Tell them about the choice you're making and the potential risks you see associated with it. Share your concerns and let them know that it's likely you're going to be needing their support as you try to navigate this new experience. This isn't only valuable if things go badly; we also need people to share joy and successful moments with, and it's great for people to know that you took on a challenge that you saw as a potential, personal, professional risk and came out on top.

But, if there *are* problems along the way, it's always good to have people who already know the story, without having to play catch-up to fill them in on the potentially more difficult details. There's no need to go back and explain things from the start – especially hard-to-see, glass things. Instead, they will already have all of the context, they'll know the narrative from the start, and they'll be ready to step in and offer support when it's needed.

Agree timelines

As we've already seen, female CEOs who are exited from roles* have shorter tenures in those roles than their male counterparts.

---

* Rather than those who choose to leave themselves, or those who leave as a result of retirement, acquisition, etc.

Women, on the whole, are given less time to find their feet, execute their strategies and turn rocky starts into moments of triumph.

Address this in your early conversations. As well as finding out what success looks like in terms of performance or business metrics, discuss the timelines associated with making these changes and achieving these wins.

◆　◆　◆

In January 2009, Carol Bartz, a predecessor of Marissa Mayer, left the business where she had worked for fourteen years and stepped into the role of CEO at Yahoo, on a set four-year contract.[26] She had been brought in to turn around the performance of the troubled internet giant, which was struggling before she arrived, and, by all accounts, she arrived with a strategic plan to reset the business and its success.[27]

In September 2011, only two years and eight months into the contract, Bartz sent the following message to the all-company email address, with the subject line 'Goodbye':

> To all,
> I am very sad to tell you that I've just been fired over the phone by Yahoo's Chairman of the Board. It has been my pleasure to work with all of you and I wish you only the best going forward.
> Carol[28]

Bartz had been fired. Over the phone.[29] And was then replaced, in what Yahoo referred to as a 'reorganization', by acting CEO Tim Morse, a white male who had been the business's CFO until Bartz's departure.*

---

* As he had only been appointed as acting CEO, Morse was later replaced by Scott Thompson, another white man, as Yahoo's next permanent chief executive.

'They didn't even let [her plan] come to fruition,' said Alison Cook, speaking to the BBC.[30] Even though a plan had been agreed, and she had been brought in on a fixed four-year contract, it wasn't enough to protect her in the role.

Bartz has since acknowledged that she might never have been given the opportunity to have such a high-profile role in a household-name company if things had been going well for the business – if the conditions hadn't been in place for her eventual fall from the Glass Cliff before she even began. As she told the Freakonomics podcast, 'it is absolutely true that women have a better chance to get a directorship, or a senior position, if there's trouble.'[31]

But understanding and recognizing those risks doesn't mean that the experience of living through a high-profile fall – framed by many, up to now, as an individual failing – isn't painful and upsetting. After the event, Bartz told *The Guardian* in the UK that Yahoo's board were 'doofuses' who 'fucked me over.'[32] And it's easy to see why someone who had been treated so coldly would feel that way.

Clearly, the time frame included in Bartz's appointment didn't protect her from falling or being pushed off the cliff. However, on the whole, those companies that are able to acknowledge the existence of the Glass Cliff and recognize that they fit the conditions that make it possible to occur are more likely to show willingness to put in the necessary guard rails, perimeters and protections around roles to minimize the Glass Cliff's potential impact.

Stepping into these roles is always intimidating and unpredictable – but there are some things that we can proactively do to reduce our chances of falling or slipping off the Glass Cliff if we do decide to take on the challenge and the risk.

Making it worth your while

While it's true that a lot of us do get more from our working lives than a pay cheque, it would be naive to imagine that being compensated as well as possible for our time isn't at least a part of the aim of the game.

Know your worth and don't offer discounts

If we're going to be taking on these highly visible positions, which involve the personal and professional risk to our reputation of falling off the Glass Cliff, it's only fair that we make it worth our while. Call it an incentive to take on a risky role. Call it danger money. Frankly, call it whatever you like, so long as you get it. And a part of the way to get it is by negotiating well.

I'm not now going to attempt to run a masterclass on negotiating – countless books, websites and podcasts cover the topic in much greater detail, and with much better authority that I can here. But I do think there are some things around negotiating as a woman that it's worth knowing, which I'll share with you now.

Men negotiate more often than women

While I presume it's no big surprise that men negotiate more often than women, it's worth reminding ourselves. Research shows us that, while 42 per cent of men were willing to initiate a negotiation for higher compensation, only 28 per cent of women self-identified as being willing to initiate the same discussion.[33] This comfort gap with negotiations is present from the very beginning of our working lives, with studies showing that only 7 per cent of women coming out of business school and stepping into their first role negotiated a starting salary, versus 57 per cent of men – leading to an average of a $7,000 gap in the first year of a woman's career, a disparity that can result in a pay gap that follows women throughout their professional lives.[34] Ultimately, this gap balloons to a loss worth almost $1 million over the average forty-five-year career.

When women do negotiate, they get better outcomes

Again, I know, no huge shock that when women *do* negotiate, it pays off. But, again, that's something really important to remember when approaching a new role, in order to end up with a better deal.

The value of being a comfortable and confident negotiator isn't limited to the interview stage of women's relationship with their employers. Once *in* roles, 'women who ask for a raise are twice as likely to receive one as women who don't'.[35] And, when women work and negotiate on behalf of one another, their successes are only multiplied.

Women get better outcomes when they advocate for one another than when they are pushing for their own wants or needs.[36] In fact, women are 14–23 per cent more successful than men when representing others in negotiations.[37]

That's probably something we have all felt intuitively to be true. It's always so much easier to help someone else than it is to help ourselves.

When a friend is looking for a new opportunity, preparing to ask for a promotion or negotiating the terms of a new role, it's so easy for us, as outsiders, to draw up a huge list of their winning qualities and the reasons that they deserve nothing but the most and the best in return for their work. It's so much easier to see the wood when we're not lost in the middle of all these trees – and this *might* be one reason that helping others feels so much easier than advocating for ourselves.

Another reason, though, may be linked to our old friend, the socialization of gender. Because, while we may be culturally cautious of a woman who advocates for her own needs with grit, ambition and determination – and so she may face a likeability backlash – we don't see women who advocate on the behalf of others in the same way. When we advocate on behalf of someone else, instead of bucking female stereotypes, we are seen as conforming to them – as being communal and collaborative, qualities much more in line with our societal expectations of women[38] – and so the fear of unlikeability doesn't hold women back from pushing for what is deserved.

Fear of being disliked stops women from negotiating

As with everything else associated with gender roles and the Glass Cliff, women's attitudes towards negotiation tell us everything about socialization and nothing about the inherent, innate qualities of being a woman. In western society, women are conditioned and expected to be conflict averse – to look for ways to end disagreements and to be reluctant to be the initiator of them.[39] This might go some way to explain any hesitation from women in asserting themselves and their needs during a negotiation.

It might also be that our collective socialization and expectations of women overall mean that women rightly fear they will be classified as aggressive and unlikeable if they choose to negotiate. This might lead them to decide it's simply not worth taking the chance. But, when dealing with a Glass Cliff scenario, there is an inherent risk in the situation which is already all on women's shoulders (or at least that's how it feels). I know I'd rather take on a well-paid risk than stay quiet and toil within a circumstance that is all risk, no potential reward.

Of course, both men and women go into negotiation situations hoping to successfully advocate for themselves and end up with an outcome that matches their goals. Women, however, are likely to have an additional cognitive load to bear during the process: the fear of taking the assertiveness necessary to successfully carry out a negotiation 'too far', and being seen to be 'unlikeable'.[40] Research shows us that remaining in line with the feminine qualities of niceness and softness that we have been socialized to expect from women takes the teeth out of women's ability to advocate for themselves effectively – too often seeing them veering towards likeability rather than successful negotiation for their needs.[41] As a result, women choose to modify their behaviour to become more agreeable and accommodating, meaning they don't ask for as much and walk away from the table with less than a man would in the same negotiation, feeling that they have pushed themselves as far into potential dislikeability as it feels safe to go.[42]

The problem is that worries about likeability aren't for nothing.

Research from Harvard Law School has shown us that, 'relative to men who ask for more, women are penalized financially, are considered less hireable and less likeable, and are less likely to be promoted', whereas 'men, by contrast, generally can negotiate for higher pay without fearing a backlash because such behaviour is consistent with the stereotype of men as assertive, bold, and self-interested'.[43]

So maybe we need to reframe what we think of when it comes to negotiations, if we want to be more successful in them.

When we change what's expected from a negotiation, women can come out on top

There is a really interesting piece of research that shows us just how much being a successful negotiator depends on our own social expectations.[44] In the study, run at Northwestern University, researchers examined the role of gender stereotypes in negotiations, and what they found was amazing.

When successful negotiation was framed in advance as relying on traditionally female-associated 'soft skills', such as communication, a high EQ* or collaboration, women outperformed men

---

* Emotional Quotient, or the level of someone's emotional intelligence (more on this in Chapter 5).

in negotiation outcomes (they got more of what they said they wanted, more of the time). However, when more traditionally male traits, such as assertiveness, determination or dominance were framed as the making of a good negotiator (as is usually the case in negotiations), men outperformed women in their respective gains.

It might be that we simply have a greater expectation that men will negotiate hard, which is in line with our socialized expectations of maleness. And so we have developed, over time, a bias towards a 'male style' of negotiation – so much so that, not only are women put off from negotiating at all, they also risk facing a likeability penalty if they do.

Maintain a personal identity outside of work

Toni Morrison wrote an incredible essay for *The New Yorker*, titled 'The Work You Do, The Person You Are', about her childhood job cleaning the house of a wealthy woman, which I think about all of the time. Here is the conclusion to the piece:

1. Whatever the work is, do it well – not for the boss but for yourself.
2. You make the job; it doesn't make you.
3. Your real life is with us, your family.
4. You are not the work you do; you are the person you are.

I have worked for all sorts of people since then, geniuses and morons, quick-witted and dull, bighearted and narrow. I've had many kinds of jobs, but since that conversation with my father I have never considered the level of labour to be the measure of myself, and I have never placed the security of a job above the value of home.[45]

I couldn't agree more, and I believe that having and maintaining a healthy work–life balance and a sense of self-identity outside of work is essential to not only happiness, but to mitigating the impact of the Glass Cliff.

Losing your job isn't any fun at all – but it's not as bad as losing yourself.

High-profile, senior-level roles are all-consuming. Or, at least, they can be if we let them. This is something I observed time and time again when I worked in a FAANG company. Like any large business, especially a tech innovator, there were very regular and very large reorgs, during which reporting lines could change within the blink of an eye, as roles flexed to meet the changing needs of the business (which in turn flexed and bent to meet the changing needs of viewers and members). This openness to change, driven by both internal and external factors, meant that employees needed to be flexible in terms of things like their titles, their remits, and sometimes even the country in which they worked.*

These large, often business-wide changes also meant that, as has very much been a theme across big tech in the 2020s, there was a constant churn of people being exited from the business, as reorgs, shifting priorities and below-expected new member sign-ups meant unforeseen changes had to be made to existing plans, which unfortunately included lay-offs.[46] Suddenly, all our jobs felt a lot more precarious than they had before.[47]

Reorgs and big changes in any business are never easy to navigate, and they can be genuinely intimidating. But it seemed to me that there were two very distinct approaches to the job that I saw in my colleagues overall, and these differing approaches appeared to have an impact on individuals' willingness to roll with the punches and feel confident and optimistic about their future.

---

* Flexibility was never my strong suit.

One group of people held their job, title and position within a FAANG business as central to their identity and sense of self,* both inside and outside of work. This meant they were often more willing to prioritize the needs of the business above their own personal needs, rather than risk the loss of that important element of their self-identity. Others, by comparison, saw their role not as an identity, but as a day job – an interaction in which they were willing to exchange a certain amount of their time and expertise for an agreed amount of compensation from the business (my approach). For this second group of people, when their working day was over, so too, largely, was their self-identity of 'belonging to' the business. And it also seemed to me that these were the people who took changes, reorgs and even exits more easily in their stride. We knew that, if the value balance or the return on investment of what we gave to a role versus what we got back from it stopped working for us, we could simply walk away, without any damage to our self-identity.

We could argue that it makes sense. We could say that those people who saw their employment as an exchange of goods and services were less *dedicated* to their roles, and so cared less if they found themselves in a precarious position. But I think something different was at play. I think those stunning colleagues[†] who saw their employment as a transactional exchange had done something really important – they had maintained a sense of identity and self, outside of their work – which had allowed them to assess if proposed changes really were the right thing for them, *as well as* the needs of the business.

Resisting the urge to merge work and self allowed them to be firmer in their boundaries, saying no and challenging decisions

---

* Working within these businesses, known for fast-growth stock, high performance, innovation and high salaries, is seen as a badge of honour to some.
† The business I worked for refers to every employee as a 'stunning colleague'; I'm not being weird!

that would create hardship for them or their families (such as being required to move country). Someone who had built a self-identity with their job role at the centre, on the other hand, couldn't do that, as they would risk not only losing a role, but losing a big part of their perception of self, if refusing meant putting their job security at risk.

I implore you to protect your identity outside of any working relationship, fiercely. Jobs come and go, particularly precarious Glass Cliff ones, and it's important to at least have yourself to fall back on, should things go wrong or something unexpected play out.*

Part of the way we can do this is in protecting a healthy work–life balance and avoiding, where possible, work–life blending.

Maintaining a healthy work–life balance

Senior roles can be intensive, particularly if we've been brought in to reset and revitalize a company and a team that's in a period of crisis.

Recently, I had a friend who had left a long-term role at Amazon to take on a new position at TikTok. She was young and ambitious, but sadly she found that, despite her high hopes and best intentions, the new role simply wasn't a good fit for her. She wanted to leave, she told me, but she didn't want to let the business down.

I listened and I nodded along, and then I told her what I thought she needed to hear in that moment. And that's really what I want to share with you, too. So here we go:

Your job isn't real, and it doesn't care about you. It's not able to. Individual people you work with do, of course, but they will also leave when the time is right for them. And the business itself? It simply

---

* I ended up leaving in a reorg in 2021, after leading the UK/EMEA arm of a staff strike in protest of transphobic content – a risk, and a stand, I never would have been able to take if I didn't have a strong sense of self and my values and identity outside of my working life.

doesn't care about you. At all. It can't, because your job isn't a person, and, no matter what you do, it's not going to love you back.

Why would we give all our time, our attention – all of *ourselves* – to something that is simply never going to love us back? I mean, sure – if we die, they'll send flowers, but not before they've had a meeting about what on earth they're going to do next, and how they're going to fill the role.

Why would we bend over backwards to make another person's business a success, at the cost of ourselves? *Especially* if we're not shareholders. (Negotiate stock, please.)

The way that we approach these roles also has an impact on the expectations and ambitions of the next generation of women entering the workforce. In the 2022 Women in the Workplace report, co-authored by McKinsey and the Lean In Foundation, two out of every three women under thirty years old said that they 'would be more interested in advancing if they saw senior leaders with the work–life balance that they want.' Most women under thirty (58 per cent) also said that advancing professionally had become more important to them in the past two years. And, in the same survey, 76 per cent of women under thirty said that flexibility has become more important.[48] Younger women are looking for workplaces to be flexible for them, rather than seeing flexibility at work as a one-way street, all give and no take.

Set boundaries. Build guard rails around yourself. Rely on your network and have difficult conversations that clearly outline the challenges you know you're likely to face from the Glass Cliff before you get going in roles.

None of it is easy. All of it feels gross, and as though we're putting ourselves at risk by being clear about exactly what we are and are not willing to give to make a role a success. But, if we're going to take on a risk and step into a precarious position in order to fix someone else's mess, we need to make sure that it works for us and our needs, too.

TL;DR: *Too Long; Didn't Read*

- If you've decided to take on a role where there's a high likelihood of facing the Glass Cliff, there are some things that can be done to mitigate the risk.

  - Acknowledge it in advance. Identifying the risk from the beginning, both in negotiations with the business and in your social circle, can help in making it feel more manageable, and can also help you to gather support. Having these discussions can be intimidating and uncomfortable – but it's better than finding yourself on the edge of a cliff, with no support or understanding.

  - Identify key relationships and support systems within the business. The Glass Cliff happens most often when there isn't a clear in-business support structure. In fact, it almost disappears in supportive environments. Find out who your closest relationships will be with, and gauge the support you can expect from them before making a decision.

  - Agree timelines in advance. Turning around a business that's in difficulty is not only challenging, it takes time. Agree timelines for key areas of progress and change in advance as a shared measure of success.

- If you're going to take on a role where there's a high likelihood you'll face the Glass Cliff, it should be worth your while. This means being unafraid to negotiate and advocate for your needs. Know your worth and don't offer discounts.

- Losing a job is hard. Really hard. But losing a job *and* yourself is much harder. Maintain and protect an identity outside of work, maintain a work–life balance, remember who you are and remember why you're already smashing it.

CHAPTER 5

Am I the Problem?

Let us never cease from thinking – what is this 'civilization' in which we find ourselves? What are these ceremonies and why should we take part in them? What are these professions and why should we make money out of them?

VIRGINIA WOOLF[1]

In October 2014, following an especially tense hearing with members of Congress, Julia Pierson resigned from her role as the first female director of the US Secret Service in its 150-year history.[2] She had taken on the position in March 2013 – just nineteen months prior.

Although her time in role had been short, her appointment – the result of a nomination by President Obama himself – was initially a cause for celebration. In his announcement of Pierson taking on the position, Obama had said, 'Over her thirty years of experience with the Secret Service, Julia has consistently exemplified the spirit and dedication the men and women of the service demonstrate every day [. . .] Julia is eminently qualified to lead the agency that not only safeguards Americans at major events and secures our financial system, but also protects our leaders and our first families, including my own.'[3]

Hopes had been high – so how had things gone so badly so quickly?

During Pierson's brief time as head of the Secret Service, there were several very serious breaches of security. Firstly, a security contractor, armed with a gun despite reportedly having three previous convictions for assault and battery, shared an elevator journey with President Obama in Atlanta, an incident that wasn't disclosed to the president himself, or his wider team, and wasn't referred to an 'investigative unit that was created to review violations of protocol and standards.'[4]

Only a few days after that incident, an intruder armed with a knife was able to gain access to the interior of the White House after jumping over a fence and making it all the way to the East Office. This was another serious breach, the severity of which the Secret Service failed to accurately disclose.*

Following these incidents, lawmakers and politicians alike expressed a lack of confidence in the agency under Pierson's watch, criticized the Secret Service for its lack of transparency and voiced serious concerns for the safety of the president, who, despite initially defending her, eventually conceded that new leadership was required, 'in light of recent and accumulating reports about the agency'.[5]

The sentiment that it was time for Pierson to step down from her role was shared by a number of political leaders from both parties, including Elijah Cummings, ranking Democrat on the House oversight committee, who said during an interview with CNN, 'I want her to go if she cannot restore trust in the agency, and if she cannot get the culture back in order. I told her that she's got a tall order there.'[6]

Speaking to Bloomberg News in light of the calls for her resignation, Pierson reportedly said, 'I think it's in the best interest of the Secret Service and the American public if I step down. Congress has lost confidence in my ability to run the agency. The media has made it clear that this is what they expected.'[7]

There were many who agreed with the decision – after all, the role of security services is to provide security, to keep people safe from potential threats and dangers, rather than putting them in harm's way and then failing to fully disclose the level of the breaches. Rosemary Plorin, president of PR firm Lovell Communications, said at the time, 'When the president learns about a major security breach moments before it is discussed in the media, I think you have to assume that your career timeline just got a lot shorter,' adding that, 'Julia Pierson is dead in the

---

* They initially reported that the intruder was unarmed and made it no further than the door of the White House building.

water. The Secret Service has experienced a more significant loss of confidence across the board than GM has.'[8]

I think we can all agree that none of this looks good, and that some very, *very* serious oversights were made. But it's worth pausing for a moment to ask the question: what was the agency like *before* the appointment of its first ever female leader, just nineteen months previously? Had the Secret Service held the confidence of Americans at large up to that point?

The answer to that question is a resounding 'no'.

President Obama's nomination of Pierson as the new leader of the Secret Service, and her subsequent stepping into the leadership role, had in fact come at a time of very public scandal for the agency.

It was reported that, under the leadership of the previous director, Mark Sullivan, eleven Secret Service employees on a trip to Colombia, while preparing for Obama's arrival, had potentially compromised security by employing twenty sex workers[9] as well as boasting to members of the public that they worked for Obama and were in Colombia to protect him, while partying at a club in Cartagena.[10] Far from being an isolated incident, this happened during the same year that three agents on a working trip to Amsterdam had to be sent home over 'a drunken incident in a hotel' the day before Obama was due to arrive.[11] The news sparked scrutiny of, and embarrassment for, the service – resulting in a very public scandal and reputational damage.[12] *The Washington Post* reported that married agents had been heard to joke during aircraft take-off about an unofficial, but very widespread, Secret Service motto – 'wheels up, rings off' – running a headline just a few days later that read, 'The Secret Service had the "Worst Week in Washington".[13]

Of those who were pushed out of their roles in the service following the reports, two were senior leaders within the agency with over twenty years of experience – leading many to wonder if this incident was a one-off lapse of judgement or an indication of more systemic issues as a result of the culture that had been allowed to develop, and eventually boil over, under the leadership of Sullivan, who had headed the service for seven years.[14] Sullivan maintained that it wasn't indicative of a wider problem or mismanagement, though.

According to *The Guardian*, in June 2002 the US News & World Report 'painted a picture of an agency "rife with problems" ranging from alcohol abuse to criminal offences, as well as allegations of extramarital relationships between agents and White House staff.' The same article added that a follow-up piece in September indicated 'a "pressure-cooker" environment where a "debilitating loss of manpower" coincided with increased responsibilities.'[15]

It was also reported that the Secret Service had, as a result of poor management, suffered from underfunding and understaffing, and had developed a culture of 'laxness and corner-cutting'.[16] Ronald Kessler, a journalist and author of the book *Inside the CIA*, who helped break the story of misconduct during the Colombia trip, claimed that 'The Secret Service is overwhelmed with more and more duties and not enough agents. They are all working overtime', which he believed led to the neglecting of 'basic security precautions'.[17]

But, you might be saying, these are different kinds of problems. A Secret Service allowing a security breach that could endanger the president is not the same as some agents getting carried away on a night out.

That might be true. Yet, Pierson's predecessor also had a security breach on his watch – in an incident in which two reality-TV stars were able to infiltrate a state dinner being held by Obama at the White House,[18] getting past 'three [separate] Secret Service checkpoints despite not being on the guest list' – an incident that Kessler describes as 'further evidence of poor standards under Sullivan's watch'.[19] The incident took place in 2009, three years before the incident in Colombia and Pierson's appointment, and *The Washington Post* reported that Jason Chaffetz, chairman of the House oversight and government reform subcommittee on national security, said that he 'fears the agency's leadership needs an overhaul [. . .] The Secret Service has a serious management problem, and they have to acknowledge it.'[20]

There was a big mess waiting for Pierson when she stepped into her role – not only in terms of reputation, but also in terms of resources (available budget) and personnel staffing – making her position as the first woman to hold the title in the agency's entire history even more challenging and noteworthy. In announcing her new role when she accepted the position in 2013, *The Guardian* wrote, 'By appointing a woman, the White House sends a message that a macho culture will not be tolerated.'[21]

Pierson inherited a Secret Service that was overstretched, 'perpetually underfunded and understaffed.'[22] Pierson said, in testimony before Congress, that the agency was 550 employees below its 'optimal level', an issue that she inherited and which may well have led to some of the problems she faced in her time as the service's leader.[23] After the second security breach, when a man was able to break into the grounds of the White House wielding a knife, *The Washington Post* reported:

> [F]ormer agents said they fear the breach may [have been] related to a severe staffing shortage [that] the agency [had] struggled with in the past year in its Uniform Division. This is the team of officers with primary responsibility for securing the White House grounds, and the service [had] been flying in agents from field offices around the country to do temporary assignments. Those agents naturally would have [had] less familiarity with the grounds and intruder response plans.[24]

While her predecessor, Mark Sullivan, was given the time and opportunity to continue in role, and potentially solve the issues the Secret Service was facing under his leadership, Pierson inherited a stack of problems and was pushed out of her position in under two years for not being able to tidy up the mess.

•　　•　　•

As part of their International Women's Day celebrations 2023, I was invited by the Women of the World Festival to host a panel discussion at the Southbank Centre on the topic of the Glass Cliff.*
I was nervous and excited – unsure what to expect. Although I'm very regularly invited into businesses to speak about the phenomenon, this would be my first time having the discussion with members of the public. Since the phenomenon has up to now been relatively overlooked, I wasn't sure what the appetite would be for the discussion, nor how many people the panel would attract.

It turned out to be the most oversubscribed session of the day.

Before the doors opened, as I was testing the microphone and making sure I didn't have lipstick on my teeth, an unexpectedly large number of women began to gather outside the room to secure a seat in the audience.

OK, I thought, *we're on to something here.*

Once the doors opened, the seats quickly filled up, but the queue didn't seem to have subsided at all, and more and more women continued to file in, finding spaces for themselves to stand at the back of the room, or sit on the floor or on the internal window ledges, with some even sneaking in while the event organizers' backs were turned, ducking under their arms as they turned to count the capacity of the room.

Despite the squeeze, dozens of women had to be turned away from the session, as there was simply no more space. We were

---

* Speaking at the Southbank Centre had always been a dream of mine, but one that I'd never really thought would come true. The invite to host came on the same day that Beyoncé announced her Renaissance tour – and, honestly, it was probably the best day of all time.

lucky enough to have a British Sign Language interpreter for the event, which meant that, while several members of the deaf community were able to secure front-row seats to the discussion, others, who had arrived later, were able to stand just outside the glass doors, watching the interpreters throughout the entire session.

The thing that really struck me, once the event was over, besides realizing for the first time the huge appetite for this discussion, was the nature of the questions in the room. I had anticipated that questions would be theoretical, based on understanding the phenomenon in an academic context – the way I had always thought of the topic up to that point. In reality, the questions from the women who had given up their Saturday afternoons to attend the session were all personal and urgent. These were women who found themselves teetering on the edge of professional cliffs – they were desperate both for advice, and to feel less alone in their experiences. They said they were grateful to have been given the words and framing to realize that what they were living through was not a personal failure. They repeatedly stressed that, although they felt sad that their experiences had taken them to the edge of the Glass Cliff, they were glad to be able to see that the issue was systemic, larger than themselves, and that they could begin to find community within that, as a shared experience.

As the event was drawing to a close, a woman who had come alone and was sitting in the front row put up her hand and I passed her the mic. She said she didn't have a question, but she wanted to thank us for talking about this important topic – a topic that she'd never heard of before – because it allowed her to understand what she was going through at work right now.

She explained that she had been brought into a new senior finance role in the business she was working for, but that things had been slowly going wrong before she even arrived (which, of course, as we've seen, is one of the conditions for the Glass Cliff) and, after a couple of years of trying to make it work, she had been forced to leave what she had thought would be her dream job, because of what she felt was the business owners' lack of support. She told us, trying to be cheerful, that it was OK – she'd been starting to feel a little better since she'd stopped trying to make the job work, because, no matter what she did or how hard she tried, it just wasn't working. She told us that she had been able to find some relief when, instead of trying to save herself and her role, which was the stressful position she'd been in for the months before, she had decided she'd had enough. She'd got a lawyer, there was a draft exit settlement, there was an end in sight. She told us that she'd been young when she'd taken the role, in her thirties, and that, although she'd thought she was ready for it, clearly she hadn't been, and she thought that was the problem.

'I really did think I was ready for it,' she said, shaking her head as she handed back the mic. She was visibly upset.

I felt bad for her, but I was in host mode, and she hadn't asked a question, so I looked around the raised hands to see who would speak next, planning to grab a moment with her once the panel was over.

To know me is to know that I'm not the most gushing in an emotional situation, but, happily, the same couldn't be said for my panel-mates, who swooped in to give this woman the reassurances she needed and deserved. They recognized the pain she was feeling as she watched what she thought was her dream job turning into a nightmare. They understood the self-doubt that was plaguing her as she tried to balance her belief that she'd been ready for the role with what seemed like indisputable evidence that she hadn't. They empathized, knowing that she was going through an internal rebranding – no longer seeing herself as a woman who could take on new challenges and win, but as someone who had bitten off more than she could chew and was now paying the price of her overambition.

She was seeing herself as the problem. And that simply was not the case. Because, to have even got into that position, she must be phenomenal. Once we remember that the Glass Cliff is a cultural phenomenon, rather than a personal, individual failing, we can see how things that we might have otherwise blamed ourselves for are actually part of something so much bigger than us.

I realized then that there must be thousands of women in the same position as the one who spoke at my talk – women who took up what seemed to be dream leadership positions and then, in lieu of any other explanation available to them, blamed themselves for the Glass Cliff they only realized they were walking along once they found themselves teetering on its edge – before, inevitably, falling off it.

To those women, I say this: it is far more likely you're experiencing the Glass Cliff phenomenon than you're bad at your job, especially if the business's outlook was in any way bleak when you took the position. Time after time, women are proven to be exceptional leaders – better than men, in many scenarios – yet we never hear those stories or statistics in our cultural conversation.

So that's what this chapter is. It's not you that's the problem, and I'll prove it.

The truth about leadership for women

It's really important that we're honest about what leadership and life above the Glass Ceiling can be like for a lot of women.

My background is mostly in advertising, and so, when I imagine a leader, a couple of things spring to mind. Firstly, in my head, a leader is default male. I know, I know. *Still*. Isn't it ridiculous? After all this work, after all the research I've read and the conversations I've had, and even despite having been a leader myself, I've not been able to escape that socialization of having a man in my mind. But I can be honest about it, at least.

When I picture leaders, what I see in my mind looks suspiciously like characters from *Mad Men* – a group of white men with smoke wafting around them, each with a tumbler of a spirit over ice in their hand.* And I picture them doing stereotypical TV 'leadership' things – talking in hushed voices, looking intently at a graph, hosting an important meeting. But that's not what leadership really looks like. For one, it's not the seventies, but, for two, the reality of leading for a woman – and particularly for a woman who has been brought in to lead a business that's facing a crisis – just doesn't fit in with any versions of leadership I've ever seen in a TV show or film. And I bet you haven't either.

◆　　◆　　◆

In 2020, Amanda Blanc joined Aviva, the international insurance company, as the UK's group chief executive. In 2023, it was widely reported that some of the company's shareholders had made 'sexist' and 'derogatory' comments about her at the business's AGM. The BBC reported that one shareholder said during the meeting that a 'speech where she highlighted returns to share-holders was at odds with Aviva's share price performance over the past ten years, which signified "she's not the man for the job"', despite the fact that, as the BBC also pointed out, 'Aviva's market capitalisation is about a third higher than when Ms Blanc joined.' A second shareholder questioned whether or not Blanc should be 'wearing trousers', before a third took a swipe at board-level women overall, reportedly saying, 'They are so good at basic housekeeping activities, I'm sure this will be reflected in the direction of the board in future.'[25]

In a statement on LinkedIn after the meeting, Blanc wrote, 'In all honesty, after thirty-plus years in financial services I am pretty used to sexist and derogatory comments like those in the AGM yesterday [. . .] I guess that after you have heard the same prejudicial rhetoric for so long though, it makes you a little immune

---

* Advertising is still suspiciously close to the tropes shown in *Mad Men*, and I've genuinely never worked in an office that *doesn't* have an open bar.

to it all'. She went on to say that, as is the case for so many other women in leadership in businesses, she had already gained her 'fair share of misogynistic scars' from the boardrooms of the businesses she'd worked at. 'The more senior the role I have taken, the more overt the unacceptable behaviour,' she added.[26]

Sadly, though, and in keeping with the thoughts shared by the secretary general of the United Nations around the rights and opportunities of women stalling and even being eroded, Blanc didn't believe the fortunes or acceptance of women in senior roles were improving. In fact, she said that she believed the opposite was true – pointing out that, while such comments might have been made privately in past years, the fact that they had been emboldened to express these sexist views and remarks publicly was 'a new development'.

In a society where it's – of course, rightly – taboo for a company to express the slightest hint of sexism, an insidious hidden consequence has developed: the sexism has gone underground, and a host of leadership issues faced by women have been swept under the rug. Because they're not part of the discourse, they're not being named or tamed, and nobody is able to prepare for them, and so the cycle of sexism continues unchecked.

That's unacceptable. So, if you're stepping into or already working in a leadership role, here are some things I want you to know about the state of our workplaces – because the more we know, the more prepared we can be, and hopefully, the more we can shape better outcomes for ourselves.

Even once they become leaders, women are expected to take on hidden work

When women take on leadership roles, even the most senior leadership roles, there are likely to be a whole host of additional hidden expectations that come along with it, which men would not be expected to perform.

It's like office housework, but at a whole new level.

In 2022, the Lean In Foundation and McKinsey published their annual Women in the Workplace report, which highlighted some interesting discrepancies in the tasks, responsibilities and expectations of female versus male leaders in the workplace. They found that:

- Women leaders are twice as likely as their male counterparts to spend 'substantial' amounts of time on diversity, equity and inclusion work, in addition to their actual job roles, even though 40 per cent of them say that it isn't acknowledged or taken into account during performance reviews.

- Women are more likely than men to be active as 'people-focused' leaders, and more likely to 'take consistent steps to promote employee well-being, such as checking in on their team members and helping them manage their workloads'.

- While 86 per cent of companies say that it's 'very or extremely' critical that managers support their team members' well-being, only 25 per cent of them formally recognize those leaders who take on this additional emotional burden.[27]

With all of this in mind, it's no wonder that 43 per cent of female leaders report experiencing burnout, compared to just 31 per cent of men at their level, and that female leaders are 50 per cent more likely than male leaders to have changed jobs because their workload was unmanageable.[28]

Even when women are capable and prepared to take on leadership roles, the reality of the additional burdens we are implicitly expected to take on is far beyond the requirements of the leadership roles on paper, and above and beyond the expectations made of our male colleagues.

Even getting fired doesn't necessarily mean you've done a bad job

All of this is unfair. Absolutely. And I'm sorry to say it – but I have one final unfair fact to share with you before we get to some good stuff. And that is, even the circumstances in which male and female leaders are fired are unequal.

In short, male leaders get fired when business performance is bad on their watch. But, while women leaders also lose their jobs when performance is poor, they are just as likely to get fired from their roles even when performance is good.[29]

Female CEOs lose their jobs even when their businesses are thriving.[30]

The research tells us that, overall, female CEOs are about 45 per cent more likely to be fired than their male counterparts, and that while, for men, improvements in self-performance can protect them from losing their jobs, no similar protections are given to women leaders.[31]

One of the study's researchers said, in a statement, 'Dismissing the CEO is usually viewed as evidence of good corporate governance as it suggests that the board is taking its monitoring role seriously, however, our research reveals there are invisible but serious gender biases in how the board evaluates CEOs and its decision to retain or fire particular CEOs.'[32]

The study's* co-author added, 'The results of this study point to the extra pressure and scrutiny directed at women in senior

---

* This study is very similar to another which looked exclusively at the experiences of financial advisers who had been found to have committed an act of misconduct. In this study, female advisers were 20 per cent more likely to lose their jobs, and 30 per cent less likely to find new jobs in the field compared to male advisers. 'Although men commit misconduct at a rate that is three times higher than women, women face substantially harsher punishments both by the firms that employ them, and other potential employers in the industry,' the study found.

leadership positions relative to their male counterparts. This is problematic because women face difficult barriers and obstacles in breaking through the proverbial Glass Ceiling, but they also seem to continue to face additional challenges even after reaching the top of the corporate hierarchy.'[33]

BUT, WHAT ABOUT . . . ?

Does the Glass Cliff mean that women should be allowed to be in roles where they are underperforming? Does it mean that women should be given unlimited time, resources and support to fail in place?

It's important to remember that the Glass Cliff is a phenomenon at a societal level, not an individual level. Seeing a small number of women take on roles that are less or even not at all susceptible to the Glass Cliff playing out doesn't mean the phenomenon isn't real. In the same way, seeing a high-profile senior woman lose her job isn't always indicative that the Glass Cliff is at play.

Sometimes women, even senior women, are bad at their jobs. Or they're not the right fit for that particular company. Or the timing is wrong. Or a million other things that we know can impact anyone's success in a role, regardless of their gender, might be going on behind the scenes.

Was Liz Truss the shortest-serving UK prime minister because of the Glass Cliff or because she wasn't right for the job? The situation isn't always clear, and there are always personalities at play.

I'm happy to say that, for once, it's not all doom and gloom. Because, although workplaces may not currently be set up to protect and respect women in leadership, there is some very good evidence to suggest that women are, in fact, really good when they're given the chance to lead. On their own terms. Particularly during a time of crisis.

Women lead better in a crisis

It takes much longer, on average, for women to be appointed to the most senior roles than men – females are on average four years older than males when they step into their first CEO role, and it takes boards a third longer to choose a woman for a CEO role than a man.[34] Despite this, however, once they're in roles, women do in fact seem to lead better than men, especially during a crisis.

In anticipation of International Women's Day 2023, Personal Finance Club put together some stats about how the female-led businesses in the S&P 500 were performing.* What they found was astonishing. Firstly, of the 500 businesses that make up the index, only 6.4 per cent – thirty-two companies – had a female CEO. But secondly, and perhaps more surprisingly, despite being a tiny minority, those firms that were led by women had 'significantly outperformed' those led by men over the past ten years; more specifically, 'the difference in returns is 384 per cent from female-led companies† vs 261 per cent from male-led companies.'[35] Not only that; women are also rated as being better leaders by the people who work with them, and this gap, both

---

* The Standard and Poor's 500 is one of the most commonly followed equity indexes – tracking the stock performance of 500 of the largest companies listed on stock exchanges in the United States.

† While not all of these companies had female CEOs for the full ten-year period, the researchers do note that, 'if you compared these companies [during] just the period when they all had a female CEO, the women-led companies still outperform the male-led companies (and the overall market as well!)'.

in terms of outcomes and approval, only seems to grow when we're facing a crisis.[36]

The Covid-19 factor

If we want to look at the impact of gender on leadership during a time of crisis, we really don't need to look far. We have all, in the past few years, endured the global crisis that is the Covid-19 pandemic. There is arguably no higher leadership position than being the prime minister or president of a country (or equivalent), and looking at data about how different countries managed the outbreak may give us some insight into how women really do perform in leadership positions during a crisis.

How did those countries headed up by women fare during the Covid-19 pandemic compared to those headed by men?

In short – female-led countries fared better. A lot better, in fact.

Researchers looked at a data set that covered 194 countries with a variety of socio-demographic variables and found that Covid outcomes were systemically and significantly better in those countries headed by women, such as Germany, New Zealand,* Denmark, Taiwan and Finland.[37] On average, each of these went into lockdown earlier than those countries with male leadership, and suffered half as many deaths.

Speaking to *The Guardian* about their work, one of the researchers noted, 'This analysis clearly confirms that when women-led countries are compared to countries similar to them along a range of characteristics, they have performed better, experiencing fewer cases as well as fewer deaths,' adding that female

---

* Even when the female leadership 'outliers' of New Zealand and Germany and the male leadership outliers of the USA were removed from the statistics, the study found that the case for the relative success of female leaders was only heightened, *The Guardian* reported.

leaders of countries during the pandemic had shown an interesting attitude towards risk, both leaning into and avoiding it. They were 'risk averse with regard to lives', and so put their countries into lockdown conditions significantly earlier than those led by men, while also being 'more willing to take risks in the domain of the economy'.

The study shows, in the words of the researchers, that 'being female-led has provided countries with an advantage in the current crisis'.[38]

This is a sentiment mirrored by Susannah Torpey, co-chair of Winston & Strawn LLP's Technology Antitrust Group, who pointed out that women leaders had disproportionately been the ones who listened to and followed the advice of scientists despite public backlash, showing the ability to 'exercise good judgement in the face of harsh criticism and concerns relating to short-term economic effects.'[39]

But does it have to be a woman making choices for an entire country during a global pandemic for us to see these disparities, or are women, overall, better suited to lead during times of crisis?

Staff prefer a female leader during turbulent times

Building on work they conducted pre-pandemic – in which they looked at assessments of over 60,000 leaders and found that women were rated as better leaders than men by those who worked with them – researchers from leadership development consultancy Zenger Folkman wanted to find out if the same remained true during the first phase of the Covid-19 crisis.[40]

When they repeated their study, albeit with a greatly reduced sample size, they found that not only did their pre-pandemic findings remain true, but the gap between positive assessments of male and female leaders by those who worked directly with them had actually widened over time – people rated their female leaders *even more* positively than they had before the pandemic – suggesting that women had done a particularly good job of leading during that incredibly difficult period. Of the nineteen 'key competency criteria' areas that the leaders were measured against, women were rated more highly in thirteen.*

As well as being assessed in their competencies, each leader was also given an 'employee engagement score' based on the responses of those who reported directly to them to questions about how satisfied and committed they felt within their roles. For those with male leaders during Covid, employee engagement was 'slightly below average', with a score of 49.2.† We all know working through Covid was incredibly hard, so really this isn't a shock. However, for those employees led by a woman, the results were 'significantly higher', with a score of 55.2 being recorded.

Employees in businesses with female leaders not only gave them higher approval ratings, they themselves were more engaged and satisfied in their work.

But why would that be?

In order to better understand, the researchers looked at which key competencies employees said mattered to them the most as the pandemic unfolded. They discovered that, during this time of high risk and fast change, employees placed a higher value on interpersonal skills – such as 'inspires and motivates', 'communicates powerfully', 'collaboration/teamwork' and 'relationship building' – all qualities that fit with the socialization of femininity, which women traditionally demonstrate higher instances of.

---

* Men were rated more highly only in one competency area – 'technical/professional expertise' – although the researchers say that the difference was 'not [large enough to be] statistically significant'.
† With fifty being average.

We undervalue emotional intelligence

In 2017, the World Economic Forum looked at the impact of EQ, or emotional intelligence, in the workplace, and what they found was incredible. When they tested emotional intelligence alongside a set of thirty-three other workplace skills, they discovered that EQ was the 'strongest predictor of performance, explaining a full 58 per cent of success in all types of jobs.' They found that 90 per cent of top performers scored highly in emotional intelligence, versus only 20 per cent of bottom performers, noting that, 'You can be a top performer without emotional intelligence, but the chances are slim.'[41]

Not only are professionally successful people likely to have a higher EQ, there is also an incredibly strong relationship between the skill set and financial rewards, with the research finding that those workers with a high EQ make, on average, $29,000 more per year than their less emotionally intelligent counterparts. The link is so strong and direct that 'every point increase in emotional intelligence adds $1,300 to an annual salary', a finding that remained true for people in all industries, at all levels, in every region of the world. The researchers noted that they 'haven't yet been able to find a job in which performance and pay aren't tied closely to emotional intelligence.'[42]

I find this surprising, because it's so different from the words and characteristics we usually use to talk about success and leadership. Yet, as we know, when the Glass Cliff comes into play, when we're in a risky or precarious position, these softer, more personable skills are those that we turn to female leaders to provide.

As we've seen, one of the reasons that businesses are more likely to bring in women in leadership positions during times of crisis is because of a belief that women have a greater abundance of soft skills, and that those soft skills are good for re-engaging a team that has gone through a difficult patch – which the research I've just mentioned seems to endorse.

So what is the value of soft skills for leaders? And are there particular sets of soft skills that really do help during times of crisis?

It seems that, especially in times of great uncertainty and fast change, rather than wanting a leader to be cold, detached or authoritative, what people want most is to feel that their leader understands and is empathetic to the difficulty of the situation and the challenges their team is likely to face. In this instance, the value of transparency becomes particularly important and desirable.

When things have gone wrong – *wrong* wrong, *big* wrong – it's easy for people at all levels to fall into survival mode, to keep their heads down, try not to rock the boat and hope that things will get better soon. Talking about things that are going wrong is difficult and can make us feel vulnerable, and so it might feel safer to adopt a 'business as usual' approach, despite you and your team all knowing that, just beneath the surface, nothing is actually as calm as it seems. But it could be that there is a real value in transparency and authenticity at times like this.

'Being transparent is critical during challenging times,' said Vanessa Akhtar of Kotter International, a management consulting firm based in Seattle and Boston, in an interview with writer Sara Connell. 'The notion of taking care of your team, being vulnerable, and creating space for others to be vulnerable as well is really important. Showing that you're human and creating as much clarity as possible will go a long way during challenging times.'[43]

Another soft skill that seems to be required of successful leaders dealing with times of crisis is empathy – so much so that *Forbes* recently reported that it is a 'strategic imperative in business.'[44] The WEC research showed that 61 per cent of people surveyed with 'highly empathic senior leaders report often or always being innovative at work, as compared to only 13 per cent of those with less empathic senior leaders'. Furthermore, 76 per cent of people surveyed 'with highly empathic senior leaders report often or always feeling engaged, compared to only 32 per cent of those with less empathic senior leaders.'[45]

Working with a leader who displays empathy allows people to be more innovative, to dream bigger and to take more risks in the hope of greater reward for the business – to such a degree that the researchers concluded that 'cultivating empathic leadership is an effective strategy to respond to crisis with the heart and authenticity that many employees crave – and boost productivity.'[46]

This is a truth that female leaders have known all along. Dr Jen Welter, the former professional football player and gold medallist who became the first female coach in NFL history (as discussed in Chapter 2), knew that she needed to be her true and authentic self if she was going to build connections with her players and earn their trust. 'One thing I knew very distinctly,' she said on an Indeed.com panel about women in leadership, 'I was never going to outman a man at being a man.' So she didn't try to. Instead, she leaned into the skills and competencies that came naturally to her, instead of trying to follow an idea of leadership which felt forced.[47]

So, while our perceived higher propensity for soft skills can land us in Glass Cliff positions – being more likely to be appointed into leadership when there is some kind of crisis to overcome – it seems that there is a real benefit to leaders, and their teams, when they take a more open, transparent and empathetic approach.

However someone feels as they find themselves in the precarious position of the Glass Cliff, whatever their involvement in leadership has been, I want to be clear – experiencing the Glass Cliff is no individual's fault. I really hope that having some language to put around it, and a fuller understanding of the elements of women's accounts of leadership to add context, can help people to see that, and can help those facing it to feel less alone in the experience.

It's not you; the system is rigged, and no one is talking about it.

As we saw in the previous chapter, even when women out-perform men, their scores for perceived potential are lower, meaning they have to prove and re-prove their leadership potential to be taken seriously and given leadership opportunities. And, as we've seen in this chapter, even after being appointed, there is very likely to be a whole host of factors, prejudices and expectations put at women's doors that it would have been difficult to anticipate and prepare for.

Even at the most senior levels, women are still being expected to take on undervalued, unsupported caring and nurturing office housework in businesses that men are not being expected to do. Is it any wonder, then, that, instead of waiting to be pushed out of leadership roles, women are falling out of love with the romance of leadership and taking matters into their own hands? Should we be surprised at the emergence of what researchers are beginning to call the Great Break-Up?

TL;DR: *Too Long; Didn't Read*

• Women are rated as better leaders by those they work with.

• Businesses led by women, in the ten years ending in 2023, outperformed their male-led counterparts and the overall market, in terms of financial returns.

• Even when women do make it to the most senior leadership positions, their experiences are often quite different from the polished, idealized vision of leadership we've come to expect and imagine. This is for reasons such as:

  – Additional office housework. Even at the most senior levels of business, women don't escape office housework, as they are disproportionately expected to take on tasks such as leading DEI initiatives and providing nurturing, pastoral care to their team members. These expectations are in addition to their on-paper job roles, are not taken into consideration in performance reviews and can lead to burnout.

  – The risk of being fired, even when things are going well. Overall, female CEOs are about 45 per cent more likely to be fired than their male counterparts. And, while male leaders tend to be at risk of losing their jobs when the business they're leading is performing poorly, women are just as likely to get fired from their roles even when performance is good.

• Women seem to lead better during times of crisis. This could be due to women demonstrating higher workplace EQ. Higher emotional intelligence is directly related to workplace success (and compensation). Female leaders tend to show higher levels of authenticity, transparency and empathy – qualities that lead to increased engagement and innovation in their employees.

– Those countries led by women during the Covid-19 crisis were 'risk averse with regard to lives' and so put their countries into lockdown conditions significantly earlier than those led by men, following the advice of scientists above pressures related to the potential impact on the economy. Ultimately, these countries experienced fewer Covid-related deaths.

– Staff prefer working for women when crisis strikes, with a study involving 60,000 leaders finding that women outperformed men in thirteen of nineteen potential competency categories.

CHAPTER 6

The Great Break-Up

Until a white man comes to any place,
nothing lives.
It's only when he comes and says, 'Boof,
I've discovered you.' Now you exist.

MIRIAM MAKEBA[1]

I n 2014, Ellen Pao became the interim CEO of Reddit.

Even before taking on the role, Pao had a strong reputation within the tech field. In 2012, she had been the plaintiff in 'Silicon Valley's most-watched gender discrimination suit'[2] when she'd sued her previous employers.*

Pao, who had trained and worked as a corporate lawyer before joining the world of Silicon Valley tech, first joined Reddit in 2013 as the head of business development and strategic partnerships, before stepping into the CEO role when previous leader Yishan Wong resigned from the position.

Pao only remained in the CEO position for eight months, suffering tremendous online abuse and harassment before finally handing in her resignation. Despite this, during her short tenure, she was able to make significant changes both inside the business and on Reddit's public platform.

Internally, Pao brought in advisers to help to diversify the business and introduced questions about candidates' attitudes towards diversity to the interview process, an action which she has said 'did weed people out'.[3] Pao banned salary negotiations during the hiring process in the belief that they disadvantaged

---

* In 2015, a jury sided with the company, and against Pao, on all counts, a decision Pao initially decided to appeal, before dropping the appeal in August of that year. Although she lost the case, in which she asserted that she was passed up for a promotion because of her gender, women in the tech industry have remained supportive of Pao. Shortly after the verdict, a group of them collectively took out a full-page ad in a Palo Alto newspaper reading, 'Thanks Ellen.'

female candidates, and instead Reddit began making all candidates two offers that the business believed to be fair (one weighted towards more cash; one that offered more equity). Later, in an interview with *The Guardian*, Pao said, about her choices, 'there are things that I was able to do at Reddit as CEO that weren't about fighting discrimination per se, but just creating a fair environment. Like, let's make sure that our pay is fair across the whole company, and that helps everybody across the board – not just women and minorities, but also men who can't negotiate, or managers who are bad negotiators whose teams aren't happy because they're not being paid the same amount.'[4]

The changes that she made to the Reddit platform, which until her arrival had been seen as a space where 'anything goes', were equally bold – and, ultimately, it seems, led to her downfall.[5]

During her short tenure as the business's CEO, Pao banned revenge porn – a stance which many other social-media platforms have since followed.[6] She and two other executives banned five controversial Reddit communities that had used the platform to harass individuals, including a subreddit called FatPeopleHate which had over 150,000 subscribers[7] – a decision some users criticized as an attempt to limit free speech. The business defended the choice by saying they were 'banning behaviour, not ideas'.[8]

As a result of the bans, dissatisfied Reddit users started multiple Change.org petitions to call for Pao's resignation – the most popular of which reached 10,000 signatures in a matter of days.[9]

Surprisingly, though, the most controversial decision Pao seemed to make during her time as Reddit's CEO was the dismissal of a member of staff – Victoria Taylor.

Taylor, a publicist who had been with Reddit since 2013 as its director of communications, was seen by many as the bridge between the users of Reddit and its management team, including Pao.[10] She is also credited with legitimizing, and helping to take mainstream, the platform's popular Ask Me Anything (AMA) format that encouraged celebrities onto Reddit.[11]

Upon the news of her dismissal becoming public, music artist Lorde tweeted, 'idc who calls the shots at reddit, they should've known rule #1 in their pr handbook was always VICTORIA STAYS'.[12] She wasn't alone in her dissatisfaction.

In protest over the decision, which at the time the public believed had been made by Pao, Reddit moderators began setting sections of the Reddit platform to 'private', locking users out of various forums and temporarily closing a number of subreddits.[13] This caused huge disruption to the site. As Vox reported, 'The affected subreddits were some of the most visited on the site. Reddit's popular Ask Me Anything forum was set to private – freezing out its more than 8 million subscribers. Other forums like Art, with 3 million subscribers, and Ask Reddit, with 8.9 million subscribers, also went dark.'[14]

Taylor, it seemed, was viewed by Reddit users as an important link between themselves and the business – the platform's users had struggled, prior to her appointment, to get information, answers or updates from the executives in charge. On 3 July, just one day after Taylor was exited, Pao apologized, both on the platform and in *Time* magazine, for 'letting down users'.[15] But it wasn't enough to save her job.

Despite having been the CEO of the business for only a matter of months at the time, Pao wrote a longer apology in an additional *New York Times* piece on 6 July, which spoke specifically to this lack of transparency over a period of several years. She wrote:

> We screwed up. Not just on July 2, but also over the past several years. We haven't communicated well, and we have surprised moderators and the community with big changes. We have apologized and made promises to you, the moderators and the community, over many years, but time and again, we haven't delivered on them. When you've had feedback or requests, we haven't always been responsive. The mods and the community have lost trust in me and in us, the administrators of reddit.[16]

Pao would later refer to what came next as 'one of the largest trolling attacks in history'. She suffered sickening abuse from users, which I won't rehash here beyond saying that she endured 'death and rape threats, racist abuse, libel, [and] her home address [being] publicized online'.[17]

A new Change.org petition was started to call for her resignation, this time ultimately reaching more than 210,000 signatures from unhappy Reddit users.[18]

On 10 July 2015, just nine months after stepping into the CEO role, and only eight days after Taylor was exited, it was announced that Pao had left Reddit 'by mutual agreement'.[19] She was replaced by the business's co-founder Steve Huffman.

Sam Altman, a member of Reddit's board at the time, released a statement which said, 'We are thankful for Ellen's many contributions to Reddit and the technology industry generally. She brought focus to chaos, recruited a world-class team of executives, and drove growth. She brought a face to Reddit that changed perceptions, and is a pioneer for women in the tech industry. She will remain as an adviser to the board through the end of 2015. I look forward to seeing the great things she does beyond that.'[20]

Two days after Pao's resignation, the business's former CEO Yishan Wong wrote a post letting people know that the decision to fire Taylor had been made not by Pao, but by a board member.[21] Pao tweeted in response to the media picking up the story, 'Thanks for not blaming me for it.'[22]

Speaking at the end of 2015 to *The Guardian*, Pao was asked, 'Why do you think people see your working towards basic fairness as an attack on them?' She responded by saying:

> I think there's a lot of fear in change. For some people, it is:
> 'The system has worked for me, so what's wrong with it?
> There can't be anything wrong with it.' There's an aspiration
> that people have that they are fair and unbiased and meri-
> tocratic, and when you start pointing out these differences,

there's this huge gap between who they aspire to be and who they really are and what they're doing. It's extremely uncomfortable, fear-inducing and disappointing to them. So I think they can't acknowledge that gap. They have to push to make sure that the people criticising it are the problem.[23]

•   •   •

Maybe you've heard of the Great Resignation. Or maybe you've read some articles about Quiet Quitting, or even Lazy Girl Jobs, and have planned how to tone down your working scope recently. But have you heard of the Great Break-Up?[24] It's the newest trend that we're seeing in workplaces, and one that's particularly related to women's experiences and expectations.

If you're in a Glass Cliff situation, the end of that experience usually means choosing to leave or losing your job – depending on how it plays out. But, however it comes about, whether the decision is made by or for you, the end of the experience almost always constitutes stepping or sliding over the edge.

We've seen that, when times are tough and crisis bites, although men are able to save their roles by making improvements to their personal performance, even when business performance remains poor, women are not offered the same safety blanket. To add insult to injury, women's likelihood of being fired remains *equally high* whether the business is performing well or performing badly. It really is a no-win scenario at times.

And so, instead of waiting for the Glass Cliff to play out to its inevitable conclusion, or trying to get buy-in or support from those who would rather deny its existence than reckon with bias, prejudice or their own experiences of systemic privilege, it's easy to see why more and more women are choosing to take matters into their own hands, make their own choices and plan their own exits, on their own terms.

What I want to talk about now is why that happens, as

increasing numbers of women are refusing to play a role in a story they no longer feel they have any control over.

It's not me, it's you

Recently, something interesting and rather remarkable has happened. Women, more than ever before, have started to make the choice to leave their jobs, on their own terms.

This is known as the Great Break-Up, and it was first identified in the 2022 edition of the annual Women in the Workplace report, produced by the Lean In Foundation and McKinsey.[25]

This report found that, over the previous year, female leaders had 'switched jobs at the highest rates we've ever seen – and at higher rates than men in leadership.'[26] They looked at a data set of 40,000 employees from 333 companies in the US and Canada, and found that 10.5 per cent of female leaders* had voluntarily left their jobs in the previous twelve months, compared to 9 per cent of male leaders.[27]

As the researchers put it, 'To put the scale of the problem in perspective: for every woman at the director level who gets promoted, two women directors are choosing to leave their company.'[28]

Rachel Thomas, the CEO of LeanIn.org, added in an interview with NPR, 'Women leaders are leaving their companies at the highest rate we've ever seen. We already know women are under-represented in leadership, and now companies are starting to lose the precious few women leaders they do have.'[29]

This was an unexpected trend, and the researchers have suggested that it could have 'serious implications' for businesses.

We already know that the Broken Rung prevents women from taking the first steps to leadership, and the Glass Ceiling artificially caps the potential of so many others. When we add to this the

---

* Historically, this figure had been between 7 and 8 per cent for female leaders.

unexpected loss of women once they do reach the most senior levels, by their own choice, the result is that instead of improving the representation and visibility of women at the most senior levels of business, we're instead looking likely to continue to run at a deficit. That is, if businesses can't, or aren't willing to, shift and evolve to become better environments for women to invest their futures into, long term.

Although new, the Great Break-Up is not confined to research papers; we've all seen several high-profile women in the world of business decide to step away from their roles. In February 2023, Susan Wojcicki, the CEO of YouTube and one of Google's earliest employees, said in a statement that she was leaving in order to 'start a new chapter focused on my family, health, and personal projects I'm passionate about'.[30]

Just days before Wojcicki left Google, Meta confirmed their chief business officer, Marne Levine, was stepping down from her role after thirteen years with the company, in order to 'recharge and prioritize some quality time with family' before beginning her 'next professional chapter'.[31] This made her the third high-profile female Meta C-suite leader to leave her position in quick succession (following the loss of Sheryl Sandberg as their COO in 2022 and the exit of their global ad chief in 2021).

In the world of politics, we saw the same thing happening, as Scotland's first minister Nicola Sturgeon resigned from her role after eight years, and New Zealand's prime minister Jacinda Ardern stepped down and said she would not seek re-election as she had 'no more in the tank' to lead the country.[32]

The loss of this cohort of senior female leaders feels jarring and at odds with the story of gains and progress that we're so used to women's roles in the workplace being framed within. Yet we also know that people don't make choices, especially risky choices, based on nothing. And so what *is* driving women, indeed the *most senior women*, to step away from and give up the roles that they have worked so hard to secure?

BUT, WHAT ABOUT . . . ?

I can almost hear it already – the voices of those people who are shouting, 'CHILDCARE! STARTING A FAMILY! *That's* why women are leaving their jobs! And not only that – that's *exactly* what we told you would happen, and that's *exactly* why women are simply not suited for leadership, and they never have been!! All of their hormones and babies swirl around and just get in the way of them doing a good job. Either they're on their period, they're pregnant or they're on maternity leave. But, whichever it is, women are simply not cut out for important senior leadership roles. And we've always known it.'

Or, you know, something to that effect.

To this argument, I simply say: childcare, or the desire to start a family, does not seem to be the reason that women are making the difficult choice to leave their roles once in place. This is despite it often being put front-and-centre in media representations and narratives around women's priorities as they age and progress through their careers, as we endlessly discuss and debate whether or not women can, in fact, 'have it all'.

A longitudinal study found that, while women left management positions in Fortune 500 companies more often than men (26 per cent versus 14 per cent), this was not a result of them having (or wanting) more family commitments than their male counterparts.[33] What they found, instead, was that 'women had become more disaffected with their working life because their career opportunities were limited and sub-optimal [. . .] Women left their jobs for exactly the same reasons as men – it was simply that they had more reason to do so.'[34]

This is backed up by additional research which found that, of both men and women who plan to leave their current roles, the vast majority are not dropping out of the workforce altogether. In fact, 80 per cent intend to look for a new job and continue working, but in a different company which better fits with their needs and priorities. Interestingly, they also found that 'just as many men as women say they'll leave to focus on family, and the number for both genders is remarkably low: 2 per cent or less.'[35]

So more women than ever are choosing to step away from roles that they've worked hard to get, and it's not because of babies. What's changed, and what's driving women to take this difficult decision? Could it be that, in the aftermath of a pandemic world, we've simply lost our infatuation with the romance of leadership? Or has living through this time of great change meant that there has also been a change in us, both in terms of what we are willing to give to the companies we work for, and what we expect from them in return?

A new set of post-pandemic priorities

Living through the Covid-19 pandemic changed everything, not least our relationship with our working lives and our expectations of our employers.

While the research that forms the Women in the Workplace study is focused on workers within the United States, the trend of the Great Break-Up can be seen much further afield than that. Consultancy firm Deloitte looked into understanding the trend of more women choosing to leave their roles (with or without the threat of the Glass Cliff), surveying 2,100 employees and C-level leaders across the US, the UK, Canada and Australia. They found that nearly 70 per cent of the C-level professionals they spoke to were 'seriously considering' quitting their current role in favour of finding a position that 'better supports their well-being'.[36]

They also found, overall and unsurprisingly, that the pandemic has had a large and negative impact on our collective mental and physical health – meaning that well-being is at an all-time low for workers at all levels in their careers. More than three quarters of C-level employees say the period negatively impacted their well-being. Not only that, but 40 per cent of C-level leaders reported feeling overwhelmed (versus 35 per cent of employees overall), 30 per cent reported feeling lonely (versus 24 per cent of employees overall) and 26 per cent reported feeling depressed (versus 23 per cent of employees overall).[37]

It's really no wonder, then, that more and more of us are making the choice to leave companies and ways of working that no longer serve us, and are looking for businesses that can support us better – with a focus on better progression opportunities, flexibility and inclusion built in from the start.[38]

Women want an ROI from their employers

Let's go back to the stat from earlier in the chapter: 'for every woman at the director level who gets promoted, two women directors are choosing to leave their company'.[39] This means that, even if businesses are making progress in recognizing the work of and promoting women, the gap that we see in female representation at the top levels of businesses isn't closing because more women are leaving than being brought in to backfill those who have been lost. And why are they leaving? Because they've found that businesses are not supporting them in the ways they need. To put it another way, 'even if a company feels they may be promoting a couple of women, the net picture is that women aren't feeling this is the environment for them to thrive.'[40]

So what do women need to thrive? What are women looking for from their employers? Of those women who are switching jobs, what are the push and pull factors that are driving those decisions?

Really, it's nothing groundbreaking.

Women report that these are the main reasons they are switching jobs:

- Forty-eight per cent of women say they want the opportunity to advance (versus 44 per cent of men).

- Twenty per cent of women report wanting flexibility (versus 13 per cent of men).

- Eighteen per cent of women want a company with a commitment to DEI* (versus 11 per cent of men).

- Twenty-two per cent say that having an unsupportive manager is a factor in them switching jobs (versus 18 per cent of men).

- Seventeen per cent of women say that an unmanageable workload is a reason for them looking for a role in a different business (versus 10 per cent of men).[41]

We're talking about this as the result of a post-pandemic period – a time in which everyone's working lives and routines underwent the biggest shake-up imaginable. It was a time when we all had to take stock of every element of our lives and decide what was important to us and what we were ready to leave behind.

It might be tempting to say that these changes to priorities are temporary, and that, if we can just ride the storm without losing too many more women along the way, we'll be fine. Yet, in reality, that's not the case. To believe that, we'd have to ignore

---

* Diversity, equity and inclusion.

the impact of an increased millennial (those born ~1977–95) and Gen Z (~1995–2010) presence in our workplaces – both generations that recognize progress has been made up to now, but demand more.[42]

What we see in reality is that the factors which are important to female leaders today are only growing in importance for the next generation of women in the workplace. Looking at those women under thirty in 2022 – specifically what they say is important to them now in a working environment versus what they thought was important just two years prior – we see the following:

- 58 per cent say that advancing is now more important (versus 31 per cent of current female leaders).

- 76 per cent say that flexibility is now more important (versus 66 per cent of current female leaders).

- 41 per cent say that a commitment to DEI is now more important (versus 31 per cent of current female leaders).

- 56 per cent say that the support of a manager is now more important (versus 42 per cent of current female leaders).

- 68 per cent say that a commitment to employee well-being is now more important (versus 55 per cent of current female leaders).[43]

The double shift has become the triple shift[44]

As we discussed in Chapter 2, the prevalence of work outside of the workplace remains a very consistent factor in working women's lives, even as they progress through their careers. Although men are able to decrease their share of domestic duties and responsibilities outside of work as they climb the professional ladder, we don't see this same reduction happening in the expectations of women's unpaid labour. As we've discussed, 58 per cent of entry-level women report being responsible for most or all of their family's housework or childcare, a number that dips ever so slightly as women progress professionally, with 52 per cent of women at senior manager level or above reporting the same.[45] This continued expectation of domestic labour and caregiving simply does not persist in the same way for men as they move forwards in their careers, with entry-level men reporting being responsible for 30 per cent of the same work – an already significantly lower number, which is slashed to 13 per cent* by the time we look at senior manager and above.[46]

Not only are the expectations we have of pastoral caregiving different in our home lives, creating an additional burden for women on top of their careers, they also look very different in terms of the expectations put on us during our *working* lives.

Both male and female workers are expected to achieve business performance results, in terms of driving revenue and growth.[47] But, as we saw briefly in the previous chapter, women who are in leadership positions are also expected to pick up and take responsibility for the vast majority of DEI work within the businesses they work for. Women in leadership do twice as much work around DEI as their male peers.[48]

'Women leaders are really stepping up as great people managers and as champions of diversity, equity and inclusion,' Rachel Thomas told NPR's *Morning Edition*. 'And we know employee companies prioritize that work, they want to see more of that being done. But interestingly enough, that important work is generally going unrecognized and unrewarded in most organizations.'[49] While 93 per cent of companies take business goals into

---

* The researchers note that this is 'data for all women and men, not just those who live with a spouse or partner.'

account in managers' performance reviews, fewer than 40 per cent do so for factors like team morale and progress on DEI goals – despite businesses recognizing their value and implicitly expecting women to invest working hours into these caregiving tasks.[50]

Again, the soft-skill-heavy nurturing, caring work, which has been expected of women since before we even joined the formalized workplace, continues to be expected of senior women in leadership today. And, as it always has been, it remains both undervalued and unrecognized.

'Call it emotional labour, call it good leadership: they [women] do far more of the sponsorship than their male peers. They disproportionately hold the diversity and inclusion responsibilities. They check in with employees more on wellness, on workload, on balance. And so they're showing up the way that companies say they want,' Alexis Krivkovich, McKinsey senior partner, told *The McKinsey Podcast*. 'But they don't get rewarded formally for it, and so many of them are looking around and saying, "There's got to be a better deal."'[51]

There *has got* to be a better deal.

This is a sentiment echoed by Sheryl Sandberg, founder of the Lean In Foundation:

We are in the midst of a Great Breakup in corporate America. Women leaders are leaving their companies at the highest rate we've ever seen [. . .] Now, senior women, who are disproportionately doing the hard work that employees want around people management and DEI, are leaving for better opportunities elsewhere [. . .] Companies need to double down to remove bias from the workplace and make serious investments in DEI, or we are in real danger of losing decades of progress toward women's equality. The time to act is now.[52]

BUT, WHAT ABOUT . . . ?

OK, OK. So you might be thinking that, since both women who are already leaders, and those women under thirty who are aspiring to be the next generation of leaders, say clearly and repeatedly that DEI is important to them, they should be the ones doing the work around diversity and inclusion. If they care so much, isn't it reasonable for them to take on more of the burden than male employees, who report valuing it less highly?

I'd say caring about something and having all of the responsibility for making it happen, on top of your real job, for no benefit or recognition, are two very different things. Especially when that thing is revenue-driving, like DEI (more on that later).[53]

The lost romance of leadership[54]

Even without the additional consideration and burden of navigating the Glass Cliff, women have been reassessing what they need and deserve from their working lives, and they're being definitive, determined and brave in setting the conditions to make the most of, and get the most from, the time investment they're making in their careers.

But, of course, the Glass Cliff *does* leave us with additional contexts and considerations – such as, what does it look like not just to switch jobs, as we're seeing a record number of women do during the Great Break-Up, but to be faced with the choice of either leaving or being fired from a role where the public perception is likely to be one of failure?

Research has found that external observers of companies in a period of crisis were more likely to blame the leaders of that business for the problems it finds itself in than to look at, acknowledge or recognize blame in external, situational factors.[55]

The research points out that, in moments of crisis, businesses and their leaderships are likely to be more visible than usual, with increased scrutiny and pressure being applied to them by shareholders and the media at large.[56] This heightened visibility means that blame attributed to leadership during Glass Cliff situations is likely to be both visible and public – and, in these doubly unusual situations in which we have both a business that is publicly seen to be in crisis and is publicly led by a woman, people may assume the relationship between the two unusual factors is a causal one, interpreting it as 'evidence' that women make worse leaders than men.

This means that, even when the odds are stacked against a leader from the start, when they were always destined to fail, the public perception of the situation may be very different. The blame that is put onto the shoulders of an exiting leader can make their next steps difficult, since a perception of personal blame tarnishes their reputation, meaning that leaders of poorly performing companies are less likely to be appointed to leadership positions in the future.

This may go some way to explaining why under-represented leaders tend to be punished more for mistakes than those who are over-represented.[57] Just like in any 'only' situation, being under-represented creates an increased burden on the trailblazers who step into these positions, as they are seen as representatives not just of themselves, but of all who share their gender. The stakes, in a lot of ways, couldn't be higher. And, sometimes, that's a bigger burden than people are willing, or able, to carry.

It's also important to remember that the choice to step down doesn't need to be framed as a failure, by any means. In reference to Susan Wojcicki's choice to step down as the CEO of YouTube, Valerie Workman, chief legal officer at Handshake, a job-search platform for college students and recent graduates, told CNBC, 'If you were the head of YouTube, how is it a fail that you decide to go and do something else when you've made it as far as you can possibly go?' She added, about the trend of the Great Break-Up overall, 'They're meeting their goals and being successful, and some are choosing to leave before they get burned out. It's a phenomenal example for young women. That's a success story.'[58]

And you know what? I think she's correct.

I don't believe anyone making the choice to step away from a role they have worked hard for does so flippantly. But it's also difficult to stay motivated when it feels as though the ground is falling away under your feet, or when you know you've taken things as far as they, and you, can go.

As we've seen in our discussions about tenure, often there is no choice to be made, anyway, since women are exited both more often and more quickly from their leadership roles than their male counterparts.

Being pushed over the edge

It's one thing if women are choosing to take their fate into their own hands, to step away from roles that aren't serving them and structure their lives around their own priorities, but that's not always the case. Sometimes, that choice is taken away from them. There are plenty of examples of Glass Cliff situations in which women haven't made the decision to step down, but have instead felt a firm shove to the small of their back as they were pushed off the cliff.

So what happens when the choice is taken out of your hands?

Research shows that, while the average tenure for a male CEO is 8.4 years, for the average female CEO that shrinks to just 6.3 years, and additional longitudinal studies show us that, over the past decade, 38 per cent of female C-level leaders who left their positions were fired, compared with 27 per cent* of their male counterparts.[59]

It could be that, in part, women's experiences in these high-level, often risky positions play out differently to men's because men find it more difficult to identify instances of, and even to believe in, the Glass Cliff as a phenomenon. And so they are less likely to be able to offer the support needed to turn the situation into a story of success.

Unfortunately, this is especially true when they don't think of themselves as sexist.[60]

If a woman is having a difficult time in a precarious position in leadership, even being believed and having her experience acknowledged can make a difference to how it feels to be in that difficult situation. We already know that internal support is one factor that's important in making a situation more or less susceptible to Glass Cliff conditions. If we know that people in senior leadership are more likely to be male, which we do, then it's also likely that the people who women need to rely on to be in their corner, rallying support for them, are also going to be male – the group that are most over-represented at that leadership level. And so, if those men are not open to recognizing the impact that gender can have on their colleagues' leadership experiences and potential outcomes, then they are unlikely to be able or willing to help in avoiding a fall.

And, of course, these factors are at play long before the Glass Cliff itself emerges as a clear and apparent threat.

Researchers have looked into factors that can lead to hiring discrimination in the workplace.[61] They found that, when it comes to hiring, managers who believe themselves to be the most objec-

---

* This finding was cited by the original Glass Cliff researchers in their follow-up study, 'The Glass Cliff, a Decade of Research'. The 'exhaustive' study looked at the world's 2,500 largest publicly listed companies over a ten-year period, with the researchers commenting: 'Such findings present concrete evidence that, rather than simply being a matter of perceived or potential risk, the precariousness of Glass Cliffs manifests itself in an increased incidence of career trauma.'

tive lean into the idea that 'I think it, therefore it's true' – which can actually amplify biased outcomes. In short, when managers believed they held a higher sense of personal objectivity, they were *more* likely to believe that their own thoughts and internally held beliefs were true, valid and 'therefore worthy of being acted on' when it came to hiring decisions – which, instead of mitigating against bias, increased gender discrimination.[62] In fact, it was found that 'evaluators shift the hiring criteria for the position in favour of male applicants for stereotypically male jobs, but do not exhibit the same favouritism toward female applicants', and those 'decision makers who flexibly change their hiring criteria to rationalise selecting male candidates believe themselves to be more objective'.[63]

But, of course, hiring managers is just the beginning of the story of inequity for under-represented leaders in our workplaces.

Once we have mitigated for bias during hiring decisions, we can look at our experiences and perceptions of our working lives. And when we do that, we see something very interesting: not only are men less motivated to be active in dismantling the Glass Cliff, they are unwilling, in great numbers, to even believe in its existence.

In an experiment, men and women were asked to read a newspaper article about the Glass Cliff – and then respond to some questions about the phenomenon. The researchers found that, while women were more likely to recognize the experience, its dangers and its unfairness, men were much more likely to 'question the validity' of the research, and were also more likely to deny that the positions the female leaders found themselves in were, indeed, risky, rather than grappling with the phenomenon and its consequences.[64]

'Intriguingly,' the researchers said, 'the most overwhelming response from male participants was to question the very existence of the Glass Cliff phenomenon, with over 50 per cent of male participants either denying that Glass Cliffs existed or maintaining that men were more likely to be affected than women [. . .] In contrast, it is striking that only 5 per cent of women expressed doubt about the phenomenon's existence.'[65]

There were also big differences, among those who did accept the phenomenon, in the ways in which men and women explained the reasons behind the Glass Cliff.[66] Women were much more likely to explain it by talking about the lack of other available options for progression, sexism and men's tendency to prefer working with other men. Men, on the other hand, were much more likely to talk about more passive causes for the Glass Cliff, such as whether or not women really did have a suitability for this kind of work, the role's perceived need for strategic decision-making (an ability which they didn't seem to think women possessed, at least not equally to men), or other business factors which overlook the role of gender.[*]

Whether we have chosen to jump from roles which no longer serve us, or have been the victim of a firm hand to our back, pushing us over the edge, the end of the Glass Cliff is usually an exit from the business we've been a part of, or the role we've held up to that point.

And, although undeniably scary for a whole host of emotional, professional and financial reasons, a fresh start can also be an opportunity. It's a chance to think about who we are and who we want to be – both inside and outside of our working lives. It's an opportunity to reset, regroup and reconsider the ways we've all worked up to now, and the ways we want to work in the future.

---

[*] Interestingly, the researchers found that these gendered differences in terms of our willingness to accept the existence, causes and impact of the Glass Cliff are most true for those in junior and mid-level roles. They noted: 'At the most senior level, women's responses were much more similar to those of men, in that they were more likely to deny the phenomenon or to endorse benign explanations. Such patterns accord with findings from a body of previous work which suggest that the women who make it to the top of (male-dominated) organizations tend to be relatively similar to their male counterparts and hence not to be the most passionate advocates for women's causes – either because they have been selected on this basis or have accommodated to the perceived ideological requirements of their role.' (Derks, Ellemers, van Laar and de Groot, 2011; Ellemers, Heuvel, de Gilder, Maass and Bonvini, 2004).

TL;DR: *Too Long; Didn't Read*

- When the Glass Cliff strikes, the usual outcome is that the woman is pushed or decides to jump over the edge – exiting the role and the business.

- The Great Break-Up is seeing female leaders switching jobs at the highest rates researchers have ever seen. This exodus means that, for every woman at the director level who gets promoted, two female directors are choosing to leave their companies.

- Reasons for the Great Break-Up include:

  - Changing priorities as a result of living through the Covid-19 pandemic, and the impact that it's had on our collective mental health.

  - Women want and expect to get something back for the work they're putting into their jobs, including flexibility, the opportunity to advance, and reasonable workloads. These expectations have become even more important to those workers under the age of thirty.

  - As well as their actual jobs and at-home responsibilities, women in senior positions are being expected to take on additional workplace tasks, such as mentoring and leading DEI initiatives. Women in leadership do twice as much work around DEI as their male peers.

  - We're not seduced by the romance of leadership any more. Women are prioritizing their well-being and mental health over an outdated view of leadership.

- When presented with research around the Glass Cliff, women are more likely to recognize the experience, its dangers and its unfairness. Men, on the other hand, are much more likely to 'question the validity' of the research and deny that the roles available to women are risky.

- Over 50 per cent of males either denied the Glass Cliff existed or claimed that men were more likely to be affected by it than women. Only 5 per cent of women expressed doubt about the phenomenon's existence.

• Managers who believe themselves to be the most objective and the least sexist are *more* likely to believe that their own thoughts and internally held beliefs are true, valid and 'therefore worthy of being acted on' – which can actually lead to *more* biased outcomes.

CHAPTER 7

The Ways We Work

You can say all are welcome, but if
wolves and sheep are both welcome then
you're only going to get wolves.

ADAM BATES[1]

In 2001, Anne Mulcahy was made the CEO of Xerox, and in January 2002 she took a seat on the company's board of directors.[2] The business was not in great shape. The exiting CEO had lasted only eighteen months in the role and, according to many reports, Xerox was on the verge of bankruptcy.[3] After six consecutive years of losses, the company was reportedly a huge $18 billion in debt, and was under investigation for its accounting practices.[4]

'It was alarming how fast things began to unravel in late 1999 and 2000,' Mulcahy later said. 'We thought we had coined the term "Perfect Storm".'[5]

On the day her appointment to the CEO role was announced, stock valuation dropped by 15 per cent.[6]

It looked like they may as well have coined the term 'Glass Cliff'.

But, unlike many under-represented leaders, although she was appointed to this role during an undeniable period of difficulty, she wasn't new to the business altogether. In fact, Mulcahy had joined Xerox back in 1976 as a field sales rep, and she would work in sales within the business for the next sixteen years – building connections and a wealth of knowledge about the company from the ground up.[7] Her journey through the ranks of the business included being appointed VP for HR in 1992 (a role in which she managed company benefits, labour relations, training and management development), taking on the position of chief staff officer in 1997 and being named a senior VP within the business.[8] She knew Xerox from all angles, had strong internal relationships, and had

had the opportunity to form her own opinions about what the real issues were and what could be done to put the business back on track.

'I certainly hadn't been groomed to become a CEO,' Mulcahy said. 'I didn't have a very sophisticated financial background, and I had to make up for my lack of formal training. I had to make up for it with intense on-the-job learning.'[9]

Perhaps because of this wealth of pre-existing internal knowledge, Mulcahy made extraordinarily quick work of changing the fortunes of Xerox, as the business went from making a $273 million loss in 2000, just before her arrival, to reporting a $91 million profit in 2003 – which, by 2004, had risen to $859 million, on sales of $15.7 billion. As well as profitability being up, Xerox's stock had also risen, 'returning 75 per cent over the past five years, compared with a loss of 6 per cent for the Dow Jones Total Stock Market Index.'[10]

The Xerox business was unquestionably back on track with Mulcahy at the helm, and, in 2005, *Fortune* ranked Mulcahy as the second most powerful woman in business.[11]

Reflecting on her early days in the role, and her lack of previous experience of leadership to draw on in order to make a success of it, she told a crowd at Stanford Business School that, 'I feel like my title should be chief communication officer, because that's really what I do.' Emphasizing the importance of listening to customers and employees, she went on, 'When I became CEO, I spent the first 90 days on planes travelling to various offices and listening to anyone who had a perspective on what was wrong with the company. I think if you spend as much time listening as talking, that's time well spent.'[12]

Instead of fighting the perception of female leaders having an abundance of soft skills, and trying to lean in to more traditionally masculine leadership stereotypes, Mulcahy embraced it – speaking to people, having conversations, gathering feedback, building relationships and finding out what was really going on inside the business, from those on the ground who knew it best. Remembering that time, she said that honesty and confidence were essential in effective communication, adding, 'When your organization is struggling, you have to give people the sense that you know what's happening and that you have a strategy to fix it. Beyond that, you have to tell people what they can do to help.'[13]

But she was also firm about what she wanted and needed for the whole business – including her senior leadership team – in order for any changes to be successful. Even the most successful leader isn't going to make transformational change alone. She needed to be able to rely on her team, particularly her most senior team members – which, as we saw in Chapter 2, isn't always easy for under-represented leaders. Mulcahy, however, took a no-nonsense approach, which may well have been fundamental in her success: 'I gave people a choice to make: Either roll up your sleeves and go to work or leave Xerox.'[14]

That's not to say that Mulcahy had an easy success story, as Alison Cook noted in an interview with Vox. 'She bled for Xerox, and everybody knew it.'[15]

'I think I am more motivated by fear of failure than a desire to succeed,' Mulcahy herself admitted, continuing her conversation at Stanford. 'My experience at Xerox has taught me that crisis is a very powerful motivator. It forces you to make choices that you probably wouldn't have made otherwise. It intensifies your focus, your competitiveness, your relentless desire to attain best-in-class status. I want to do everything I can to make sure that we don't lose that now that we're back on track.'[16]

Having successfully led Xerox through its difficulties, Mulcahy made the choice to step down from the role of CEO in 2009 – handing the leadership of the business over to another under-represented leader, Ursula Burns, who became not only the first Black woman to take the top role at a Fortune 500 company, but the first to succeed the role from another woman.[17]

Burns held the role from 2009–16, as well as serving as the business's chairman from 2010–17.

•   •   •

I hope that, as you've read this book, you've come to recognize the hallmarks of the Glass Cliff, as well as the circumstances that come together to create the conditions for the phenomenon to occur. I hope you will have had a chance to reflect on your own professional lived experiences, and maybe even to reframe some of those experiences in a whole new context – now that you know about the previously invisible peril.

And, while all of that is incredibly valuable, both on a personal and cultural level, in order to take away the stigma associated with women in leadership positions – especially when they're going through a bumpy period – I don't think that should be the end of the story.

Instead of learning to individually identify and then protect ourselves one by one from falling victim to the Glass Cliff phenomenon, I'd much rather be in a position of imagining and trying to create a world where we look for ways to stop it playing out altogether.

For all of us.

I know I've spent this book up to now talking about just how real the Glass Cliff is, and just how strongly it can impact on the careers of under-represented leaders. But I hope I've also been clear in another way. The Glass Cliff is a phenomenon that relies on a whole host of factors coming together to make the conditions needed for it to play out. And so, if we can remove, or at least make less common, some of those factors, maybe we can start to imagine a world beyond the Glass Cliff.

One thing we need to agree to do, collectively and right away, is to stop blaming under-represented people as a default when we see things going badly in businesses. The article in *The Times* that accused women of 'wreaking havoc', and sparked the research that led to the conception of the Glass Cliff phenomenon, may have been all the way back in 2003, and it's tempting to say that we as a society have moved on from then, that we simply wouldn't see a piece like that running now – but, unfortunately, that's not the case.[18]

On 10 March 2023, Silicon Valley Bank, the $212 billion tech world's lender of choice, collapsed. Seemingly overnight. It was a collapse that *The Guardian* referred to as 'triggering the most significant financial crisis since 2008'[19] and *The Economist* also noted that it was 'the biggest lender to collapse since the global financial crisis of 2007–09'.[20]

Of course, it didn't take long for newspaper articles and think pieces to start picking over the bank's downfall and pointing fingers towards possible scapegoats.

On 11 March, *The Wall Street Journal* released its take on the situation in an article written by Andy Kessler, journalist, author and ex hedge-fund founder, titled 'Who Killed Silicon Valley Bank?'[21] Unlike most other news sources, which were interested in looking at the wider context, economic landscape, financial factors and political policies that may have led to the bank's sudden demise, *The Wall Street Journal* focused on the people at its helm – an unusual angle to take when looking for a cause of the collapse.

'Was there a regulatory failure?' the article asked. 'Perhaps. SVB was regulated like a bank but looked more like a money-market fund. Then there's this; in its proxy statement, SVB notes that besides 91 per cent of their board being independent, and 45 per cent women, they also have "1 Black," "1 LGBTQ+" and "2 Veterans." I'm not saying that twelve white men would have avoided this mess, but the company may have been distracted by diversity demands.'[22]

Now, I don't know about you, but that feels like a really wild take to me. And several other news sources agreed with me. *Vanity Fair* ran a counter piece with the headline, 'The Wall Street Journal Goes Full White Supremacist, Blames Silicon Valley Bank Collapse on "1 Black" and "1 LGBTQ+",[23] the *San Francisco Chronicle* made its stance abundantly clear when it went with, 'No, "wokeness" isn't the reason Silicon Valley Bank collapsed',[24] and the Daily Beast pushed back with a piece titled, 'WSJ Makes Ludicrous Suggestion "Diverse" Board May Have Doomed SVB'.[25]

Even *Vice*'s Motherboard published a piece titled 'WSJ Wonders: Did Silicon Valley Bank Die Because One Black Person Was on Its Board?' in which it pointed out that 'the implosion of one of the least diverse banks in America is being blamed on its "wokeness"'.[26] It's an interesting idea, as the piece went on to explain that, despite what sounded like an unusually diverse leadership team, the reality of the bank's leadership before its collapse was a lot more homogenous:

> One does not have to do much to imagine how a board of twelve white men would have acted; ten of SVB's eleven directors are white, all of them are rich, and the youngest is fifty-three years old. SVB's board, it should be noted, is less diverse than any of the United States' top five banks, according to their own annual reports. There is, of course, literally no evidence whatsoever to suggest that SVB was 'distracted' by diversity demands, and less than zero evidence that any token corporate interest in diversity led to its downfall.[27]

A whole host of politicians also joined the discussion, blaming the bank's 'woke' policies and inclusive leadership, including Florida governor Ron DeSantis, who told Fox News that Silicon Valley Bank was 'so concerned with DEI and politics and all kinds of stuff. I think that really diverted from them focusing on their core mission'.[28] The chair of the Republican House oversight committee also referred to them as 'one of the most woke banks' (not in a good way).[29]

Despite the evident ridiculousness of looking to blame the bank's failure on the gender, ethnicity, sexuality, or veteran status of its board members, and despite the pushback that *The Wall Street Journal* received, it was absolutely not alone in mentioning the make-up of the board in its reporting of the potential reasons behind the surprise collapse. The *New York Post* chose to run with the headline 'While Silicon Valley Bank collapsed, top executive pushed "woke" programs',[30] and even *The Guardian* dedicated a section of its SVB 'Explainer' article* to the bank's management make-up.[31]

The Guardian's coverage, however, did make an interesting point, which may give a better indication of personnel issues linked to the bank's downfall. As the article explained it, 'The bank didn't have a chief risk officer (CRO) for some of 2022, a situation that's now being looked at by the Federal Reserve, according to reports'. The CRO is a key role in any business tasked with making and taking informed risks that pay off for its members and their investments. The article goes on:

> The narrative [that the bank collapsed because of its 'wokeness'] fed into a larger conflict over ESG, or environmental, social and corporate governance-driven investing, that has become a target of conservatives. But the bank's loans to community and environmental projects were not central to its collapse nor are its diversity, equity and inclusion (DEI) policies dissimilar to other banks. The argument also fails to take into account all the banks that existed in 2008, before DEI or 'woke' became a part of corporate or political discourse.

---

* Though this was a week after the collapse, and several days after the *WSJ* piece, so it may have been in reaction to the existing public conversation.

BUT, WHAT ABOUT . . . ?

There are some people who try to frame the Glass Cliff through a political lens, as we've already seen in Ron DeSantis's Fox News analysis of the SVB collapse. But to frame the Glass Cliff in terms of party politics is to misunderstand it. There is no evidence to suggest that the phenomenon is more apparent under any political party, or that people who vote one way or another are more or less likely to succumb to its trap.

In many ways, the Glass Cliff is bigger than politics.

Although we've been focusing on women's experiences in this book, I want to remind you that the Glass Cliff has a very similar impact on racially marginalized men, too. And those with more than one area of intersectional marginalization (think race plus gender, for example) suffer its impact even more strongly. Again, irrespective of which party they vote for, or where they source their morning news.

When we think bigger than just ourselves, we can begin to see the structural inequities that impact all of us. And, in a similar way, when we work and plan together, we can begin to design and shape worlds that work for the many, rather than the few.

It would be great to say I believed that we've come a long way since 2003, but the truth is, I don't *really* think we have. People are still being blamed for things outside of their control simply because they deviate from the archetypes of whiteness and maleness that we still expect to be represented front and centre in positions of power and authority.

But that's not to say things can't change. Not at all. We just each need to be mindful in understanding, putting words to and committing to playing our own parts in making that change. We need to recognize when the dream of meritocracy we've been sold is not being equally applied to everyone – if it exists at all.

With that in mind, I want to take a moment to discuss the other side of the Glass Cliff – the mirror experience of white men, resulting from the same factors that create the Glass Cliff, except in reverse. Before I dive into that, I need to point out that, of course, just as there is no singular female experience, no singular Black or neurodivergent experience, there is not a singular way that white men experience the workplace. Just as with all the other points raised in this book, the purpose of this coming discussion is not to say, 'This is universally true,' because it simply isn't, in the same way that the Glass Cliff is not a universal truth. Instead, the purpose is to shine light on factors that can and should form a part of our understanding of the Glass Cliff as a cultural phenomenon, rather than an individual shortcoming.

What's the opposite of the Glass Cliff?

So here we are. We've understood the Glass Cliff, and I hope that we're ready to set about, together, in playing our part in dismantling it. But, of course, things are never quite as simple as that. Because, while the Glass Cliff is a phenomenon that impacts and limits the professional experiences of under-represented leaders, we all know that we don't exist in a vacuum. Where there is a push, there is usually a pull. So, if the Glass Cliff is the experience for under-represented leaders, what is the equivalent for *over-represented* leaders?

We can't be aware of and work against the Glass Cliff and its impact without also being aware of the impact of its counter-balancing brother, the final part of our Glass Menagerie.

That would be the Glass Escalator.

The Glass Escalator

The Glass Escalator is the final part of the trio that makes up our Glass Menagerie.* Unsurprisingly, while the glass metaphors that we use to explain women's journeys through the workplace – the Glass Ceiling and the Glass Cliff – are related to limiting factors and hidden falls from the top, the glass metaphor we use for men's experiences as they progress through their careers is altogether more advantageous.

Just as the Glass Cliff plays out most often in businesses that are not only in some form of crisis, but which have also had a history of being led by males, the Glass Escalator is especially prevalent for those men who work in traditionally female industries† such as teaching or nursing.[32] However, unlike women, who must pay the penalty of increased visibility, responsibility and scrutiny for stepping outside of our society's expectations for them, men are met with a boost.[33]

We can all think of industries within which the majority of those on the ground, doing the day-to-day work, are women, yet, once we look at the most senior roles, they are all held by men. This is one major cause of the gender pay gap – women remain clustered at low-level, low-paying roles while men rise to the top. It is a discrepancy that reinforces our belief that, even in industries where women are better represented, they're still not the right fit when it comes to the most senior leadership spots.

---

* So sorry, my degree is in theatre and I really had to.

† The initial research looked at nursing, teaching, librarianship and social work. It's worth noting that, while these are traditionally 'feminized' work areas (being for the most part linked to caregiving work), there is not an equivalent subset of 'masculinized' roles, since the entire domain of paid work outside of the home has, traditionally and historically, fallen into that category. Therefore, when we talk about women entering any profession that isn't directly related to caregiving, we should presume she is entering an equivalently 'othering' industry to the men in this study.

Although men who choose to enter what is seen as a traditionally female industry may face a social stigma outside of the workplace, once they're in, instead of discovering themselves to be in a risky position ending in a potential drop, the Glass Escalator metaphor refers to the invisible helping hands that pull men up through their careers, seeing them progress both more smoothly and more quickly than their female counterparts. There are many factors that make up the Glass Escalator, but most often they are the same as those we've seen at play in our discussion of the Glass Cliff – but in reverse. Men are more likely to be promoted for their perceived potential than women, and they are less likely to be expected to take on undervalued office housework and DEI tasks; they are also advantaged by traditional negotiation styles being weighted towards stereotypically male characteristics.

The Glass Escalator is the cliff in reverse. Maleness is uplifted in all kinds of subtle ways in our workplaces, which were made with them in mind first and foremost. Men in these traditionally female industries, the research shows, 'tend to fare better even than men in male-dominated jobs, and they typically earn higher salaries, receive more promotions and achieve higher levels within organisations than their female counterparts.'[34]

Caren Goldberg, Ph.D., has researched the Glass Escalator phenomenon at the Kogod School of Business. Speaking to *Forbes*, she said, 'Men that enter female-dominated professions tend to be promoted at faster rates than women in those professions [. . .] When you look at senior management, you tend to see men disproportionately represented. So while there may be less than 5 per cent of all nurses who are male, you see a much larger percentage than 5 per cent in senior-level positions like hospital administrators.'[35]

This is reinforced by a 2021 study, also looking at nursing, which found that, although males represent 10 per cent of the nursing workforce, they hold close to half of top leadership positions in nursing.[36] This shows a clear and huge chasm between the demographic make-up of those on the ground, and those in better-paying, arguably more secure senior positions.

We can see something very similar when we look at the 11,449 people employed by the NHS in England. In 2022, women represented 68.7 per cent of NHS employees, compared to 31.3 per cent men.* Despite this, men in the organization held 42.2 per cent of the highest-paying jobs, while women made up 77.6 per cent of the *lowest*-paying roles. Notably, this is an improvement on the 2019 data, at which time men represented just 23 per cent of the NHS workforce, but held 53 per cent of 'very senior manager' roles – but, either way, it's not great reading.[37]

The research around the Glass Escalator makes a point of noting that the phenomenon doesn't apply equally to all men, explaining that, 'while the impact of the Glass Escalator is clear for white males, it does not appear to apply to minority males or persons of colour equally or equitably'.[38]

Just as understanding invisible barriers is essential in reframing our thoughts about and relationship to women in leadership positions, it's important to get the fullest sense of the invisible factors that add important context to the other side of the conversation, if we want to clear the way for a more equitable future.

In order to build the most equitable future of work possible, together, we need to both understand and recognize the importance of diversity within businesses, both morally and as a key factor of business success. Only then can we make sure not only that everyone is treated equally, but that businesses are able to benefit from the truest value of diversity.

Why diversity matters

One of the early questions I got when I went into a business to talk about the Glass Cliff was a surprise to me.

---

* No other genders were mentioned in the NHS's reporting.

'So if, even when women get to the top, it's still not good – doesn't that really just mean we should give up on them? Hire men, and stop all of these unnecessary problems?'

You won't be surprised to hear that my answer was a resounding 'No!' I would hope that the evident unfairness of everything we've spoken about up to this point is enough to make us consider the true meritocracy of the systems in which we work, and to convince people that something needs to change when it comes to the ways in which we think about women's place in leadership. But if – somehow – none of that has moved you, I want to share some information on why having more inclusive workplaces, from the most senior levels to the most junior, is *literally* good for business, and why we all benefit when we take the needs of the widest possible range of people into account when we're building tools, services, products and plans.

So where does the real benefit of inclusion lie?

Over the past few years, brands and businesses have heard – and in some cases responded to – increased calls to diversify their talent pipelines. However, instead of focusing on the slightly more difficult senior management and leadership layers of business, their efforts have mostly increased what often feels to be tokenistic representation of more junior and entry-level cohorts. Perhaps consequently, these employees are often brought into businesses without equal investment in their long-term futures, or access to the kinds of sponsorship that can lead to pay rises and promotions. This often means that under-represented talent has not yet been able to make it beyond the Broken Rung to the most senior levels of businesses, where the real impact of their points of view can be the most valuable.

I'm sure we can all remember the early steps in our careers, the jobs we had when we were just starting out. When we are at the very beginning, it can feel massively intimidating and over-whelming, especially if we are marginalized and under-represented in the working environments in which we find ourselves. Rather than feeling empowered to speak out and share our valuable opinions, we often consider ourselves lucky to have been given the opportunity to be in our role in the first place, and so are unlikely to be willing to go against the grain, to 'rock the boat' or risk unlike-ability by asserting our views and beliefs, especially if they are different from those of the leaders above us.

An influx of under-represented talent that doesn't permeate to the very top of a business means that, while we may have created a workplace in which under-represented talent has been able to physically access previously closed spaces, we have not even begun to come close to creating the conditions necessary for them to feel safe in bringing their full selves into their working lives. Businesses may have made steps towards diversity, but the equity and inclusion that are essential to making those efforts a success – and which deliver the most value to the business – remain overlooked.

But this doesn't have to be the case – and when we ensure that we have both diversity and inclusion at the most senior levels, we can begin not only to open up opportunities more fairly and equitably, but businesses can also begin to reap the benefits of having a wider range of viewpoints and perspectives interrogating their ideas, plans and products before they reach customers.

In 2014, McKinsey looked at the performance of businesses in the top quartile for gender diversity at an executive level, compared to those businesses in the bottom quartile, and found that those businesses in that top group were 15 per cent* more likely to experience above-average profitability than companies at the bottom.[39] They repeated this study in 2017 and found that the stat of 15 per cent had risen significantly, to 21 per cent, and when they revisited it in 2019 the gap had grown once again – this time reaching 25 per cent.[40]

This financial premium for diversity at the most senior level may seem surprising, but it makes a lot of sense.

By the time people reach a senior leadership level, they are

---

* For ethnic and cultural diversity, rather than gender, the 2014 finding was a huge 35 per cent likelihood of outperformance.

much more likely to be secure in themselves, their identities and their roles in the workplace – and so they are more likely to feel empowered to bring their true perspectives and lived experiences to the fore in decision-making processes.

The real value of diversity is not in bringing in tokenistic, overlooked, unheard and disempowered junior team members who are good for the optics of a team photo* but are too afraid to speak out and share their real opinions about decisions being made. The value in diversity also doesn't come from simply pulling together a group of people who all *look* different from one another. The value comes from bringing together and hearing the opinions of people who *think* differently from one another. Since our race, gender, disability status, class background – and all of the intersectional elements that make us ourselves – impact our lived experiences, then bringing together a wide range of people who look different is a pretty good place to start, but visual diversity is not, and has never been, the end goal here.

Instead, the real value comes from having leaders with a wide range of lived experience and perspectives which they feel comfortable bringing to the table in order to stress-test and assess the ideas, propositions or products being made by their business. It is, then, the role of leaders, from any and all backgrounds, to foster a feeling of psychological safety for their entire team, regardless of their level, in order to allow them to express their true opinions informed by their actual lives.

The logic goes that, the wider the range of different perspectives held by people who feel safe and empowered to share their true thoughts and opinions, the earlier any potential mistakes or oversights will be caught. The wider and more varied the range of

---

* Which is performative and box-ticking at best, and, more often than not, nothing more than short-sighted and offensive. I can't tell you the number of times I've 'happened to be' OOO on days where office photography is planned because I'm not interested in being ushered to the front of a photo to act as an embodiment of 'diversity' in a business that is failing in that regard.

answers and solutions that are put forward, the more likely that at least one of them will lead to a final output which is good and resonates well with the widest possible consumer base – ultimately making the business more money and avoiding potential mistakes.

Homogeneity is natural and comfortable for humans – we are most drawn to those people who remind us of us. We find it easier and quicker to develop a shorthand and work smoothly with others with whom we have a shared background and similar experiences, people who value the same things as us and who are most likely to agree with our ideas and points of view with minimal friction. It's easy, it's smooth – and unfortunately it's a breeding ground for creative stagnation, rather than innovation.

When we only hear and take on the opinions and feedback of people who are similar to us, who share our expectations, values and cultural touchpoints, the problem is that they are likely to share our blind spots, too. They're likely to misinterpret, overlook or undervalue the exact same things that we are – things that someone with a different identity and lived experience might have picked up on immediately.*

Remember when Apple launched their health-tracking app back in 2014, with the promise that 'with Health, you can monitor all of your metrics that you're most interested in'? Users could track their blood alcohol levels, sodium intake and steps in a day.[41] But there was no way to track a menstrual cycle, since it simply wasn't on the list of things that were important to the people who made up their development team.

How about when NASA was preparing to send a female astronaut into space and asked if a hundred tampons would be enough for the week-long trip, during which she wasn't expecting her period?[42]

---

* This is also why, when we're hiring, we should always be looking for culture *adds*, rather than culture *fits*. We should be recruiting to fill gaps in knowledge and skill sets, but also in experience, perspective and background, to get the most out of the teams we're building.

Maybe you remember when automatic soap dispensers were launched for public bathrooms, but, because of the make-up of the teams working on them, it wasn't until they were finalized, installed and in public use that people started noticing they didn't work for everyone, because they simply couldn't detect Black people's hands?[43]

Or, speaking of public bathrooms, how about the anecdotal story of an all-male team who developed self-flushing toilets, eliminating the need to touch a handle or press a button to flush manually? Surprisingly for the developers, the toilet flushes in women's public bathrooms were repeatedly flagged as malfunctioning, despite the fact that, when technicians were sent out, everything seemed to be in working order. The 'fault' wasn't resolved until a member of the team happened to be complaining about the issue to his wife one evening, and she casually mentioned that many women squat or hover above public toilet seats – something that is obvious to most women, but had been a knowledge gap in the all-male team, resulting in them developing a flush that relied on a person fully sitting down and then standing up to trigger it.

If you know, you know. But if you don't, the chances of realizing you're missing knowledge, let alone then going on to intuit an effective solution, are tiny.

Examples of these kinds of oversights really are endless. Sometimes, they cost businesses a lot, either in terms of revenue from products needing to be recalled or pulled from shelves, or in reputational damage.

Think back to any public brand slip-up. Take H&M's 2018 release of the 'Coolest Monkey in the Jungle' hoodie, modelled by a young Black boy;[44] or Gucci's $890 'Blackface jumper', which looked suspiciously like a golliwog face and had to be pulled by the brand in 2019;[45] or even an influencer trip organized by Mango in 2022, which generated online backlash due to the fact that, of the sixty guests invited by the brand, 'one was a mixed-race journalist, one was an Asian influencer and the rest were white'.[46]

Regardless of the details of the case, one of the first cries that always goes up from the public on learning about these brand mishaps – that seem so clear, obvious and avoidable from the outside – is: 'But don't they have any Black people/women/ whatever-the-oversight-has-been-this-time on the team? HOW could this have been allowed to happen!?'

People instinctively know that having the right people in the room, sharing authentically and openly, is essential.

In truth, the answer is usually that, yes, there are marginalized people on the teams who could have saved brands from expensive and embarrassing snafus. But, all too often, these under-represented team members are too junior, and so too intimidated to feel that it's their place to raise their hand and say, 'I'm sorry, but I think we might be in for a problem if we do this, in this way.' Their potentially extremely valuable, potentially reputation-saving insight is lost, and so brands and businesses continue to make the same mistakes they always have.

In her 2019 TEDx Talk, 'When we design for disability, we all benefit', Elise Roy, who is a lawyer, activist and human rights advocate, discusses design thinking and the benefits that come from it.

Design thinking, says Roy, operates on the basic assumptions that:

- Everyone is creative, since we all problem-solve throughout our lives, depending on our personal needs.

- Everyone has a valuable perspective, usually building on their own lived experiences moving through the world.

- If you bring together people from multiple disciplines and perspectives, you can build something brand new, and better than you would have been able to achieve alone.[47]

While studying for her master's degree, Roy, who is profoundly deaf, fell in love with woodworking. As she was practising the skill, she quickly came to learn that most woodworkers rely on sound to warn them when a piece of wood or a tool is going to 'kick back' at them – a warning that she couldn't access without hearing. To compensate for this, Roy designed and made a new tool – a pair of safety glasses that visually alerted the wearer to changes in pitch in the tool, indicating an upcoming kickback *before* it could be detected by human ears.

'Why had tool designers not thought of this before?' Roy asked during her talk. Well, one of the reasons she puts forward is simply, 'I was deaf. My unique experience of the world helped to inform my perspective.'

Roy is not alone in leveraging her often overlooked needs, perspectives and experiences to create tools and solutions that otherwise wouldn't exist, and which we all benefit from.

Text messaging, for instance, was initially developed as a tool to allow deaf people to communicate without speaking, but its adoption outside of that community has transformed the way we communicate.[48] And I for one know I'm not going to answer a call – if you want to get hold of me, it needs to be through some kind of text medium.

Automatic doors, an innovation that was initially intended to help physically disabled people to access spaces more easily, have been widely adopted throughout the world. Businesses have found that installing them has led to unexpected benefits, such as reduced heating costs, as the doors only open as needed, and reduced cleaning costs, as the doors are rarely, if ever, touched by fingers and hands.

Closed captions and subtitles on TV and film were also pioneered as an accessibility feature. However, in 2006, research from Ofcom found that 7.6 million people in the UK – around 18 per cent of the entire population at the time – had used them. Ofcom notes that, of that figure, only around 1.4 million people reported having a hearing impairment, which means the vast majority – around 6.2 million users of subtitling – can hear perfectly well.[49] And it seems that the popularity of the service is only growing. In 2021, a study found that 80 per cent of people aged between eighteen and twenty-five used subtitles 'all or part of the time', compared to just a quarter of those aged fifty-six to seventy-five, despite people in the older age bracket being almost twice as likely to say they are deaf or hard of hearing.[50]

Things which begin as accessibility adaptations, arising from listening to and valuing the needs and experiences of differently abled people, become not only accepted, but useful additions to all of our lives.

In my last book, I wrote about Vernā Myers' well-known quote: 'Diversity is being invited to the party; inclusion is being asked to dance.' I won't rehash my thoughts here, beyond saying – I think we can do better. Whether we're waiting to be invited to the party, or waiting to be invited to dance, we're always *waiting* – never calling the shots, making the playlist, or cutting the cake. We're relying on permission from someone else to allow us to step in, participate and take up space. It's essential that we move beyond being grateful for being tolerated in spaces, for being able to access organizations and environments that would have historically been closed to us, and move into being treated, and treating others, as collaborators, friends and equals.

'Nothing about us without us' is a central tenet of the disability manifesto. I find it to be beautiful, powerful, essential – and a framing that I think we can all benefit from. No laws, policies, decisions or choices about the lives of disabled people should be made without input from people who belong to the community. It's so simple, and is clearly the way we should approach conversations around disability, as well as all other areas of marginalization – but I wonder, again, if we can take it further.

I wonder if we can try to make a world where there's nothing for *any* of us that doesn't work for *all* of us. I know, at least now, it's not going to be possible all of the time – but, if we set that up as the expectation, or at least the ambition, then we can work towards a world where things are built, by default, to be inclusive for the largest possible number of people. When we have the widest possible range of voices included as equal, respected and valued parts of the conversation – interrogating, widening and improving our own perspectives and starting points – then we build solutions and businesses that work for the many, not the few, from the start. That's when we can really begin to unlock the truest value of diversity.

It's less a question of needing more people, and more one of needing more *types* of people, who are made to feel safe and whose perspectives are valued as we are invited into and involved in discussions and key decisions.

We can see that a commitment to increased diversity, including women being represented at the most senior levels, has a real business benefit. And so we need businesses to see and understand the value that traditionally under-represented leaders can bring to them all of the time, not only during moments of crisis.

I find that people sometimes have a difficulty in quantifying the value of diversity; they think of it as a nice-to-have, and it ticks a box on their mental morality list. At times when things feel uncertain, or difficult, like during the cost-of-living crisis, or while recovering from the impact of the Covid-19 pandemic, diversity can be quickly dismissed as businesses enter 'panic mode' and default to how things have always worked in order to, theoretically, safeguard their assets. But it's important to remember that diversity and inclusion are so much more than a nice-to-have – and making and fostering a truly inclusive team is essential for businesses' ongoing success. In fact, research has shown that, in the period of recovery after the 2008 global financial crash, banks with a higher share of women on their boards were more stable than their peers who lacked the same representation.[51]

Businesses with more female representation at the most senior levels make more money. Research commissioned by the Peterson Institute, a US economic think tank, found that businesses which go from having a zero per cent female share of corporate leadership*

---

* The CEO, the board and other C-suite positions.

to a 30 per cent female share gain a one-percentage-point increase in their net margins – which translates to a 15 per cent increase in profitability for a typical firm.[52]

The same research points out that the benefit of having multiple women in senior roles is greater than having a stand-alone female CEO or single female board member. In fact, those businesses with more than 30 per cent of board seats held by women showed 54 per cent revenue growth in 2020, compared to those with 20 per cent or fewer board seats held by women, which showed a 45 per cent revenue growth.[53] In turn, companies with at least 20 per cent female representation at senior levels were more likely to outperform those businesses with lower gender representation or none at all, with McKinsey[54] finding that 'a substantial differential likelihood of outperformance – 48 per cent – separates the most from the least gender-diverse companies'.[*]

When considering the Glass Cliff and its impact, we should of course be thinking about women's experiences. But we should also be thinking, seriously, about its impact on businesses and their performance.

If we stop thinking of female representation, and inclusion overall, as a nice-to-add fluffy business extra and begin to acknowledge it as the revenue-driving force for change that it really is, we can work towards businesses recognizing the value of women in leadership all of the time – not only when soft skills are in demand after a period of crisis. We can also begin to be more mindful, and intentional, about designing workplaces that truly work for everyone, with everyone's needs and interests in mind, and begin to break the cycle of the Glass Cliff.

---

[*] The research also notes: 'In the case of ethnic and cultural diversity, our business-case findings are equally compelling: in 2019, top-quartile companies outperformed those in the fourth one by 36 per cent in profitability, slightly up from 33 per cent in 2017 and 35 per cent in 2014. As we have previously found, the likelihood of outperformance continues to be higher for diversity in ethnicity than for gender.'

TL;DR: *Too Long; Didn't Read*

- The opposite to the Glass Cliff is the Glass Escalator – an invisible force that raises white men quickly through the ranks, towards leadership positions. Particularly in female-dominated industries.

  - In the UK's NHS, men make up only 31 per cent of employees. Despite this, men in the organization held 42.2 per cent of the *highest*-paying jobs. Women, by contrast, represent 68.7 per cent of NHS employees and make up 77.6 per cent of the *lowest*-paying roles.

  - Black and Global Majority men do not receive the same benefits or advantages from the Glass Escalator as their white peers.

- The benefit of inclusion doesn't lie in bringing together a wide range of people who only look different from one another. The benefit comes from bringing together a wide range of views, perspectives and lived experiences – and creating environments in which they feel safe to express their true thoughts and opinions.

- Businesses that are the most diverse in terms of gender at an executive level significantly outperform those which are the least diverse, in terms of profitability and EBIT (earnings before interest and tax) margins.

- Expensive and embarrassing business mistakes can be avoided by not only having the right people in the room, but making sure they feel safe and able to share their authentic views and concerns.

- A large number of tools and innovations that were developed with increased accessibility needs in mind, from text messaging to subtitles, have been adopted by a much wider group than initially anticipated. When we design for diversity, we all benefit.

CHAPTER 8

Breaking the Cycle

Don't tell me the moon is shining; show me the glint of the light on broken glass.

ANTON CHEKHOV[1]

In May 2014, Jill Abramson stood before the graduating class of Wake Forest University to give the commencement speech that would hopefully help them in finding their paths through the world, as graduates.

'First of all, congratulations,' she told them.

After making some reflections about her own graduation day from Harvard, she continued, 'Very early last Thursday, my sister called me and she said, "I know Dad would be as proud of you today as he was the day you became executive editor of *The New York Times*." I had been fired the previous day, so I knew what she was trying to say. It meant more to our father to see us deal with a setback and try to bounce back than to watch how we handled our successes. "Show what you are made of," he would say.'[2]

This was the first time that Abramson, who up until the previous week had held the role as the first female executive editor of *The New York Times* in the newsroom's 160-year history, had spoken publicly after being abruptly fired from the paper.[3]

'We human beings are a lot more resilient than we often realize. Resilient and perseverant', she told the crowd of graduates, their parents and the assembled press. 'Some of you have faced danger or even a soul-scorching loss, but most of you haven't. And leaving the protective cocoon of school for the working world must seem scary. You will have a dozen different jobs and will try different things. Sure, losing a job you love hurts, but the work I revere, journalism that holds powerful institutions and people accountable, is what makes our democracy so resilient. And this is the work I will remain very much a part of.'

She was, it seemed, speaking to the press, who had gathered, somewhat unusually at the commencement ceremony, in similar numbers to the graduates themselves. These were her first public statements about her time as the leader of *The New York Times*, and she joked that she had no plans to have the (real) *Times* 'T' tattoo on her back removed, reflecting on her experiences with colleagues during her tenure as their leader.

Abramson had taken on the role of executive editor at *The New York Times* in 2011, following a series of highly publicized crises at the paper.[4] Under the leadership of her predecessor (who led the paper from 2003 until mid-2011), the newspaper had faced financial difficulties that meant they needed to take out an extremely high-interest loan of $250 million to keep the struggling business afloat.[5] During the same period, the business had also faced a plagiarism scandal,[6] widespread criticisms of the paper's coverage of foreign policy and national security under the Bush and Obama administrations, and declining competitiveness on the digital-news front.[7]

Abramson, like far too many women stepping into leadership roles, had taken the helm of a business in need of some support.

During her short-lived leadership of the newspaper, Abramson was instrumental in turning the tide in a period that was widely regarded as being a disaster area for the newspaper industry overall.[8]

Just before she took on the executive director role, *The New York Times* had implemented an online paywall for its articles – a revenue-driving exercise. Under her watch, the news outlet's digital-only subscriber base for the initiative grew to almost 800,000 subscribers, and was profitable.[9]

'When she was brought on, anyone who was going to be the next editor of *The New York Times* was going to be taking *The New York Times* in this brave new era of information,' Rachel Sklar, founder of Change the Ratio and TheLi.st, which promotes women in media, told Vox. 'That's widely seen across the industry as a big challenge.'[10]

But it seems to have been a challenge that Abramson rose to, admirably.

The first-quarter accounts for the *Times*, published in April 2014, just weeks before Abramson was fired, tell the story of a business that was performing well – the paper had shown a $22 million operating profit on $390 million in revenue. That revenue figure 'represented a 2.6 per cent increase from the previous year's quarter, including a 3.4 per cent increase in ad revenue'.[11] It was also noted in the same month that the *Times* reported a 4 per cent print ad revenue increase for the first quarter, despite the entire newspaper industry losing 8.6 per cent of its print revenue during the same period.[12] With revenue from both print and digital on the rise, it's reasonable to say that, in that respect, Abramson was doing all of the right things as a leader, during what was a difficult time for the newspaper industry overall.

In fact, Abramson helped the paper turn an operating profit nearly every quarter she was in charge, and, in every quarter of 2013, those profits had increased from the previous year.[13]

She had also been able to retain a full staff of close to 1,100 employees, which was no small feat for a newspaper at the time, when so many others were being forced to cut back on expenses such as staffing. While other newspapers were fighting for survival during the period that Abramson was in role, her organization had fourteen national and six regional bureaus, plus twenty-five foreign bureaus – more than at any moment in the paper's history. (*The Washington Post*, by contrast, closed all its domestic bureaus and slashed the head count in its newsroom, once totalling more than 900, by nearly a quarter).[14]

Of course, beyond paywalls and profitability, a huge part of any newsroom's ambition is great reporting, an area that also flourished under Abramson's leadership, with *Times* staffers earning no fewer than eight Pulitzer Prizes during her short time as the paper's leader.[15]

Abramson, it seemed, was auspiciously leading a business that was successfully changing to meet the adapting demands of an increasingly online audience. Part of the plan for this future-proofing exercise was to create a new senior editor position, reporting to the *Times*' managing director, Dean Baquet, to handle growing the paper's online audience.[16]

It was common knowledge that Baquet did not have the most harmonious working relationship with the executive editor. An incident was reported widely in which Baquet, frustrated by a meeting with Abramson, 'burst out' of her office, 'slammed his hand against a wall and stormed out of the newsroom', not returning for the rest of the day, missing his afternoon meetings.[17]

This wasn't the only tense internal relationship that Abramson was said to have had with her team during her time as leader. A controversial piece published by *Politico* said that many team members had characterized her as 'stubborn and condescending, saying they found her difficult to work with.' It added that, 'at times, [staffers] say, her attitude toward editors and reporters leaves everyone feeling demoralized; on other occasions, she can seem disengaged or uncaring'.[18]

There have been multiple reports that Abramson's leadership style clashed with other leaders within the business.[19] Even her supporters admit that Abramson could be 'high-handed, impatient, sarcastic, judgmental, and obstinate' – all qualities, by contrast, likely to be praised in a man leading one of the top newsrooms in America, tasked with investigative journalism and uncovering the truth.[20]

Abramson herself says she admitted in her interview for the role of executive editor that she had an occasional brusqueness, though those who had worked with her when she was at the *Legal Times* recalled giving her the nickname '"Mama" because she used to look after everybody [. . .] Jill is the one who visits you when you're in the hospital.'[21]

As with any of us, the truth about her personality and relationships with colleagues is likely to be a mixed bag, but I think we can agree that, had it been Abramson who stormed out of a meeting and didn't return for the day, it would have sparked a lot more discussion than it did for Baquet.

One factor that may have led to Abramson being removed from her role is the fact that, in the weeks before the decision was taken, she discovered that her pay and pension benefits, as both executive editor and, before that, as managing editor, were considerably less than the pay and pension benefits of Bill Keller, the male editor whom she replaced in both jobs.[22] Naturally, she instructed a lawyer to speak to the *Times'* leadership team about the issue, a move that some have speculated may have fed into the management's narrative that she was 'pushy'.[23]

The *Times*, after news of this reported disparity came to light, was quick to issue a memo on what it said was misinformation about the pay issue, claiming, 'It is simply not true that Jill's compensation was significantly less than her predecessor's,' and that, 'Her pay is comparable to that of earlier executive editors.'[24] Though, 'comparable' and 'equal' are not necessarily the same thing.

While we will probably never know the full story behind Abramson's firing, we do know that it was not a mutual decision, and that, even by the *Times'* own estimation, it was a shock. The announcement that Abramson was being replaced due to 'an issue with management' was made to a 'stunned' newsroom.[25] No details were given beyond the publisher saying, 'I chose to appoint a new leader of our newsroom because I believe that new leadership will improve some aspects . . .'[26]

It was noted that Abramson didn't choose to attend the announcement, nor did she offer any suggestion that she had been consulted about the decision in advance.[27]

It's also notable, as Glass Cliff researchers speaking about Abramson's dismissal pointed out, that 'at an organization where the executive editor has traditionally remained in the position until retirement, the first woman in this role was fired fewer than three years into her tenure and replaced by a man, all in the name of saving the paper.'[28]

Abramson was replaced in her role by Dean Baquet.

Speaking to the Wake Forest University graduating class, Abramson said, 'What's next for me? I don't know. So I'm in exactly the same boat as many of you. And like you, I'm a little scared but also excited.'[29]

◆ ◆ ◆

We've spoken a lot about the Glass Cliff – we've looked at what it is, how to spot it, the circumstances that make it most likely, and why, despite being fully aware of its risks, some women still choose to take on roles which have a high chance of being impacted by it. But I don't want to leave it there. Because one thing that's important about the phenomenon is that it's neither a necessary fact nor part of nature. It's a consequence of socialization, and that means that it's changeable – it's possible for us to be part of breaking the cycle and to make workplaces and cultures where the Glass Cliff simply doesn't occur. In dreaming that dream, there's a lot that we can learn from the places where it already doesn't exist.

When we're looking at the steps we can take to break the cycle of the Glass Cliff and reduce the likelihood of women encountering it during their careers, we are trying to imagine a world where the Glass Cliff doesn't exist. But it might be that we don't need to use our imaginations as much as we may expect – because there is evidence to suggest that, around the world, there are several places where this is already the case.

This doesn't mean that the Glass Cliff isn't real anywhere, or that the phenomenon is any less impactful for the lives and careers for those who it does touch. But it does mean that we can see, from research on the Glass Cliff, Ceiling and Escalator, that none of them are inevitable, because none of them are related to an intrinsic set of abilities in leaders of different genders. Instead, they are all a result of the way that we have structured our societies and workplaces, the value we have given to different team members and the expectations we have socialized in relation to gender. And while those are all *huge* things to try to unpack on their own, let alone combined, they're much easier for us to try to work against than anything that's a fundamental fact of nature. And so – let's look at some things we can learn from places where the risk seems to have been taken away.*

As we get closer to gender equality, the likelihood of the Glass Cliff occurring, and the level of impact it has on women's careers, should be reduced, and there is research to show that's exactly what happens.[30]

When looking at the prevalence of the Glass Cliff as a phenomenon in countries that rank higher in gender equality, such as Switzerland and Germany, researchers have found that its impact is smaller than in less gender-equal countries, like the US and the UK. As Thekla Morgenroth, the Purdue researcher, commented, 'These countries are fairly similar culturally. It's surprising and maybe encouraging that even small differences in gender inequality can really make a difference.'[31]

There is also evidence from Turkey showing that managers did not opt for a female executive candidate as CEO in scenarios in which the 'company performance is poor', leading the researchers to conclude that 'in consideration of contextual fundamentals, it can be suggested that the concept of the Glass Cliff, a term coined . . . in the United Kingdom, where masculinity is predominant, may not be valid for Turkey, where the level of masculinity is relatively low'.[32]

We have already discussed the ways in which both a more feminized society and a society with less emphasis on individualistic

---

* As Rita Dove, Poet Laureate consultant in poetry to the Library of Congress, said, 'one does not look a muse in the eye and say, Ah, forget it.'

values may be key in reducing the impact of the Glass Cliff. While there still needs to be more research into a great range of locations and cultural factors, once this is done, we are likely to be able to better identify the likelihood of women facing Glass Cliff scenarios, and use these as models to inform our own ways of working. If we're willing to look at our own values, expectations and ways of working, we may be able to shape workplaces to work better for women, and reduce the risk of them experiencing the Glass Cliff.

Changing our expectations of leaders

One of the reasons that we see the Glass Cliff playing out time and time again is that having women in the most senior positions is still seen as a risk by so many businesses – one that they only become willing to take when they feel they have tried everything else, or when there has been a prolonged problem which they believe a woman's soft skills are better suited to address.

But, of course, that's not what they say. Since most people haven't been aware of the Glass Cliff as a phenomenon up to this point, it's interesting to look at the reasons business leaders give when asked about the lack of female representation at their most senior levels.

To find out what attitudes and beliefs have held women back from being able to take their places on boards up to now, the UK government's Department for Business, Energy and Industrial Strategy commissioned research in which they interviewed CEOs and chairs from a range of FTSE 350 companies about why they thought there were so few women in board-level positions.* They

---

* This research was part of the Hampton-Alexander Review, which in 2017 introduced the requirement for businesses in the private and voluntary sectors with 250 employees or more to report their gender pay-gap differences, and challenged large firms to have at least one third female representation on boards and non-leadership by 2020.

published their findings on the government's website with the heading, 'Revealed: The worst explanations for not appointing women to FTSE company boards' – and I'm going to share some of their findings with you here.

The explanations the male CEOs and chairs gave for not having women on their boards included:

1. 'I don't think women fit comfortably into the board environment'
2. 'There aren't that many women with the right credentials and depth of experience to sit on the board – the issues covered are extremely complex'
3. 'Most women don't want the hassle or pressure of sitting on a board'
4. 'Shareholders just aren't interested in the make-up of the board, so why should we be?'
5. 'My other board colleagues wouldn't want to appoint a woman on our board'
6. 'All the "good" women have already been snapped up'
7. 'We have one woman already on the board, so we are done – it is someone else's turn'
8. 'There aren't any vacancies at the moment – if there were I would think about appointing a woman'
9. 'We need to build the pipeline from the bottom – there just aren't enough senior women in this sector'
10. 'I can't just appoint a woman because I want to'[33]

Truly, absolutely absurd and outdated thinking. And, as Jemima Olchawski, the policy head at the gender equality campaign group the Fawcett Society, pointed out to *The Guardian*, 'these are just the things they were prepared to say out loud'.[34]

'As you read this list of excuses you might think it's 1918 not 2018. It reads like a script from a comedy parody but it's true', chief executive of Business in the Community, Amanda Mackenzie, said as part of the report.[35] 'Surely we can now tackle this once and for all. Maybe those that give credence to these excuses are the ones that are not up to sitting on boards and should move over: we are in the 21st century after all.'*

It's a good point. Instead of debating where all of the 'good' women are, presuming the issues to be tackled are too complex for women to grapple with or self-congratulating on having one sole woman on the board and so deciding that 'it is someone else's turn', it's time to consider whether having homogenous boards without a range of backgrounds, beliefs and lived experiences really is appropriate for businesses attempting to navigate the changes and challenges of the modern workplace.

The report continues: 'Boards made up of just men, from the same socioeconomic backgrounds, cannot be the optimal forum for challenging debates.'[36] This sentiment was endorsed by Brenda Trenowden, global chair of the 30% Club, who expressed her concerns about the suitability of those interviewed to lead FTSE companies, telling *The Guardian*, 'If they're so out of touch with the real world, I wonder if they're really qualified to be doing those jobs. It's backwards thinking, it's wrong and if they honestly believe what they say, they're not doing justice to the companies they're chairing because they're missing out on a huge talent pool and they're going to get left behind.'[37]

I know I keep saying that things aren't real – but I really do mean it. I really do mean that there is nothing at all that is intrinsic

---

* It's also worth noting that this lack of women in the most senior roles was also identified by the Hampton-Alexander Review team as a key reason given by companies as they reported on their pay-gap figures – noting that 'the pay gap was due to insufficient women in senior roles, and/or a predominance of women in lower paid work. Ensuring women are selected in more equal numbers for senior roles, significantly reduces the pay gap.' The study's authors noted that, 'According to research by McKinsey bridging the gender pay gap could add £150 billion to the UK economy by 2025 and it could translate into 840,000 additional female employees.'

about our images or our expectations of leaders or leadership that is based on hard fact – it's all based on what we've come to expect from what we've seen so far.

But the world isn't the same as it was twenty, ten, or even five years ago. Our working lives have been forever changed by technology, by the pandemic and by our own shifting cultural values and norms – and that means we can reimagine our vision of leadership too, as something that's a better fit for the world we live in now.

And so, if the old-fashioned, tried-and-tested make-up of boards isn't what we believe is going to set us on the path for success in a quickly changing world, and challenging economy, what do we think has a better chance of success? What do we need to look for in the next generation of leaders – particularly as they navigate challenges and crises?

If we're to go by the FTSE 350, today's idea of a good leader is so blinkered that it risks overlooking and excluding those viewpoints that would give businesses a competitive edge. It's time we rethought the idea that leaders as we traditionally know them are giving businesses what they need to remain successful in the long run, especially in a world that is fast-paced and increasingly unpredictable.

So what should we be prioritizing as we plan to build future-facing businesses? And how can the changing needs of a fast-paced, always-on, super-connected culture alter our expectations of what to look for in a leader, and open up more opportunities for women to take on leadership roles, without the threat of the Glass Cliff looming large?

Making workplaces that work
for women

So much of what we've spoken about throughout this entire book has been, in one way or another, the ways in which businesses are not giving women what they want and need. Whether it's the pay gap, lack of access to promotions thanks to the Broken Rung, or finding yourself on the edge of the Glass Cliff once you've finally broken through the Glass Ceiling – at no stage has the workplace been set up by women, or with women in mind.

We know, at this point, that one of the main factors that indicates we're likely to face a Glass Cliff scenario is stepping into a leadership role in a business that has only had men holding top positions up to that point. This is likely a result of status-quo bias, which essentially means 'if it's not broken, don't fix it'.[38] If a business has been run successfully by men (and only men) in the past, the appointment of a woman is seen as being an unnecessary risk to what is perceived as a proven winning formula. This means that, when things go well, the maleness of the leadership is understood as being a contributing factor, and it's only when that proven 'winning formula' goes badly that we shake things up by seeing if a woman can solve the mess.[39]

In their reporting on the Glass Cliff, *Harvard Business Review* pointed out that they were 'especially struck by the finding that the phenomenon does not seem to apply to organizations with a history of female leaders. This suggests that as people become more used to seeing women at the highest levels of management, female leaders won't be selected primarily for risky turnarounds – and will get more chances to run organizations that have good odds of continued success.'[40]

So, since the Glass Cliff phenomenon and its impacts do not seem to apply to organizations when they have a history of female leaders, what can we all do to make sure that, even when there's not a crisis, more and more women are able to take on and be successful in leadership roles?[41] How can we create a proven model for successful female leadership and remove the novelty of under-represented leadership (and, hopefully, stop them from being under-represented at even the most senior levels in the long term)?

I want to say that I'm aware, since women are not a homo-genous group, that there is no single, unified answer to what women want. I'm also aware that that question alone – what do women want from their workplaces and how can we give it to them? – is more than enough to fill a whole library's worth of books. And so please don't imagine this to be a fully comprehensive list of all the ways that workplaces are failing women, and all the things we can do to change that. I am focusing on the issues that we can most clearly see impacting women's experiences of susceptibility to the Glass Cliff phenomenon, and offering very top-line suggestions around righting or beginning to address them – particularly where there is research to back things up.

I'm also aware that it's something of a chicken-and-egg problem. How do we get more women into these spaces in order to create the conditions and environments where more and more women can flourish, if those initial women face a hostile reception and an eventual fall from the Glass Cliff? But it feels like something that needs to be considered, especially since research has shown that 'gender stereotypes form subtle systemic barriers to the advancement of significant numbers of women into these roles at the group level. To circumvent these stereotypes, increasing the representation of women in senior leadership roles is a necessary first step, not an eventual outcome.'[42]

It turns out that, even in the very first moments in a new role, from the way that a new female leader's appointment is announced, we may be unintentionally limiting her potential for success.

Researchers from Penn State examined the ways in which new female CEOs were announced to their companies, looking at the appointments of ninety-one women between 1995 and 2012. They analysed the language used in both internal and public press announcements – referring to the outgoing and the new, female, incoming CEOs – and then looked at how long the newly announced women ended up remaining in role.

Surprisingly, they found that the more companies praised and touted the past accomplishments of their incoming female CEOs when announcing their hiring, the more likely it was for these women to have shorter tenures in the CEO role. They put this down to the idea that these early endorsements, internally and externally, increased the likelihood that new female CEOs would be at the receiving end of stereotypes and biases in their new role.[43]

As we saw in Chapter 6, gendered stereotypes play a huge role in women's professional experiences, both when we are seen as living up to them and when we are seen to be deviating from them. It's a no-win scenario, as identified in the Penn State research, which found that 'Women are stereotypically seen as being sensitive and nurturing and thus not fit for leadership roles, but when women show that they are competent enough for leadership roles, they are then judged as not fulfilling the stereotypical expectations for what women should be.' A researcher in the project specifically noted, 'Organizations may want to help women by touting their accomplishments, but as soon as they do, it can trigger a backlash. They're trying to help, but it may actually end up hurting.'[44]

They did, however, find a few things that lessened the impact of such a backlash, including the new female CEO being promoted from within the company, rather than being completely new to the business, and – you've guessed it – other women already being on the leadership team and on the board.

Promote, don't recruit

Consistently, and in so many different forums, we've seen the question coming up of promotion versus moving company in order to secure a better role. We've seen in our discussions, from the Broken Rung to the Great Break-Up, that women's promotions can be slow and difficult to secure, and so women are taking their progression into their own hands and changing roles in order to secure better prospects for themselves.

But we've also learned that women who are hired in as new leaders to a business are seen as outsiders, more likely to struggle to get buy-in and support for their ideas and directions once in place, and therefore more likely to face a Glass Cliff.

Female CEOs are also more likely than their male counterparts to be brought in externally, rather than as the result of a promotion.[45] In fact, 35 per cent of female CEOs entered their roles as outsiders, versus just 22 per cent of male CEOs – making the position a much more difficult one to turn into a story of success.

'Being CEO as an outsider is a tougher job,' Gary Neilson, a researcher and senior partner at management consultancy Strategy&, told *The Washington Post*. 'They don't have as many connections in the company to understand how things work, and their performance is not as high as those who've been groomed in-house.' The *Post* article goes on to mention that 'research has shown, for instance, that external CEOs are 6.7 times more likely to be dismissed with a short tenure than home-grown ones.'[46]

And so, with this in mind, why do so many businesses choose to go through the time-consuming and costly process of hunting for external talent instead of nurturing the teams they already have?

We can get a good idea from thinking back to the reasons male CEOs gave for not having women represented on their boards. In particular, 'We need to build the pipeline from the bottom – there just aren't enough senior women in this sector', and, of course, everyone's favourite: 'All the "good" women have already been snapped up'.

While these comments are specifically about board membership, they are exactly in line with the sentiments I hear from businesses when discussing their inability to retain under-represented talent once they have been appointed to roles. They can bring people in, but they're failing at the next steps of retention and promotion – and they always blame the pipeline. And it's simply untrue.

If Beyoncé can find twenty-four Black trombonists *and* a mirrorball horse, you can find a woman in your business who is ready to be promoted.

If there are women who are impressive and qualified enough to bring in externally to fill senior roles, there are women in your business who are qualified, too.

And if there aren't – if there are only internal men or external women – the problem with the pipeline doesn't lie with anything women are or aren't doing. No, on the contrary, it's down to the business's investment in them – as far back as their first promotions and the old issue of the Broken Rung.

One other reason we see businesses overlooking their own internal talent and instead deciding to search externally is Tall Poppy Syndrome.* In the first research project of its kind, The Tallest Poppy study interviewed thousands of women in a range of professions in 103 countries around the world to hear about their experiences of being 'attacked, resented, disliked, criticized, or cut down because of their achievements and/or success', rather than being celebrated. This is an experience that 86.8 per cent of the women surveyed felt they had experienced in their careers.[47]

In a statement accompanying the release of the research, Dr Rumeet Billan, author of the study, said:

Our data tells an eye-opening story about how Tall Poppy Syndrome negatively impacts ambitious, high-performing

---

* Tall Poppy Syndrome occurs when a person's success causes them to be attacked, resented or criticized. In cutting down tall poppies, we devalue the achievements of others by suggesting that they did not deserve the attention or success they received. Interestingly, this is an idea common around the world – in Japan, the equivalent phrase is said to translate as, 'The nail that sticks up gets hammered down', while in the Netherlands it's expressed as the warning, 'Don't put your head above ground level.'

women, and what this means for organizations [. . .] Not only does our data reveal the negative effects of being cut down because of one's achievements, it helps us understand how the cutting is being done, who is most likely to do the cutting, and most importantly, legitimizes the experiences of women who, in many cases, have experienced this throughout their careers [without having a name to put to it].[48]

The types of 'cutting' the study found were very similar to the microaggressions we discussed in Chapter 2:

- 77 per cent of respondents had their achievements down-played.

- 72.4 per cent of respondents were left out of meetings and discussions or were ignored.

- 70.7 per cent said they were undermined because of their achievement(s).

- 68.3 per cent had their achievement(s) dismissed.

- 66.1 per cent said others took credit for their work.[49]

As a response to the experience of being 'cut down', 73.8 per cent of women reported it having a negative impact on their mental health, 90 per cent reported increased stress, and 66.2 per cent reported lowered self-confidence.[50]

'Organizations often talk about the "war for top talent," when instead, there should be a focus on retaining top talent,' said Dr Billan. 'As a result of Tall Poppy Syndrome, high-performers are minimizing their skills and accomplishments, 60.5 per cent of those who responded to our survey believe they will be penalized if they are perceived as ambitious at work. When ambitious workers find themselves in an environment where excelling is penalized, their productivity will be impacted, and they will have one foot out the door. This not only negatively impacts the individual, but the organization as well.'[51]

We need businesses to invest in women, to see and nurture their potential, to open up opportunities for glamour work (rather than office housework) which would give them the chance to showcase their abilities and to form bonds with the most senior stakeholders – increasing their likelihood of being top-of-mind when decisions about opportunities for progression are happening.

What about quotas?

Quotas are always a difficult subject to broach – and, to be honest, I've changed my thoughts and opinions about them several times over the years. But, the more I learn about the Glass Cliff, the more I find myself leaning in favour of them.

I've come to think of quotas as a stick in the ground, a stated intention that we can measure against, and I think the more transparent we can be in recognizing both the shortcomings we have in our businesses and in our plans to overcome them, the better. And quotas can be a really good way of helping to avoid bias in making hiring decisions.

'If you have some form of quotas it is much harder to have these biased decision processes, that's a very practical thing that organisations can implement', Thekla Morgenroth told the BBC.[52] This is backed up by Michelle Ryan and her colleagues in their report looking back on ten years of research and data around the Glass Cliff. In the conclusion to their paper, they noted that, 'as work on the topic has progressed, we have been struck by the persistent framing of the Glass Cliff as "a woman's problem". And yet, if one looks at the data which give rise to the effect, it is apparent that it is driven as much, if not more, by the fact that men are given preferential access to cushy leadership positions as by the fact that women are appointed to precarious ones.'[53]

In 2022, following a decade of discussion, the European Parliament passed the Women On Boards law in an attempt to break the Glass Ceiling.* It stipulates that listed companies in the EU must have a minimum of 40 per cent female representation of non-executive board members by mid-2026, and at least a third of all company directors must be women. But the new law doesn't stop there. Also included is the requirement that 'where two candidates for a post are equally qualified, priority must go to the under-represented sex, with those businesses who don't follow the new requirements facing penalties including fines, or even the annulment of the contested director's appointment.'[54]

'After ten years since its proposal by the European Commission, we will now have an EU law to break the Glass Ceiling of listed companies' boards,' said Ursula von der Leyen, president of the European Commission. 'There are plenty of women qualified for top jobs and with our new European law, we will make sure that they have a real chance to get them.'[55]

'We are removing one of the main hurdles for women to get the "top jobs": informal male networks,' said Evelyn Regner, an Austrian lawmaker who helped the new rules pass through parliament. 'From now on, competence will count more in a selection procedure than ever before, as will transparency.'[56]

So, if men have been given preferential treatment in the workplace so far, and we have called it a meritocracy, maybe setting out some clear intentions around women's participation can only be a positive next step. And we can learn things from countries who have already put gender-based workplace quotas in action.

Norway introduced the first quota law of its kind in Europe in 2005 when it introduced a 40 per cent female quota for the boards of listed companies in the country. Adoption was quick, and while female representation on public Norwegian boards

---

* Companies with under 250 employees are exempt.

stood at just 3 per cent in 1992, it had risen to 40 per cent by 2009.[57]

Seventeen years after it was initially put in place, in 2022, the Norwegian government proposed expanding the policy, putting forward a bill that would mean large public *and* private Norwegian companies whose boards weren't made up of at least 40 per cent women would be shut down.[58]

Discussing the plans to expand the requirement to the private sector, Norway's Industry Minister Jan Christian Vestre said in a statement, 'Companies are not good enough in using the skills of both genders. It is high time this changes.'

'It has taken 20 years to increase the share by 5 percentage points. If we continue at this tempo, we will never reach our goal (of having gender balance),' Equality Minister Anette Trettebergstuen added.[59]

Once gender-based quotas for board-level representation are in place, they not only open up the opportunities for women to be appointed, they also allow those women, once in place, to push and advocate for change, policies and decisions that help other women to be successful in the workplace. Research published in the *American Journal of Political Science* looked at gender equality in almost a thousand businesses, comparing those in Italy (where a mandated gender-representation requirement for business boards was introduced in 2011) and Greece (a country with a similarly sized economy and no gender-based board-level quotas). They found that, in the first eight years after Italy introduced the workplace quotas, female representation on Italian boards grew from 5 per cent to 36 per cent; while there was also an increase in Greece during the period, it was much smaller, going up from 6 per cent to just 9 per cent.[60]

As well as looking at women's ability to access board-level appointments, the researchers were interested in the impact that women were able to make in these roles once appointed. They observed that 'boards with quotas for women create more gender inclusive and equity-oriented policies that have a meaningful impact not only on women's working conditions, but also on the men they work with – ultimately improving workplace culture for everyone.' *Forbes*, reporting on the research and the impact of quotas, added that, 'yes, quotas in board composition have real and measurable impacts on conditions for women throughout the company. The impact is stark; by their measurements, attention to gender equality issues increased by upwards of 50 per cent, even increasing the importance that both women and men within an organization assign to these issues.'[61]

Of course, not all of us live in countries where government-mandated quotas are likely to be put in place any time soon. Which is OK, because research[62] has found that, whether quotas are issued at a governmental level or put in place by individual businesses, they function in the same way, are equally effective and can reap the same benefits.*

Change the rules

In Chapter 4, we learned about the differences in both expectations and outcomes in negotiations led by men and women. We saw that women often negotiated less successfully, and those who did negotiate well were often forced to pay a likeability penalty for their efforts.

So what if, instead of teaching women to 'negotiate better', or how to remain pliable while pushing for what they want and deserve, we change the rules of the game altogether?

This is something Ellen Pao did during her time at Reddit, when she banned salary negotiations.

---

* As well as increasing representation, increased female presence at the highest levels results in businesses implementing a greater number of policies that better reflect women's needs, such as improved provisions for childcare, and even addressing pay inequity.

Explaining the decision to PBS, Pao said, 'We come up with an offer that we think is fair. If you want more equity, we'll let you swap a little bit of your cash salary for equity, but we aren't going to reward people who are better negotiators with more compensation.'[63]

In discussing this choice in an interview with Yahoo, Joan Williams, a professor of law at UC Hastings, observed, 'Does [ending salary negotiations] mean it will be better for every single woman? No, that's not how things work. But if you want to eliminate an advantage men have because of these prescriptive stereotypes, then this is a clear way to do it.'[64]

The more we can be aware of the old ways of working, to see them as choices rather than necessities and challenge them to see whether they really do still serve us, the more we can all work together to rebuild and reshape workplaces that work for us all. Equally.

What women want

Having more women in top leadership positions isn't an end goal in and of itself – it's also an essential part of paving the way for more and more women to see high-flying positions as an option for themselves. We've all heard that you need to see it to be it, and, as we know, the more history of successful female leadership a business has, the less likely future female leaders are to succumb to the Glass Cliff when they take their place in that business's leadership roles.

As we've also seen in the quota conversation, more women in senior leadership means that women's voices are better heard and their interests are pushed forwards.

Everyone wants to feel that they are dedicating their time and efforts to relationships that are at least in some ways reciprocal. It can't be all give and no take. But, following the pandemic, the balance of our relationships with our workplaces is feeling out of sync. Research shows that 'only 56 per cent of employees believe that [the executives at their companies] care for their well-being, despite 91 per cent of C-level leaders' saying they think their teams believe they care.[65]

So what do employees want in order to feel motivated and productive in the workplace?

Meaning and purpose

Meaning, it seems, has never been more important to us in the workplace. In fact, over 90 per cent of workers across age and salary groups, surveyed in 2018, stated they would give up a percentage of their salaries in exchange for a greater sense of meaning at work.[66] That is a huge, unexpected figure.

And they don't just mean a tiny percentage of their salaries. Of over 2,000 American workers asked, the average amount that someone would be willing to sacrifice from their entire future earnings in exchange for a job that was 'always meaningful' was 23 per cent.[67] People were willing to give up almost a quarter of everything they could earn for the rest of their lives in exchange for that work feeling meaningful. It's quite the trade.

Additional research has also shown that nearly 80 per cent of people would rather have a boss who cared about them finding meaning and success in work than receive a 20 per cent pay increase. When we consider that the average American spends around 21 per cent of their income on housing, we can really start to see just how high a value people put on meaning in their work.[68]

Aside from employee happiness, feeling the work that's being carried out has meaning is good for motivation – and, in turn, good for business. Employees who feel their work has meaning produce more, work more and stay with their companies longer.[69] In fact, employees who find their work highly meaningful stay in their roles for an average of 7.4 months longer than employees who find their work lacks meaning. This seems to be especially impactful at leadership levels; when managers report finding their jobs highly meaningful, staff turnover rates fall to only 1.5 per cent. Meaning, or purpose, is deeply motivating, and so employees doing work that feels meaningful to them put in, on average, an additional one hour of work per week and take two fewer days off per year – figures that show us that raising one employee's experience from average to highly meaningful generates an extra $9,078 in labour output per year.[70] A truly phenomenal amount when replicated throughout a company.

It's not only employees that respond well to purpose-led businesses, though more than 70 per cent of millennials expect their employers to focus on societal or mission-driven problems; consumers also want to engage with businesses that they feel stand for something, or put something good into the world. It's been found that those businesses that lead with purpose can achieve continued loyalty, consistency and relevance in the lives of consumers, while those that don't have purpose embedded into their operating principles are likely to fail to meet the needs and expectations of their consumers in the longer term. As Deloitte reported in a 2020 study on global marketing trends, 'Today's consumers often identify with a brand's purpose, seeking to connect at a deeper level even as the brand reciprocally aligns with who they are and who they want to be.'[71]

Brands and businesses that are purpose-focused, Deloitte found, grow on average three times faster than their competitors, gain higher employee satisfaction scores and are able to retain their staff for longer. Furthermore, the staff of purpose-driven businesses perform better, with Deloitte's research finding that those businesses reported 30 per cent higher levels of innovation and 40 per cent higher levels of workforce retention than their competitors.[72]

Purpose could be a key to unlock not only employee productivity and retention, but consumer spending and positive brand associations.

Deloitte use Unilever's brand portfolio as an example, saying that its twenty-eight 'sustainable living' brands* – which include Dove, Vaseline and Lipton – 'delivered 75 per cent of the company's growth and grew 69 per cent faster on average than the rest of its businesses in 2018 [. . .] Soap, petroleum jelly and tea are everyday household essentials, but by promoting sustainable living, these products became differentiated as they embody the company's purpose.'[73]

Flexibility

In 2022, the UK government announced legislation to give all workers, not only parents, the right to request flexible working hours from their employers from the moment they begin a new job, and for good reason.[74]

One thing that comes through time and time again in research around what women value in the workplace is flexibility – whether that's in terms of where, when or how they work, flexibility is key and something that we are prioritizing as we think about which businesses we want to join, or remain within. Over half of all women say that a lack of flexibility at work has pushed them to leave or consider leaving a job, 21 per cent say they feel a lack of flexibility has negatively impacted their career progression, and a quarter of women have taken a career break as a result of lacking flexibility.[75]

McKinsey senior partner Alexis Krivkovich, speaking on *The McKinsey Podcast*, had the following to say:

> The number-one thing women cited pre-pandemic that would help them be more all-in in the workplace was flexibility in a number of different forms. The hours we expect, where you

---

* Brands focused on reducing Unilever's environmental footprint and increasing social impact.

physically get the job done, what we mean by face time, and the value attributed to that.

In this moment, half of women are saying, 'It's a top three criteria when I think about a job opportunity. I value it, and I evaluate it the same way I do benefits and other factors.' They care about it tremendously.[76]

As well as being essential for businesses who want to attract and retain female talent going forward, there is a huge potential business benefit unlocked by increased workplace flexibility. A recent 'Flexonomics' report shared by flexible-working campaigner Anna Whitehouse* estimates that the economic contribution of flexible working is a huge £37 billion, and a 50 per cent increase in current flexible-working rates could result in a net economic gain of £55 billion, alongside the creation of 51,200 new jobs.[77]

While the business benefits are interesting and compelling for any business owners who need convincing that this flexible way of working is a worthwhile shift for their businesses to make, it's unlikely to be the reason that so many women now see flexibility in their working lives as a non-negotiable requirement, particularly with regards to the location of their work. When talking about their next career moves, 69 per cent of men and 80 per cent of women have reported that remote working options are in the top factors they would consider when making a choice.[78]

So why is flexible working so important to women?

In part, the increased desire for flexible working shown by women will be because of gendered expectations of caregiving – meaning they are more likely than their male counterparts to need to take on caregiving duties, to either children or elderly family menders – which can be made a lot simpler by being able

---

* AKA @mother_pukka, who was the public face of the Flex Appeal Campaign.

to have some flexibility and room for change in our working commitments.

'Women may feel responsible for handling family-related matters and being away from home may create a feeling of guilt,' Dr Seulki 'Rachel' Jang, an assistant professor of industrial-organizational psychology at the University of Oklahoma, told the BBC when discussing gender differences in workers' appetites to return to the physical workplace.[79]

But that, of course, is not the only reason – it may also be that women are demanding better flexibility in the workplace, especially favouring virtual or remote working more highly than men, because it gives them the opportunity to break away from workplaces which were never optimized for them in the first place.

It could be that women, particularly women who are othered and who face an increased number of microaggressions during their day-to-day lives, see working from home as an opportunity to avoid the burden of these unwanted interactions.

McKinsey's Krivkovich continued: 'When you look at the experience for women, particularly women of colour, particularly those with disabilities, what they describe is an in-person work environment that has more bias, that has more othering and more microaggressions associated with it. So they value certain elements of virtual interaction because they minimized aspects of that bias they face day in and day out in a way that their male peers don't.'[80] Indeed, only one in ten women report wanting to work 'mostly on site', and 71 per cent of HR managers say that remote working has allowed the businesses they work for to not only hire, but retain talent from 'more diverse backgrounds.'[81]

Continuing her earlier point, Jang added, 'Researchers also found that women experienced more psychological stress during the pandemic as compared to men, so women may not feel ready to return to the office, where they need to hide that stress as a working professional.'[82]

Whether it's escaping the impacts of microaggressions or just finding relief in not having to wear a mask of 'professionalism' that was made in someone else's image, women are choosing flexibility and looking to find their places in businesses that share that value.

It's important to note that men and women's differing attitudes to returning to the physical workplace may have some unintended effects on our leadership prospects in the long term. 'Working from home may dilute one's presence at work and attachment to the workplace by limiting interactions and hindering learning, collaboration and creativity,' say researchers from the University of Oxford who have looked into the impact of Covid on gender roles in the workplace. Jang added to their concerns, saying that she believes 'men who return to the office are likely to show higher job performance and recognition, more favourable HR decisions like promotions and raises, more social interactions, more influence and power than women who are working from home. These factors can certainly exacerbate gender inequality at work and home.'[83]

Although the long-term impact of women working from home in increased numbers compared to their male peers remains to be seen, we can learn some things from previously existing research. In 2015, a study found that, although remote workers were 13 per cent more productive than their in-office colleagues, they were only half as likely to be promoted. The researchers attributed this promotions gap to the availability of face time with senior leadership. 'Leadership is in the office generally. So, if you're going in, you have access to leadership. You see them in the halls, and you're visible to them,' says Jessica Reeder, an expert on remote work who focuses on strategy at GitLab, the world's largest all-remote company. 'That applies to promotions.'[84]

This is a dilemma that businesses will need to face quickly if they're going to future-proof themselves. How do they balance women's increased demand for flexibility with the possibility that those who have less time in the office are likely to have a slower opportunity to progress, thanks to getting in less face time with senior leaders?

I suggest changing the rules of engagement – make sure that senior leaders are available in virtual contexts, and recognize that the next generation of leaders, and workers, are expecting more from the businesses they are choosing to work with and for.

Understanding the needs of the next generation of workers

As is so often the case when we discuss the changing face of the workplace, millennials and Gen Z workers are leading the charge in rewriting the rulebook, throwing our long-held preconceptions and working practices out of the window and remaking things, step by step, to be closer to the world of work they want.

We know that two thirds of women under thirty want to take on senior leadership roles during the course of their careers, and, instead of being put off by the challenges of the Covid-19 pandemic, young women are rising to them, with 58 per cent of women under thirty saying in 2023 that advancement has become *more* rather than less interesting to them.[85]

Yet, as Krivkovich warns, 'they're also saying, "I expect something different to place that bet with you, with your company."' And what is it that they expect? They are looking for businesses whose body language matches their words – they expect *greater* flexibility, a stronger commitment to DEI, and equal opportunities for advancement.[86]

While purpose and meaning in our work is important to people of all ages, to one degree or another, it feels especially pressing and essential to younger workers. In 2023, after twelve years of looking into the 'priorities, concerns, and motivations of the youngest generations in the workforce', Deloitte – a business in which over 80 per cent of employees are representative of those generations[87] – released their annual Gen Z and millennials survey,[88] which found that 'Young employees want their employers' values to be aligned with their own – and they want to drive societal change through purposeful and meaningful work.'[89]

Young workers are taking these preferences beyond the hypothetical and putting them into practice. I know when I worked for advertising agencies as a creative producer, and then head of production, I was deliberate and firm about the clients I would work on – no gambling, no tobacco, no oil – you get the gist. Every time I took a stand like that, I felt nervous, and more than once I had warnings from colleagues about 'damaging my career' by taking stances that could be seen as difficult.

So I'm heartened to know, now, that this is a behaviour – and a risk – that more people in my generation are willing to take. According to *Fortune* and Deloitte, almost 40 per cent of millennial and Gen Z workers reported that they had rejected work assignments due to ethical concerns.[90] In addition to that, over 30 per cent have turned down offers of jobs altogether if they felt their potential new employer wasn't doing enough on matters such as the environment, DEI or mental health.

To return to our conversation about meaning and purpose, millennials and Gen Z are more likely to stay in their roles when they feel that the business they work for empowers them to drive change through their individual work.

But what about those young people who are already in leadership positions? How are they approaching things differently from their predecessors? A study from Deloitte found that millennial and Gen Z leaders are taking matters into their own hands not only when it comes to how they approach and prioritize their own work, but also in how they manage their teams. The research found that these young leaders were significantly more likely than their older counterparts to report that they're prioritizing well-being and work–life balance for themselves and their people, and they were also more likely to say that they're transparent with their workforce.

It seems that a great deal of millennial and Gen Z leaders'

attention is focused on well-being, supporting their team members and increased transparency – all elements that we've seen reduce the risk of a Glass Cliff playing out. Deloitte analytics found that:

- 72 per cent of millennial and Gen Z leaders cap their working weeks at forty hours (compared to 65 per cent of Gen Xers and 39 per cent of boomers).

- 71 per cent take breaks during the working day (compared to 61 per cent of Gen Xers and 53 per cent of boomers).

- 83 per cent are transparent with their teams about their own well-being (compared to 65 per cent of Gen Xers and 38 per cent of boomers).

- 88 per cent have taken steps to help their employees to disconnect (compared to 77 per cent of Gen Xers and 65 per cent of boomers).

- 90 per cent are increasing their focus on well-being benefits (compared to 79 per cent of Gen Xers and 54 per cent of boomers).

- 89 per cent characterize themselves as health-savvy (compared to 75 per cent of Gen Xers and just 49 per cent of boomers).[91]

Twenty-five per cent of the world's population is under twenty-five – but the chances that younger people have to make a tangible impact on the world can be limited, as we can see by the fact that only 2.5 per cent of politicians are in that same age bracket. In the workplace, around 38 per cent of the global workforce is millennial or Gen Z, but, despite this, the average age for board members of FTSE 150 companies is almost sixty.[92]

This is a disparity that The Body Shop* not only recognized, but tried to address by bringing on a group of youth advisers to the business.

'We had the realization that, if we're lacking the voices of young people [on our board], how can we really honestly say we're building a business that we can pass down to the next generation – which is, of course, what we plan to do,' Chris Davis, board member of The Body Shop and the business's international director of sustainability and activism, told *Fortune*.[93]

And so the business set up a secondary board – on which all members needed to be thirty and under – which they called a 'Youth Collective', to run in parallel with their existing board.

After some initial teething problems of finding potential board members who were opposed to capitalist businesses overall, 'he quickly learned that in order for criticisms from a board comprising bright young minds to actually be constructive, they'd need to be less radical,' *Fortune* reported. Davis himself noted, 'The activists that were working with us were pretty critical of commerce [. . .] We live in a world of trying to balance profit and principles. It's not so straightforward.'[94] They landed on a make-up for the board that worked for them – 50 per cent internal employees of the business, 50 per cent employees of other B Corps – those young people most likely to be sympathetic to balancing the needs of a business with its CSR† goals and ambitions.

'It wasn't just a question of getting young people who are interested, who are smart, who care about the world, who want to make a difference – that's actually not enough. On top of those things, you've got to bring people in who are on the side of wanting business to succeed, but succeed on sustainable terms.'

The Body Shop's Youth Collective has helped the business in modernizing their social-media strategies and output, and in

---

* One of the world's largest B Corp companies.
† Corporate social responsibility.

communicating large business initiatives – mostly linked to the area of inclusion.

Mindful of not wanting the members of the Youth Collective to feel as though they are being exploited, or treated unfairly as unpaid consultants, Davis says he doesn't turn to the group unless a problem needs out-of-the-box thinking that the older leadership team can't crack, in which case the perspectives of these so-often-overlooked youth voices are invited into the conversation.

Davis told *Fortune* that working with this unusual group of leaders and thinkers has brought 'life, insight, and energy' to the business's discussions and decisions. But he's also keen to point out that he believes a large part of this is because, in turn, the business has been clear about the terms and rules of their engagement. As Davis said: 'The way that we've set it up has been quite a safe operating environment and one where trust is built up over time because everyone knows the rules of the game.'

One of the most important rules is that every voice counts. While not every suggestion that is made is taken on board or put into action, the business says they are all listened to and taken as seriously as suggestions or comments from the traditional board – and, whether ideas are taken forward or not, the reasons behind the choice are always communicated.

'Do we always listen? Yes. Do we always act? No. When we don't, we explain why. When we do, we explain why – that's part of the deal,' he adds. 'There will always be feedback and full transparency so it's clear that everybody is heard.'

Of course, this is only one business, and the long-term benefits of working in this way, with an eye towards the needs and expectations of those under thirty, remain to be seen in full – but directly asking consumers what they want, need and value, and then acting on it – or explaining why you're not able to – feels like an exciting step for a large business to be taking in this area.

I believe that we can all be a part of rewriting the future, and making sure that what comes next works better, and for more of us, than what we're leaving behind. There are more of us who want to change the world than there are those who currently rule it – those who have a vested interest in maintaining the status quo – which means that, together, we can change how our society and our workplaces operate. We can create more flexible, fulfilled lives that allow us to be whole and happy humans. We can choose our own leaders, and we can make them whoever we want them to be and be an active part of their success stories – modelling what's possible for those who come next.

And, together, now that we have the language we need and the ability to bring what was once invisible into the light, we can shatter the glass around us.

TL;DR: *Too Long; Didn't Read*

- The Glass Cliff is a cultural and social phenomenon that doesn't exist everywhere in the world. It occurs most often, and most strongly, in countries that rank low in gender equality scores – such as the UK and US.

- Because the Glass Cliff isn't a natural fact of life, there are things we can do to work towards breaking its cycle, such as:

  - Updating our ideas about what good leadership looks like in the modern workplace, placing greater emphasis on more traditionally female-coded skills such as adaptability, and empowering others to step into their own leadership potential.

  - Adapting businesses to meet the needs of working women, especially given that we know those businesses with a history of female leadership are less susceptible to the Glass Cliff. The more successful women we see, the more successful women we're likely to see in the future.

  - Promoting, rather than recruiting. Thirty-five per cent of female CEOs (versus just 22 per cent of male CEOs) entered their roles as new hires. This makes achieving success more difficult because, as well as doing the job you were hired to do, new hires need to spend time learning about a whole new business. External CEOs are 6.7 times more likely to be dismissed with a short tenure than those who are promoted internally.

- Leaning into quotas. Quotas have proven successful in increasing female representation at the most senior levels of business, and in 2022 the European Parliament passed the Women On Boards law, requiring that listed companies in the EU have a minimum of 40 per cent female representation of non-executive board members by mid-2026. Similar schemes have been successfully trialled, and then expanded, in places such as Norway. Quotas have been proven to be just as impactful when mandated by governments as when mandated by businesses.

• In order to retain female talent, we need to recognize what is important to women, and adapt our workforces to be truly inclusive of those needs, which include:

- Creating a great sense of meaning and purpose in work. Over 90 per cent of workers say that they would give up a percentage of their salary in exchange for a greater sense of meaning at work.

- Increased flexibility. Over half of all women say that 'a lack of flexibility at work has pushed them to leave or consider leaving a job'.

• It's also essential to understand and be adaptive to the needs of the youngest working generations. We want to attract and benefit from their talents – which means even more purpose-driven, flexible businesses aligned with the values of the cohort, and allowing them to feel that they are driving and contributing to societal change.

Conclusion

Hope has two beautiful daughters; their
names are Anger and Courage. Anger at
the way things are and Courage to see
that they do not remain as they are.

AUGUSTINE OF HIPPO

S o there we have it. The story of the Glass Cliff – what it is, the conditions that make it most likely to happen, and some things that might help us to break the cycle – leaving future generations with better opportunities for success in leadership than we ourselves inherited.

I think we owe them that.

I also hope that, now we have the shared language, the words we've needed to identify and frame the Glass Cliff, two important things can happen.

Firstly, I hope we're able to redefine and better navigate our own experiences – cutting ourselves some slack for things that, although we may not have been able to see it at the time, were beyond our control.

The second thing I hope this understanding offers us is the chance to be more empathetic. To spot the impact of the Glass Cliff in our own lives and to be more tuned into and to recognize more easily the phenomenon when we see it playing out in front of us – not only in the businesses we work for, but also on a public stage.

It just so happens that, as I write this in June 2023, there is an unusually high-profile example of what many believe, or at least suspect, will *become* an example of the Glass Cliff playing out on a *very* public stage: the appointment of Linda Yaccarino as X's (formerly Twitter's) new CEO, in replacement of Elon Musk.

Here's the story up to now:

In October 2022, Elon Musk completed his purchase of social-media platform Twitter, and stepped into the role of the business's CEO – an acquisition for which he paid a reported $44 billion.

In December 2022, Musk tweeted: 'I will resign as CEO as soon as I find someone foolish enough to take the job!'[1]

In March 2023, Musk stated that Twitter had lost over 50 per cent of its value since he had acquired it, and was now worth $20 billion[2] – although mutual-funds giant Fidelity, which also owns shares in Twitter and so has a vested interest in its value, set its own valuation of the business at just $15 billion, leading newspapers around the world to report that Twitter was now worth only one third of its 'pre-Musk value.'[3]

In May 2023, Musk claimed that ad spend, which represents the main revenue stream for the business, was returning to normal, saying that 'almost all advertisers have come back.'[4] However, an internal document obtained by *The New York Times* told a very different story. Instead of a triumphant return, the document showed that ad revenue on the platform had fallen by 59 per cent, and that 'The company has regularly fallen short of its US weekly sales projections, sometimes by as much as 30 per cent.'[5]

Also in May 2023, Twitter was named number four in the index of most-hated US businesses.[6]

On 5 June 2023,* Elon Musk stepped down as Twitter's CEO, and Linda Yaccarino stepped into that most senior role in Twitter – two weeks earlier than had been expected.[7]

While I wouldn't wish for anyone to experience the Glass Cliff, it seems that, with the odds being so firmly stacked against her – as the business's stock price crumbles, public sentiment against the company (so closely and personally associated with Musk)

---

* Or, in my own personal timeline, yesterday.

continues to fall and as advertisers leave the platform – Yaccarino's chances of success may well be limited from the outset.

That being said, it could also be that Yaccarino has taken on the role fully aware of the challenge she's stepping into. It would be hard to not be aware of it – this is an unusual occasion where the Glass Cliff's threat is not only visible, but *hyper*visible in the public media's commentary and reporting around the appointment. And it's very possible that both this framing and our collective knowledge of the challenges she's likely to face will allow her the time and the understanding to make the changes needed to successfully lead the business through a time of crisis.

Another thing that may, perhaps unintuitively, make her chance of success stronger is her predecessor, Musk, who is still very much involved in and, many would argue, remains the face of the business. By his own estimation, working as Twitter's CEO is a 'painful' job that anyone would be 'foolish' to take on.[8] However, we now know that having internal stakeholders who are aware of and sympathetic to the Glass Cliff's potential harms can do a good deal in mitigating its likelihood and reducing its impact. So perhaps, instead of warning signs of impending doom, Musk's comments are a blessing in disguise?

Of course, so much depends not only on public sentiment, but on internal politics that we're never likely to understand the true dynamics of, and, realistically, Musk's close involvement may well prove to be yet another hurdle for Yaccarino to overcome, rather than any kind of saving grace.*

'There was quite a bit of cautious optimism when it was announced that Yaccarino was going to take over – that optimism has now faded,' Jasmine Enberg, a top social-media analyst at the market-research firm Insider Intelligence, told *The Guardian*. 'It

---

* I do suspect this is more likely to be the way it plays out. I do not trust that little spaceman. 🚀

was clear from the start that Musk wasn't going to step away, and now it's clear that he isn't going to step to the side either.'

Luckily, there is another factor which may go some way to protect Yaccarino from falling off the Glass Cliff – which is simply herself, her own background and experiences up to this point. Currently aged fifty-nine, Yaccarino has a well-established career, having started as an intern at NBC Universal before returning to the business in 2011 as chair of advertising for the broadcaster, running its $13 billion annual ad sales business. She has built a reputation for working with a silky but tough negotiating style, and many believe, while the role is certain to have its challenges, there are few people who would have a better chance of success at Twitter's helm than her.[9]

'Her history has given her massive credibility within the advertising world and in digital media, and she is not one to back down from a challenge,' said Dan Ives, an analyst at investment firm Wedbush Securities, in an interview with *The Guardian*. 'She recognizes that this is an uphill battle, but she also recognizes the opportunity for turnaround.'[10]

It may be that Yaccarino's appointment will be successful, and I really hope that it is. I hope that she is able to play an important role in reversing the business's fortunes and driving a recovery and even a resurgence – not because I care about the app, but because it would be amazing to have a success story to point to. But, it's a tall order for anyone to take on, successfully, long-term.

Then again, maybe that desire to look for individual stories of success, or falls, and hold them up as examples is, at its base, part of what we should be working against, if we *really* want to break the cycle of the Glass Cliff. So much of the problem with the Glass Cliff is that, because female leaders are so few and far between, we as a society have treated individuals as though they were statistically significant groups. We have looked at individual female leaders to tell us everything we think we know about women's capabilities and aptitude for successful leadership, and maybe it's time we learned from that mistake and started looking bigger, thinking more structurally and pushing for systemic rather than individual changes.

Without wrangling with the existence and impact of the Glass Cliff at a structural level, we're overlooking a major factor in the story of what *really* stops us from seeing more successful women in long-term leadership roles.

And, although the impact on women is huge, we mustn't forget that the impact of the Glass Cliff is even bigger than it might appear.

We know women are not the only group impacted by the Glass Cliff; it also affects racially marginalized men and has a compounding impact on anyone who doesn't hold the identities of *either* whiteness *or* maleness.

It's essential that we don't overlook that in our discussions of the phenomenon.

We must recognize and remember the role that intersectionality has on all of our lived experiences, inside and outside of the workplace.

None of us are able to take out individual elements of ourselves or each other and present them, piece by piece, for inspection and hopeful acceptance. I will never be able to cut myself into parts and hand you only my Blackness *or* my womanness, only my cisness *or* my neurodivergence – I present myself in full, and that is what you see, whether I, or you, like it or not. And all of that fullness, the mixture of all of those hues, come together to have an undeniable – but little researched – impact on how the world treats us.*

---

* Although, there are some non-visible parts of ourselves that we may have the option of hiding, or disguising, in situations or contexts where we have made the strategic, self-preserving assessment that they are not safe for us to reveal. This is known as code-switching and is particularly common for racially marginalized people as they move through worlds and spaces that weren't created for them.

It seems likely that there will always be one crisis or another that we are all trying to navigate through successfully. Trying to survive.

We owe it to women to do more than leave them in charge of failure. We deserve better than being brought in to clean up the mess we didn't make, and to take the blame for things that happened before we even arrived.

I hope that the information shared here about the traits of leadership that lead to success during difficult times – emotional intelligence, openness, transparency, collaboration – can help to change some of the expectations we all hold about leadership, and what it does, can and should look like to be successful.

I hope that we are able to learn to recognize, name and overcome systemic societal issues instead of defaulting to blaming those who are impacted by them. I hope that we learn to offer grace and compassion and time and support as we look to those under-represented leaders who are breaking new ground. And I hope we help them to do so on their own terms, and to step away when those positions and roles no longer serve them, personally.

I hope that language is as powerful as I believe it to be. I hope that now we have the language to identify and understand the Glass Cliff, we can be part of making a society that not only recognizes it, but moves beyond it.

BUT WHAT ABOUT . . . ?

Even now, after we've come so far and hopefully thought about things through lenses and frameworks we might have overlooked before, I know there will be some pushback. I know there will be, as there always are, some people who have been successful in their own careers, who haven't been impacted by or had to navigate their way around the Glass Cliff, who will still be reluctant to acknowledge its existence. There will be people who feel that those who succumb to it are in some way worse, weaker, less talented or less intelligent than they are themselves. If this is the case, let me ask you a very simple question:

If you're so clever, why aren't you kind?

Not just in an EQ-is-linked-to-high-performance way, but in a basic, human way. In a way that recognizes, just because someone has been lucky enough to avoid an experience, that doesn't mean it doesn't exist and doesn't have a real impact on the lives and experiences of others.

It's time for me to leave you, but I'm going to do so by sharing some words from Toni Morrison: 'I tell my students, "When you get these jobs that you have been so brilliantly trained for, just remember that your real job is that if you are free, you need to free somebody else. If you have some power, then your job is to empower somebody else. This is not just a grab-bag candy game."'[11]

It's an unusual thing to say – but I can't wait for the day that this book becomes irrelevant. I'd love for people in the future to look at this story of structural social inequity in the workplace and think of it as a relic of a way of working they can't imagine. I hope we are able to learn from the places where the Glass Cliff doesn't exist, and eventually join their number. But, until then, we need to work together. All of us.

Now you know about the Glass Cliff, your job is to spread the word. To share the knowledge (and this book) far and wide. Help other people to gain the language to frame their experiences. Be someone's safe person, and offer them the support they need to turn a challenging story into one of success.

Become part of breaking the cycle.

And just know that I'm going to be here, right alongside you, trying to do the same.

Acknowledgements

I treat this section like a MySpace Top 8 from book to book, but without the music I've coded in that you can't stop playing – so you'll just have to imagine that part. I'd suggest you go with: 'Rhinestone Cowboy' (Glen Campbell), truly an underrated bop, especially if you dance like a horse while you listen to it; 'Dancing in the Dark' (Bruce Springsteen and Hot Chip, one after the other); and 'Sabrina (i am a party)' (Fred Again), which I listened to on repeat in my headphones so much during the final week of writing this book that, although it's only June at the moment, I'm sure it's going to show up in the number-one spot on my 2023 Spotify Wrapped, no matter what else I discover this year – whichever feels most like you today.

I want to say thank you to some of the people who made this project possible.

Thank you to the researchers who spent their careers working on understanding the phenomenon of the Glass Cliff. Thank you for digging deeper, for realizing that the problem wasn't simply that women were naturally limited, and for giving us the language to understand our shared experiences.

Thank you to everyone who has been supportive and encouraging during the writing period. Thanks to everyone who encouraged me to live joyfully – to take the time to rest, to make the worst kitsch foods, to dance to Elton John in a field, to go on day trips to Costco just for the sheet cake, and to drink Aperol on terraces.

Thank you, especially for the Aperol on the terraces. 🍷

Thank you to Emily in America, who is always silent, but vibrating.

Thank you to my Style Council for giving endless thoughts and feedback on cover designs – look how beautifully everything turned out in the end!

Thank you to *The Artist's Way* for reminding me that creativity is the natural order of things – and for helping me to unblock what felt unblockable.

Thank you to TEDx London, to Maryam and the team for taking a chance on letting a Black woman talk about businesses – something you said at the time hadn't happened before my talk, but which you supported me through anyway. That really was the beginning of all of this.

Thank you to my agent, Milly, who has been kind, calm, smart and supportive throughout.

Thank you to my partner, Lawrence. For reading countless early versions of this. For keeping me sane during the publishing process. For your unwavering trust and support. Life is long and various, and I'm so glad I get to do mine with you. You're the best thing I know about. You and Miffin are lovely and grongus.

With my weak organs, I am very fond of you.[1] All of you.

Now, until we meet again, you be good. I love you.[2]

Notes

Introduction

1. Bertolt Brecht, 'Motto', *Poems 1913–56* (London: Methuen, 1987).
2. Transcript available at 'Secretary-General Rejects "Male Chauvinist" Domination of Tech Sector, Calls for Overhaul of "Patriarchal Structures", at Women's Civil Society Town Hall' (press release), United Nations (website), 13 March 2023, https://press.un.org/en/2023/sgsm21723.doc.htm
3. Ibid.
4. 'Gender pay gap in the UK: 2022', Office for National Statistics, https://www.ons.gov.uk/employmentandlabourmarket/peopleinwork/earningsandworkinghours/bulletins/genderpaygapintheuk/2022
5. Alexandra Topping, 'UK gender pay gap for higher-educated parents has grown since 1970s – study', *The Guardian*, 7 March 2023, https://www.theguardian.com/world/2023/mar/07/gender-pay-gap-for-higher-educated-uk-parents-has-grown-since-1970s-study
6. Ibid.
7. Ibid.
8. 'Name It to Tame It: Label Your Emotions to Overcome Negative Thoughts', Mindfulness.com (website), https://mindfulness.com/mindful-living/name-it-to-tame-it

9   Bruce Freeman, 'Name It to Tame It: Labelling Emotions to
    Reduce Stress & Anxiety', Oral Health (website), 5 March 2021,
    https://www.oralhealthgroup.com/features/name-it-to-tame-it-
    labelling-emotions-to-reduce-stress-anxiety

FYI

1   Alison Cook and Christy Glass, 'Above the glass ceiling: When are
    women and racial/ethnic minorities promoted to CEO?', *Strategic
    Management Journal*, 35(7), 10 June 2013, pp. 1080–9, https://
    onlinelibrary.wiley.com/doi/abs/10.1002/smj.2161
2   Christine L. Williams, 'The Glass Escalator: Hidden Advantages
    for Men in the "Female" Professions', *Social Problems*, 39(3),
    August 1992, pp. 253–67, https://www.jstor.org/stable/3096961
3   Sebahattin Yildiz, Mehmet Fatih Vural, 'A Cultural Perspective of
    The Glass Cliff Phenomenon', *Ege Akademik Bakis* (*Ege Academic
    Review*), 30 July 2019, pp. 309–21, https://dergipark.org.tr/tr/
    download/article-file/766390
4   'Women in the Wokplace, 2022', McKinsey & Company, https://
    www.mckinsey.com/~/media/mckinsey/featured%20insights/
    diversity%20and%20inclusion/women%20in%20the%20
    workplace%202022/women-in-the-workplace-2022.pdf
5   Women have leadership aspirations: 'Young women care deeply
    about opportunity to advance – more than two-thirds of women
    under 30 want to be senior leaders, and well over half say
    advancement has become more important to them in the past two
    years', Women in the Workplace 2022, Lean In and McKinsey &
    Company, https://leanin.org/women-in-the-workplace/2022/
    why-women-leaders-are-switching-jobs
6   Michelle K. Ryan, S. Alexander Haslam, et al., 'Getting on top of
    the glass cliff: Reviewing a decade of evidence, explanations, and
    impact', *The Leadership Quarterly*, 27(3), June 2016, pp. 446–55,
    https://www.sciencedirect.com/science/article/abs/pii/
    S104898431500123X

Chapter 1

1 Quote widely circulated online and referenced by Derien Nagy, 'From Multi-Tasker to Free Woman', Medium.com (website), 21 June 2023, https://medium.com/illumination/from-multi-tasker-to-free-woman-aed817e2a3c5; see also @mother_pukka Instagram post, May 2023, https://www.instagram.com/p/CsuB8DFLrkt/?utm_source=ig_web_copy_link&igshid=MzRlODBiNWFlZA==

2 Joe Hagan, 'Only the Men Survive', *New York* (magazine), 25 April 2008, https://nymag.com/news/business/46476

3 Andrew Clark, '$3.7bn loss brings down one of the top women in Wall Street', *The Guardian*, 1 December 2007, https://www.theguardian.com/business/2007/dec/01/cruz

4 Hagan, 'Only the Men Survive', *New York* (magazine), 25 April 2008.

5 Ibid., and Miles Costello, 'Glass ceiling is wiped out as Cruz missile hits Old Mutual', *The Times*, 7 January 2014, https://www.thetimes.co.uk/article/glass-ceiling-is-wiped-out-as-cruz-missile-hits-old-mutual-0f8n06wxjwc

6 'The World's 100 Most Powerful Women', 6 December 2022, https://images.forbes.com/lists/2005/11/V9JO.html

7 Hagan, 'Only the Men Survive', *New York* (magazine), 25 April 2008.

8 Andrew Clark, '$3.7bn loss brings down one of the top women in Wall Street', *The Guardian*, 1 December 2007, https://www.theguardian.com/business/2007/dec/01/cruz

9 Hagan, 'Only the Men Survive', *New York* (magazine), 25 April 2008.

10 Ibid.

11 Ibid.

12 Ibid.

13 Costello, 'Glass ceiling is wiped out as Cruz missile hits Old Mutual', *The Times*, 7 January 2014.

14 Hagan, 'Only the Men Survive', *New York* (magazine), 25 April 2008.

15 Costello, 'Glass ceiling is wiped out as Cruz missile hits Old Mutual', *The Times*, 7 January 2014.

16 Hagan, 'Only the Men Survive', *New York* (magazine), 25 April 2008.

17 Costello, 'Glass ceiling is wiped out as Cruz missile hits Old Mutual', *The Times*, 7 January 2014.

18 Hagan, 'Only the Men Survive', *New York* (magazine), 25 April 2008.

19 Andrew Clark, '$3.7bn loss brings down one of the top women in Wall Street', *The Guardian*, 1 December 2007, https://www.theguardian.com/business/2007/dec/01/cruz

20 Hagan, 'Only the Men Survive', *New York* (magazine), 25 April 2008.

21 Ibid.

22 'Last Woman Standing: The Firing of Zoe Cruz', Glass Hammer, 7 May 2008, https://theglasshammer.com/2008/05/last-woman-standing-the-firing-of-zoe-cruz

23 Hagan, 'Only the Men Survive', *New York* (magazine), 25 April 2008.

24 Ibid.

25 Ibid.

26 Costello, 'Glass ceiling is wiped out as Cruz missile hits Old Mutual', *The Times*, 7 January 2014.

27 Hagan, 'Only the Men Survive', *New York* (magazine), 25 April 2008.

28 Clark, '$3.7bn loss brings down one of the top women in Wall Street', *The Guardian*, 1 December 2007.

29 Ibid.

30 C. Hymowitz and T. D. Schellhardt, 'The Glass-Ceiling: Why Women Can't Seem to Break the Invisible Barrier that Blocks Them from Top Jobs', *The Wall Street Journal*, 1986.

31 European Commission, 2011, 2014; International Labour Organization, 2015, cited here: Clara Kulich and Michelle K. Ryan, 'The Glass Cliff', in *Oxford Research Encyclopaedia of*

Business and Management, ed. R. Aldag (Oxford: Oxford University Press, 2017), https://www.researchgate.net/publication/310799724_The_glass_cliff

32 Singh and Vinnicombe, *The 2005 Female FTSE Index. New Look Women Directors Add Value to FTSE 100 Boards* (Cranfield: Cranfield University School of Management, 2005), quoted in S. Alexander Haslam, Michelle K. Ryan et al., 'Investing with Prejudice: The Relationship Between Women's Presence on Company Boards and Objective and Subjective Measures of Company Performance', *British Journal of Management*, vol. 21, 2010, pp. 484–97, http://www.bbcprisonstudy.org/includes/site/files/files/2010%20BJM%20Tobin's%20Q.pdf

33 Joseph R. Cimpian, Sarah T. Lubienski et al., 'Have Gender Gaps in Math Closed? Achievement, Teacher Perceptions, and Learning Behaviors Across Two ECLS-K Cohorts', *AERA Open*, 2(4), 2016, https://journals.sagepub.com/doi/full/10.1177/2332858416673617

34 'COVID-19 cost women globally over $800 billion in lost income in one year', Oxford International Press Release, 29 April 2021, https://www.oxfam.org/en/press-releases/covid-19-cost-women-globally-over-800-billion-lost-income-one-year?

35 Simon Goodley, 'Dagenham sewing machinists recall strike that changed women's lives', *The Guardian*, 6 June 2013, https://www.theguardian.com/politics/2013/jun/06/dagenham-sewing-machinists-strike

36 Ibid.

37 Heather Stewart, 'Why, even now, do we think a woman's work is woth less?', *The Guardian*, 11 August 2023, https://www.theguardian.com/world/2023/aug/11/why-even-now-do-we-think-a-womans-work-is-worth-less

38 Ibid.

39 Kim Elsesser, 'The Gender Pay Gap And The Career Choice Myth', *Forbes*, 1 April 2019, https://www.forbes.com/sites/kimelsesser/2019/04/01/the-gender-pay-gap-and-the-career-choice-myth

40 'Make your workplace work for women: a conversation with Indeed CMO Jessica Jensen, Lena Waithe, Reshma Saujani and Jen Welter', Indeed, 3 January 2023, https://uk.indeed.com/lead/make-your-workplace-work-for-women-a-conversation-with-indeed-cmo-jessica-jensen

41 Jess Huang, Alexis Krivkovich, Ishanaa Rambachan and Lareina Yee, 'For mothers in the workplace, a year (and counting) like no other', McKinsey & Company, 5 May 2021, https://www.mckinsey.com/featured-insights/diversity-and-inclusion/for-mothers-in-the-workplace-a-year-and-counting-like-no-other

42 Alexis Krivkovich, Kelsey Robinson, Irina Starikova, Rachel Valentino and Lareina Yee, 'Women in the Workplace 2017', McKinsey & Company, October 2017, https://www.mckinsey.com/~/media/McKinsey/Industries/Technology%20Media%20and%20Telecommunications/High%20Tech/Our%20Insights/Women%20in%20the%20Workplace%202017/Women-in-the-Workplace-2017-v2.ashx

43 Women in the Workplace 2022, Lean In, https://leanin.org/women-in-the-workplace/2022/were-in-the-midst-of-a-great-breakup

44 Alexis Krivkovich, Kelsey Robinson, Irina Starikova, Rachel Valentino and Lareina Yee, 'Women in the Workplace 2017', McKinsey & Company, October 2017, https://www.mckinsey.com/~/media/McKinsey/Industries/Technology%20Media%20and%20Telecommunications/High%20Tech/Our%20Insights/Women%20in%20the%20Workplace%202017/Women-in-the-Workplace-2017-v2.ashx

45 Women in the Workplace 2022, Lean In and McKinsey & Company, https://leanin.org/women-in-the-workplace

46 Women in the Workplace 2022, Lean In and McKinsey & Company, https://leanin.org/women-in-the-workplace/2022/companies-need-to-hold-on-to-the-leaders-shaping-the-future-of-work

47 Women in the Workplace 2022, Lean In and McKinsey & Company, https://leanin.org/women-in-the-workplace

48 Women in the Workplace 2021, Lean In and McKinsey & Company, https://leanin.org/women-in-the-workplace

49 Maria Minor, 'Women In The Workplace: Why They Don't Get Recognized As Much As Men', *Forbes*, 5 December 2020, https://www.forbes.com/sites/mariaminor/2020/12/05/women-in-the-workplace-why-they-dont-get-recognized-as-much-as-men

50 Meredith Somers, 'Women are less likely than men to be promoted. Here's one reason why', MIT Management Sloan School, 12 April 2022, https://mitsloan.mit.edu/ideas-made-to-matter/women-are-less-likely-men-to-be-promoted-heres-one-reason-why

51 Alan Benson, Danielle Li and Kelly Shue, '"Potential" and the Gender Promotion Gap', 22 June 2022, https://danielle-li.github.io/assets/docs/PotentialAndTheGenderPromotionGap.pdf

52 Alexis Krivkovich, Kelsey Robinson et al., 'Women in the Workplace 2017', McKinsey & Company, October 2017, https://www.mckinsey.com/~/media/McKinsey/Industries/Technology%20Media%20and%20Telecommunications/High%20Tech/Our%20Insights/Women%20in%20the%20Workplace%202017/Women-in-the-Workplace-2017-v2.ashx

53 Belle Rose Ragins, 'Diversified Mentoring Relationships in Organizations: A Power Perspective', *The Academy of Management Review*, vol. 22, no. 2, April 1997, pp. 482–521, https://www.jstor.org/stable/259331

54 Herminia Ibarra, 'A Lack of Sponsorship is Keeping Women from Advancing into Leadership', *Harvard Business Review*, 19 August 2019, https://hbr.org/2019/08/a-lack-of-sponsorship-is-keeping-women-from-advancing-into-leadership

55 Rajashi Ghosh, 'Diversified mentoring relationships: contested space for mutual learning?', *Human Resource Development International*, 21(3), 2018, pp. 159–62, https://www.tandfonline.com/doi/full/10.1080/13678868.2018.1465670

56 Ragins, 'Diversified mentoring relationships', pp. 497–8, as quoted in David A. Thomas and John J. Gabarro, *Breaking Through: The*

Making of Minority Executives in Corporate America (Brighton, MA: Harvard Business Review Press, 1999), p. 27.

57 Thomas and Gabarro, *Breaking Through*, p. 28.

58 Ibid., referencing the work of D. Thomas, 'Strategies for managing racial differences.'

59 Christina Friedlaender, 'On Microaggressions: Cumulative Harm and Individual Responsibility', *Hypatia*, 33(1), Winter 2018, pp. 5–21, https://onlinelibrary.wiley.com/doi/abs/10.1111/hypa.12390. Also referenced in Bianca Barratt, 'The Microaggressions Still Prevalent In The Workplace', *Forbes*, 28 October 2018, https://www.forbes.com/sites/biancabarratt/2018/10/28/the-microaggressions-still-prevalent-in-the-workplace

60 Paola Peralta, '"Death by a thousand cuts": For working women, microaggressions are leading to burnout', *Employee Benefit News*, 1 April 2022, https://www.benefitnews.com/news/microaggressions-at-work-are-burning-out-women-at-work

61 'Women in the Workplace: Insights from 5 Years of Research', Lean In, https://leanin.org/about-the-women-in-the-workplace-report

62 Sheryl Sandberg and Adam Grant, 'Speaking While Female', *The New York Times*, 12 January 2015, https://www.nytimes.com/2015/01/11/opinion/sunday/speaking-while-female.html

63 Leonard Karakowsky, Kenneth McBey and Diane L. Miller, 'Gender, perceived competence, and power displays: examining verbal interruptions in a group context', *Small Group Research*, 35(4), 2004, pp. 407–39, https://gap.hks.harvard.edu/gender-perceived-competence-and-power-displays-examining-verbal-interruptions-group-context

64 Paola Peralta, 'Women don't feel comfortable at work. Here's how to fix your culture', *Employee Benefit News*, 21 March 2022, https://www.benefitnews.com/news/women-dont-feel-confident-about-their-role-in-the-workplace

65 Leslie Shore, 'Gal Interrupted, Why Men Interrupt Women And How To Avert This In The Workplace', *Forbes*, 3 January 2017,

https://www.forbes.com/sites/womensmedia/2017/01/03/
gal-interrupted-why-men-interrupt-women-and-how-to-avert-
this-in-the-workplace

66 Sandberg and Grant, 'Speaking While Female', *The New York Times*, 12 January 2015.

67 Victoria L. Brescoll, 'Who Takes the Floor and Why: Gender, Power, and Volubility in Organizations', *Administrative Science Quarterly*, 56(4), February 2012, https://journals.sagepub.com/doi/abs/10.1177/0001839212439994

68 Ibid.

69 Women in the Workplace 2022, Lean In and McKinsey & Company, https://leanin.org/women-in-the-workplace

70 Lydia Smith, 'Women less likely to get their ideas endorsed at work than men', Yahoo! News, 1 April 2021, https://uk.news.yahoo.com/women-less-likely-to-get-their-ideas-endorsed-at-work-than-men-230124841.html

71 Sunny Rosen, 'Credit Where Credit Is Due', University of Delaware (website), 12 December 2017, https://www.udel.edu/udaily/2017/december/kyle-emich-gender-in-workplace-research

72 Women in the Workplace 2022, Lean In and McKinsey & Company (see the orange infographic on the page), https://leanin.org/women-in-the-workplace/2022/why-women-leaders-are-switching-jobs

73 Barratt, 'The Microaggressions Still Prevalent In The Workplace', *Forbes*, 28 October 2018.

74 Caroline Castrillon, 'Why Women Leaders Are Leaving Their Jobs At Record Rates', *Forbes*, 7 May 2023, https://www.forbes.com/sites/carolinecastrillon/2023/05/07/why-women-leaders-are-leaving-their-jobs-at-record-rates

75 Ella F. Washington, 'Recognizing and Responding to Microaggressions at Work', *Harvard Business Review*, 10 May 2022, https://hbr.org/2022/05/recognizing-and-responding-to-microaggressions-at-work

76 'Edward Enninful: British Vogue editor "racially profiled" at work',

BBC News (website), 16 July 2020, https://www.bbc.co.uk/news/uk-53425148

77 'Black barrister mistaken for defendant three times gets apology', BBC News (website), 24 September 2020, https://www.bbc.co.uk/news/uk-england-essex-54281111

78 Washington, 'Recognizing and Responding to Microaggressions at Work', *Harvard Business Review*, 10 May 2022, and Women in the Workplace 2022, Lean In and McKinsey & Company, https://leanin.org/women-in-the-workplace

Chapter 2

1 Saeed Jones, 'Alive at the End of the World', published in *The New Yorker*, 28 February 2022, https://www.newyorker.com/magazine/2022/03/07/alive-at-the-end-of-the-world

2 Helaine Olen, 'Marissa Mayer and the Glass Cliff', *Forbes*, 16 July 2012, https://www.forbes.com/sites/helaineolen/2012/07/16/marissa-mayer-and-the-glass-cliff

3 Sharon Gaudin, 'After rocky tenure, Mayer to leave Yahoo "tarnished"', Computerworld, 13 March 2017, https://www.computerworld.com/article/3180384/after-rocky-tenure-mayer-leaves-yahoo-tarnished.html

4 Andrew Ross Sorkin and Evelyn M. Rusli, 'A Yahoo Search Calls Up a Chief From Google', *The New York Times*, 16 July 2012, https://archive.nytimes.com/dealbook.nytimes.com/2012/07/16/googles-marissa-mayer-tapped-as-yahoos-chief

5 Ibid.

6 Olen, 'Marissa Mayer and the Glass Cliff', *Forbes*, 16 July 2012.

7 Nicholas Carlson, 'The Day Marissa Mayer's Honeymoon At Yahoo Ended', Insider, 2 January 2015, https://www.businessinsider.com/marissa-mayer-yahoo-nicholas-carlson-book-excerpt-2014-12?curator=MediaREDEF&r=US&IR=T

8 Sorkin and Rusli, 'A Yahoo Search Calls Up a Chief From Google', *The New York Times*, 16 July 2012.

9   Ibid.

10 Olen, 'Marissa Mayer and the Glass Cliff', *Forbes*, 16 July 2012.

11 Sorkin and Rusli, 'A Yahoo Search Calls Up a Chief From Google', *The New York Times*, 16 July 2012.

12 Olen, 'Marissa Mayer and the Glass Cliff', *Forbes*, 16 July 2012.

13 Nicholas Carlson, 'What Happened When Marissa Mayer Tried to Be Steve Jobs', *The New York Times Magazine*, 17 December 2014, https://www.nytimes.com/2014/12/21/magazine/what-happened-when-marissa-mayer-tried-to-be-steve-jobs.html?_r=0

14 Olen, 'Marissa Mayer and the Glass Cliff', *Forbes*, 16 July 2012.

15 Carlson, 'The Day Marissa Mayer's Honeymoon At Yahoo Ended', Insider, 2 January 2015.

16 Carlson, 'What Happened When Marissa Mayer Tried to Be Steve Jobs', *The New York Times Magazine*, 17 December 2014.

17 As told to Mark King, 'Karren Brady: my greatest mistake', *The Guardian*, 4 May 2012, https://www.theguardian.com/money/2012/may/04/karren-brady-my-greatest-mistake

18 Maureen Dowd, 'Get Off of Your Cloud', *The New York Times*, 26 February 2013, https://www.nytimes.com/2013/02/27/opinion/dowd-get-off-your-cloud.html?_r=2&

19 D. G. McCullough, 'Women CEOs: Why companies in crisis hire minorities – and then fire them', *The Guardian*, 8 August 2014, https://www.theguardian.com/sustainable-business/2014/aug/05/fortune-500-companies-crisis-woman-ceo-yahoo-xerox-jc-penny-economy; Hanna Rosin, 'Why Doesn't Marissa Mayer Care About Sexism?', Slate, 16 July 2012, https://slate.com/human-interest/2012/07/new-yahoo-ceo-marissa-mayer-does-she-care-about-sexism.html

20 Carlson, 'What Happened When Marissa Mayer Tried to Be Steve Jobs', *The New York Times Magazine*, 17 December 2014.

21 Carlson, 'The Day Marissa Mayer's Honeymoon At Yahoo Ended', Insider, 2 January 2015.

22 Stu Sjouwerman, 'A Single Spear Phishing Click Caused The Yahoo Data Breach', KnowBe4 (Security Awareness Training Blog),

18 March 2019, https://blog.knowbe4.com/a-single-spear-phishing-click-caused-the-yahoo-data-breach

23 Michael Grothaus, 'Yahoo now says all 3 billion of its accounts were breached in 2013 hack', Fast Company (website), 4 October 2017, https://www.fastcompany.com/40476884/yahoo-now-says-all-3-billion-of-its-accounts-were-breached-in-2013-hack

24 Sophie Kleeman, 'Here's What Happened To All 53 of Marissa Mayer's Yahoo Acquisitions', Gizmodo (website), 15 June 2016, https://gizmodo.com/heres-what-happened-to-all-of-marissa-mayers-yahoo-acqu-1781980352

25 Gaudin, 'After rocky tenure, Mayer to leave Yahoo "tarnished"', Computerworld, 13 March 2017.

26 Carlson, 'The Day Marissa Mayer's Honeymoon At Yahoo Ended', Insider, 2 January 2015.

27 Ibid.

28 Nicholas Carlson, 'The Three Times Marissa Mayer Refused To Fire Thousands Of Yahoo Employees', Insider, 3 January 2015, https://www.businessinsider.com/marissa-mayer-refused-to-fire-thousands-of-yahoo-employees-2015-1?r=US&IR=T

29 Carlson, 'The Day Marissa Mayer's Honeymoon At Yahoo Ended', Insider, 2 January 2015.

30 Ibid.

31 Ibid.

32 Ibid.

33 Carlson, 'What Happened When Marissa Mayer Tried to Be Steve Jobs', The New York Times Magazine, 17 December 2014.

34 Ibid.

35 Ainsley Harris, 'Yahoo CEO Marissa Mayer Nears Decision On $37 Billion Alibaba Stake', Fast Company, 20 January 2015, https://www.fastcompany.com/3041128/yahoo-ceo-marissa-mayer-nears-decision-on-37-billion-alibaba-stake

36 Carlson, 'What Happened When Marissa Mayer Tried to Be Steve Jobs', The New York Times Magazine, 17 December 2014.

37 Brian Womack and Kelly Gilblom, 'Starboard Boosts Pressure on

Yahoo to Unlock Alibaba Value', Bloomberg, 8 January 2015, https://www.bloomberg.com/news/articles/2015-01-08/starboard-pushes-yahoo-ceo-mayer-for-more-value-in-new-letter?leadSource=uverify%20wall

38 Jon Russell, 'Yahoo spin-out Altaba is selling its entire Alibaba stake and closing down', TechCrunch (website), 3 April 2019, https://techcrunch.com/2019/04/03/altaba-alibaba-sale

39 Sue Decker, 'An Insider's Account of the Yahoo–Alibaba Deal', *Harvard Business Review*, 6 August 2014, https://hbr.org/2014/08/an-insiders-account-of-the-yahoo-alibaba-deal

40 Matt Weinberger and Paige Leskin, 'The rise and fall of Marissa Mayer, the once-beloved CEO of Yahoo now pursuing her own venture', Insider (website), 11 February 2020, https://www.businessinsider.com/yahoo-marissa-mayer-rise-and-fall-2017-6?r=US&IR=T

41 Ibid.

42 Ibid.

43 Gaudin, 'After rocky tenure, Mayer to leave Yahoo "tarnished"', Computerworld, 13 March 2017.

44 Elizabeth Judge, 'Women on board: help or hindrance?', *The Times*, 11 November 2003, https://www.thetimes.co.uk/article/women-on-board-help-or-hindrance-2c6fnqf6fng

45 The archived version on the *Times* website no longer has the quote, but it is referenced in the following articles: Kelly Oakes, 'The invisible danger of the "glass cliff"', BBC (website), 7 February 2022, https://www.bbc.com/future/article/20220204-the-danger-of-the-glass-cliff-for-women-and-people-of-colour; Michelle Ryan and Alexander Haslam, 'The glass cliff: women left to take charge at times of crisis', *The Times*, 12 November 2018, https://www.thetimes.co.uk/article/the-glass-cliff-women-taking-charge-but-at-times-of-crisis-czlvzzrns

46 'Make your workplace work for women: a conversation with Indeed CMO Jessica Jensen, Lena Waithe, Reshma Saujani and Jen Welter', Indeed, 3 January 2023, https://uk.indeed.com/lead/

make-your-workplace-work-for-women-a-conversation-with-indeed-cmo-jessica-jensen

47 'What being an "Only" at work is like', in Women in the Workplace 2018, Lean In, https://leanin.org/women-in-the-workplace/2018/what-being-an-only-at-work-is-like

48 Michelle K. Ryan, S. Alexander Haslam, Tom Postmes, 'Reactions to the glass cliff: Gender differences in the explanations for the precariousness of women's leadership positions', *Journal of Organizational Change Management*, 20(2), pp. 182–97, https://www.researchgate.net/publication/235284109_Reactions_to_the_glass_cliff_Gender_differences_in_the_explanations_for_the_precariousness_of_women%27s_leadership_positions

49 Ibid.

50 Emily Stewart, 'Why struggling companies promote women: the glass cliff, explained', Vox (website), 31 October 2018, https://www.vox.com/2018/10/31/17960156/what-is-the-glass-cliff-women-ceos

51 S. Alexander Haslam, Michelle K. Ryan, Clara Kulich, Grzegorz Trojanowski and Cate Atkins, 'Investing with Prejudice: The Relationship Between Women's Presence on Company Boards and Objective and Subjective Measures of Company Pergormance', *British Journal of Management*, vol. 21, 2010, p. 485, referencing Haslam and Ryan, 2008; Ashby, Ryan and Haslam, 2007; and Bruckmüller and Branscombe, 2007, http://www.bbcprisonstudy.org/includes/site/files/files/2010%20BJM%20Tobin's%20Q.pdf

52 Alison Cook and Christy Glass, 'Above the glass ceiling: When are women and racial/ethnic minorities promoted to CEO?', *Strategic Management Journal*, 35(7), July 2014, pp. 1080–9, https://onlinelibrary.wiley.com/doi/abs/10.1002/smj.2161

53 Christy Glass and Alison Cook, 'Leading at the top: Understanding women's challenges above the glass ceiling', *The Leadership Quarterly*, 27(1), February 2016, pp. 51–63, https://daneshyari.com/article/preview/10439499.pdf

54 Michael L. McDonald, Gareth D. Keeves and James D. Westphal,

'One Step Forward, One Step Back: White Male Top Manager Organizational Identification and Helping Behavior Toward Other Executives Following the Appointment of a Female or Racial Minority CEO', *Academy of Management Journal*, 17 April 2017, https://www.semanticscholar.org/paper/One-Step-Forward%2C-One-Step-Back%3A-White-Male-Top-and-McDonald-Keeves/1262 48f6ebac18c26ca0746588a251fa9fc1f6b2?p2df

55 Glass and Cook, 'Leading at the Top: Understanding women's challenges above the glass ceiling', *The Leadership Quarterly*, 27(1), February 2016, pp. 51–63.

56 Ryan, Haslam and Postmes, 'Reactions to the glass cliff: Gender differences in the explanations for the precariousness of women's leadership positions', *Journal of Organizational Change Management*, 20(2), pp. 182–97.

57 Susanne Bruckmüller and Nyla R. Branscombe, 'How Women End Up on the "Glass Cliff"' *Harvard Business Review*, January–February 2011, https://hbr.org/2011/01/how-women-end-up-on-the-glass-cliff

58 Ibid.

59 Ryan, Haslam and Postmes, 'Reactions to the glass cliff: Gender differences in the explanations for the precariousness of women's leadership positions', *Journal of Organizational Change Management*, 20(2), pp. 182–97.

60 Haslam, Ryan et al., 'Investing with Prejudice: The Relationship Between Women's Presence on Company Boards and Objective and Subjective Measures of Company Performance', *British Journal of Management*, vol. 21(2), June 2010, pp. 484–97.

61 Ibid.

62 Ibid.

63 V. E. Schein, 'Think Manager – Think Male? From Gender Bias to Gender Balance', presentation at University of Edinburgh Business School, 14 January 2019; see also Schein's original research, 'The relationship between sex role stereotypes and requisite management characteristics', *Journal of Applied Psychology*, 57(2), 1973, pp. 95–100,

https://psycnet.apa.org/record/1975-04236-001 and 'The relationship between sex role stereotypes and requisite management characteristics among female managers', *Journal of Applied Psychology*, 60(3), 1975, pp. 340–4, https://psycnet.apa.org/record/1975-24377-001

64 Michelle K. Ryan, S. Alexander Haslam et al., 'Getting on top of the glass cliff: Reviewing a decade of evidence, explanations, and impact', *The Leadership Quarterly*, 27(3), June 2016, pp. 446–55, https://www.sciencedirect.com/science/article/abs/pii/S104898431500123X

65 M. K. Ryan, S. A. Haslam, M. D. Hersby and R. Bongiorno, 'Think crisis – think female: The glass cliff and contextual variation in the think manager – think male stereotype', *Journal of Applied Psychology*, 96(3), 2011, pp. 470–84, https://psycnet.apa.org/record/2010-26139-001

66 Glass and Cook, 'Leading at the top: Understanding women's challenges above the glass ceiling', *The Leadership Quarterly*, 27(1), February 2016, pp. 51–63.

67 Jack Zenger and Joseph Folkman, 'Research: Women Are Better Leaders During a Crisis', *Harvard Business Review*, 30 December 2020, https://hbr.org/2020/12/research-women-are-better-leaders-during-a-crisis?ab=at_art_art_1x4_s01

68 Ibid.

69 Ryan, Haslam, Hersby and Bongiorno, 'Think crisis – think female: The glass cliff and contextual variation in the think manager – think male stereotype', *Journal of Applied Psychology*, 96(3), 2011, pp. 470–84.

70 Ryan, Haslam et al., 'Getting on top of the glass cliff: Reviewing a decade of evidence, explanations, and impact', *The Leadership Quarterly*, 27(3), June 2016, pp. 446–55.

71 Kirstin J. Anderson, 'Are Katie Couric and Diane Sawyer Perched on a Glass Cliff?', Fifteen Eighty Four, Cambridge University Press blog, 11 January 2010, https://www.cambridgeblog.org/2010/01/glass-cliff

72 Ryan, Haslam, Hersby and Bongiorno, 'Think crisis – think
    female: The glass cliff and contextual variation in the think
    manager – think male stereotype', *Journal of Applied Psychology*,
    96(3), 2011, pp. 470–84.

73 'If women are less able to demonstrate leadership success, or are
    apportioned blame for negative outcomes evident before their
    appointment, this may reinforce the pernicious stereotypes that
    women are not suited to leadership positions.' Michelle Ryan, 'The
    glass cliff: why women lead in a crisis', BroadAgenda (website), 11
    March 2022, https://www.broadagenda.com.au/2022/the-glass-
    cliff-why-women-lead-in-a-crisis

74 Glass and Cook, 'Leading at the top: Understanding women's
    challenges above the glass ceiling', *The Leadership Quarterly*,
    27(1), February 2016, pp. 51–63.

75 Kelly Oakes, 'The invisible danger of the "glass cliff"', BBC
    (website), 7 February 2022, https://www.bbc.com/future/
    article/20220204-the-danger-of-the-glass-cliff-for-women-and-
    people-of-colour

76 Ibid.

77 Jena McGregor, 'Here's why women CEOs are more likely to get
    sacked from their jobs', *The Washington Post*, 2 May 2014, https://
    www.washingtonpost.com/news/on-leadership/wp/2014/05/02/
    heres-why-women-ceos-are-more-likely-to-get-sacked-from-their-
    jobs, and Vishal K. Gupta, Sandra C. Mortal et al., 'You're Fired!
    Gender Disparities in CEO Dismissal', *Journal of Management*,
    46(4), 2020, pp. 560–82, https://journals.sagepub.com/
    doi/10.1177/0149206318810415

78 Glass and Cook, 'Leading at the top: Understanding women's
    challenges above the glass ceiling', *The Leadership Quarterly*,
    27(1), February 2016, pp. 51–63.

79 'When Wall Street Needs Scapegoats, Women Beware', Thomson
    Reuters Foundation (website), 2 November 2013, https://news.
    trust.org/item/20131103084828-93enz?view=print

80 Anderson, 'Are Katie Couric and Diane Sawyer Perched on a

Glass Cliff?', Fifteen Eighty Four, Cambridge University Press blog, 11 January 2010.

81 Glass and Cook, 'Leading at the top: Understanding women's challenges above the glass ceiling', *The Leadership Quarterly*, 27(1), February 2016, pp. 51–63.

82 McGregor, 'Here's why women CEOs are more likely to get sacked from their jobs', *The Washington Post*, 2 May 2014.

83 Marianne Cooper, 'Why women are often put in charge of failing companies', PBS News Hour (website), 22 September 2015, https://www.pbs.org/newshour/economy/women-often-put-charge-failing-companies

84 Ryan, Haslam and Postmes, 'Reactions to the glass cliff: Gender differences in the explanations for the precariousness of women's leadership positions', *Journal of Organizational Change Management*, 20(2), pp. 182–97.

85 Stewart, 'Why struggling companies promote women: the glass cliff, explained', Vox (website), 31 October 2018.

86 Julia Kagan, 'Glass Cliff: Definition, Research, Examples, Vs. Glass Ceiling', Investopedia (website), 7 December 2022, https://www.investopedia.com/terms/g/glass-cliff.asp

87 Cook and Glass, 'Above the glass ceiling: When are women and racial/ethnic minorities promoted to CEO?', *Strategic Management Journal*, 35(7), July 2014, pp. 1080–9.

88 Alison Cook and Christy Glass, 'Glass Cliffs and Organizational Saviors: Barriers to Minority Leadership in Work Organizations?', *Social Problems*, 60(2), May 2013, pp. 168–87, https://www.researchgate.net/publication/259732880_Glass_Cliffs_and_Organizational_Saviors_Barriers_to_Minority_Leadership_in_Work_Organizations

89 S. Alexander Haslam and Michelle K. Ryan, 'The road to the glass cliff: Differences in the perceived suitability of men and women for leadership positions in succeeding and failing organizations', *The Leadership Quarterly*, 19(5), October 2008, pp. 530–46, https://www.sciencedirect.com/science/article/abs/pii/S1048984308000957

90 Ibid.

91 Michael L. McDonald, Gareth D. Keeves and James D. Westphal, 'One step forward, one step back: White male top manager organizational identification and helping behavior toward other executives following the appointment of a female or racial minority CEO', *Academy of Management Journal*, 61(2), 2018, pp. 405–39, https://leeds-faculty.colorado.edu/dahe7472/mcdonald.pdf

92 Ibid.

93 Ibid.

94 Ibid.

95 Ibid.

96 Ibid.

97 Ibid.

98 Ibid.

Chapter 3

1 F. Scott Fitzgerald, *The Great Gatsby*, 1925.

2 Jena McGregor, 'Congratulations, Theresa May. Now mind that "glass cliff"', *The Washington Post*, 12 July 2016, https://www.washingtonpost.com/news/on-leadership/wp/2016/07/12/congratulations-theresa-may-now-mind-that-glass-cliff

3 Brian Wheeler and Gavin Stamp, 'The Theresa May story: The Tory leader brought down by Brexit', BBC News (website), 24 May 2019, https://www.bbc.co.uk/news/election-2017-4622594

4 McGregor, 'Congratulations, Theresa May. Now mind that "glass cliff"', *The Washington Post*, 12 July 2016.

5 Michelle K. Ryan, S. Alexander Haslam et al., 'Getting on top of the glass cliff: Reviewing a decade of evidence, explanations, and impact', *The Leadership Quarterly*, 27(3), June 2016, pp. 446–55, https://www.sciencedirect.com/science/article/abs/pii/S104898431500123X

6 Marianne Cooper, 'Why women are often put in charge of failing companies', PBS News Hour (website), 22 September 2015, https://www.pbs.org/newshour/economy/women-often-put-charge-failing-companies

7 Michelle Ryan and Alexander Haslam, 'The glass cliff: women left to take charge at times of crisis', *The Times*, 12 November 2018, https://www.thetimes.co.uk/article/the-glass-cliff-women-taking-charge-but-at-times-of-crisis-czlvzzrns

8 McGregor, 'Congratulations, Theresa May. Now mind that "glass cliff"', *The Washington Post*, 12 July 2016.

9 Wheeler and Stamp, 'The Theresa May story: The Tory leader brought down by Brexit', BBC News (website), 24 May 2019.

10 Ibid.

11 Emily Stewart, 'Why struggling companies promote women: the glass cliff, explained', Vox (website), 31 October 2018, https://www.vox.com/2018/10/31/17960156/what-is-the-glass-cliff-women-ceos

12 Wheeler and Stamp, 'The Theresa May story: The Tory leader brought down by Brexit', BBC News (website), 24 May 2019.

13 'Brexit: Theresa May's deal is voted down in historic Commons defeat', BBC News (website), 15 January 2019, https://www.bbc.co.uk/news/uk-politics-46885828

14 Wheeler and Stamp, 'The Theresa May story: The Tory leader brought down by Brexit', BBC News (website), 24 May 2019.

15 'Theresa May resigns over Brexit: What happened?', BBC News (website), 24 May 2019, https://www.bbc.co.uk/news/uk-politics-48379730

16 McGregor, 'Congratulations, Theresa May. Now mind that "glass cliff"', *The Washington Post*, 12 July 2016.

17 Andrew Woodcock, 'Brexit: Theresa May tells MPs that her deal was better than Boris Johnson's', *Independent*, 30 December 2020, https://www.independent.co.uk/news/uk/politics/brexit-theresa-may-boris-johnson-trade-deal-b1780329.html

18 Kelly Oakes, 'The invisible danger of the "glass cliff"', BBC (website), 7 February 2022, https://www.bbc.com/future/article/20220204-the-danger-of-the-glass-cliff-for-women-and-people-of-colour

19 Jena McGregor, 'Here's why women CEOs are more likely to get sacked from their jobs', *The Washington Post*, 2 May 2014, https://www.washingtonpost.com/news/on-leadership/wp/2014/05/02/heres-why-women-ceos-are-more-likely-to-get-sacked-from-their-jobs

20 Ibid.

21 Michelle Ryan, 'The glass cliff: why women lead in a crisis', BroadAgenda (website), 11 March 2022, https://www.broadagenda.com.au/2022/the-glass-cliff-why-women-lead-in-a-crisis

22 Ben Mattison, 'Women Aren't Promoted Because Managers Underestimate Their Potential', Yale Insights (website), 17 September 2021, https://insights.som.yale.edu/insights/women-arent-promoted-because-managers-underestimate-their-potential

23 Alan Benson, Danielle Li and Kelly Shue, '"Potential" and the Gender Promotion Gap', 22 June 2022, https://danielle-li.github.io/assets/docs/PotentialAndTheGenderPromotionGap.pdf

24 Ibid.

25 Linda Babcock, Maria P. Recalde, Lise Vesterlund and Laurie Weingart, 'Gender differences in accepting and receiving requests for tasks with low promotability', *American Economic Review*, 107(3), January 2017, pp. 714–47, https://gap.hks.harvard.edu/breaking-glass-ceiling-"no"-gender-differences-declining-requests-non%E2%80%90promotable-tasks

26 Joan C. Williams and Marina Multhaup, 'For Women and Minorities to Get Ahead, Managers Must Assign Work Fairly', *Harvard Business Review*, 5 March 2018, https://hbr.org/2018/03/for-women-and-minorities-to-get-ahead-managers-must-assign-work-fairly

27 Mattison, 'Women Aren't Promoted Because Managers

Underestimate Their Potential', Yale Insights (website), 17 September 2021.

28 Women in the Workplace 2017, McKinsey & Company / Lean In, https://wiw-report.s3.amazonaws.com/Women_in_the_Workplace_2017.pdf

29 Ibid.

30 'Gender Equality in the Workplace: Pipeline of Promotion', The Women's Foundation (website), 4 October 2016, https://www. twfhk.org/blog/gender-equality-workplace-pipeline-promotion

31 Women in the Workplace 2017, McKinsey & Company / Lean In, https://wiw-report.s3.amazonaws.com/Women_in_the_Workplace_2017.pdf

32 'COVID-19 cost women globally over $800 billion in lost income in one year', Oxfam press release, 29 April 2021, https://www. oxfam.org/en/press-releases/covid-19-cost-women-globally-over-800-billion-lost-income-one-year

33 Anu Madgavkar, Olivia White et al., 'COVID-19 and gender equality: Countering the regressive effects', McKinsey Global Institute, 15 July 2020, http://www.mckinsey.com/featured-insights/future-of-work/covid-19-and-gender-equality-countering-the-regressive-effects?cid=eml-web

34 'COVID-19 cost women globally over $800 billion in lost income in one year', Oxfam press release, 29 April 2021, https://www. oxfam.org/en/press-releases/covid-19-cost-women-globally-over-800-billion-lost-income-one-year

35 Judith Woods, 'Are women being made to walk the plank?', The Age, 18 September 2004, https://www.theage.com.au/business/ are-women-being-made-to-walk-the-plank-20040918-gdynkm.html

36 Oakes, 'The invisible danger of the "glass cliff"', BBC (website), 7 February 2022

37 Christy Glass and Alison Cook, 'Pathways to the Glass Cliff: A Risk Tax for Women and Minority Leaders?', Social Problems, 67(4), November 2020, pp. 637–53, https://academic.oup.com/ socpro/article-abstract/67/4/637/5637806?redirectedFrom=fulltext

38 Oakes, 'The invisible danger of the "glass cliff"', BBC (website), 7 February 2022.

39 Ibid.

40 Stewart, 'Why struggling companies promote women: the glass cliff, explained', Vox (website), 31 October 2018.

41 Ibid.

42 Ryan, Haslam et al., 'Getting on top of the glass cliff: Reviewing a decade of evidence, explanations, and impact', *The Leadership Quarterly*, 27(3), June 2016, pp. 446–55.

43 Ibid.

Chapter 4

1 Franz Kafka, *The Metamorphosis*, 1915.

2 Michelle K. Ryan, S. Alexander Haslam et al., 'Getting on top of the glass cliff: Reviewing a decade of evidence, explanations, and impact', *The Leadership Quarterly*, 27(3), June 2016, pp. 446–55, https://www.sciencedirect.com/science/article/abs/pii/S104898431500123X

3 Jessica Grose, 'General Motors Names First Female CEO Without Shoving Her Off a "Glass Cliff"', *Elle*, 11 December 2013, https://www.elle.com/culture/career-politics/news/a24095/mary-barra-named-general-motors-ceo

4 'GM 363 Asset Sale Approved by U.S. Bankruptcy Court', GM (website), https://news.gm.com/newsroom.detail.html/Pages/news/us/en/2009/Jul/0706_AssetSale.html

5 Grose, 'General Motors Names First Female CEO Without Shoving Her Off a "Glass Cliff"', *Elle*, 11 December 2013.

6 Richard Feloni, 'GM CEO Mary Barra said the recall crisis of 2014 forever changed her leadership style', Insider (website), 14 November 2018, https://www.businessinsider.com/gm-mary-barra-recall-crisis-leadership-style-2018-11?r=US&IR=T

7 Ben Klayman, 'GM recalls 1.5 million more vehicles; CEO says "terrible things happened"', Reuters (website), 17 March 2014,

https://www.reuters.com/article/us-gm-recall-idUSBREA2G15220140317

8   Dominic Rushe, 'GM fined $35m over recall scandal in deal with Department of Transportation', *The Guardian*, 16 May 2014, https://www.theguardian.com/business/2014/may/16/gm-car-recall-faulty-ignition-department-of-transport-agreement

9   Feloni, 'GM CEO Mary Barra said the recall crisis of 2014 forever changed her leadership style', Insider (website), 14 November 2018.

10 Jena McGregor, 'Honeymoon interrupted for GM's Mary Barra', *The Washington Post*, 14 March 2014, https://www.washingtonpost.com/news/on-leadership/wp/2014/03/14/honeymoon-interrupted-for-gms-mary-barra

11 'GM boss Mary Barra "deeply sorry" for ignition fault', BBC News (website), 2 April 2014, https://www.bbc.co.uk/news/business-26844494

12 Bill Vlasic and Christopher Jensen, 'Something Went "Very Wrong" at G.M., Chief Says', *The New York Times*, 17 March 2014, https://www.nytimes.com/2014/03/18/business/gm-chief-barra-releases-video-on-recalls.html

13 Klayman, 'GM recalls 1.5 million more vehicles; CEO says "terrible things happened"', Reuters (website), 17 March 2014.

14 Tom McCarthy, 'GM chief Mary Barra dodges question of responsibility for recall flaws – live', *The Guardian*, 1 April 2014, https://www.theguardian.com/business/2014/apr/01/gm-chief-executive-mary-barra-recalls-congress-hearing-live

15 Vlasic and Jensen, 'Something Went "Very Wrong" at G.M., Chief Says', *The New York Times*, 17 March 2014.

16 Dominic Rushe, 'GM chief Mary Barra: "pattern of incompetence" caused fatal recall delay', *The Guardian*, 5 June 2014, https://www.theguardian.com/business/2014/jun/05/gm-mary-barra-fatal-recall-incompetence-neglect

17 McCarthy, 'GM chief Mary Barra dodges question of responsibility for recall flaws – live', *The Guardian*, 1 April 2014.

18 Hilary Burns, 'A case study on the hot seat: Why some execs stay

cool while others get burned', BizWomen, The Business Journals (website), 9 October 2014, https://www.bizjournals.com/bizwomen/news/profiles-strategies/2014/10/a-case-study-on-the-hot-seat-why-some-execs-stay.html?page=all

19 Geoff Colvin, 'Mary Barra's (unexpected) opportunity', Fortune, 18 September 2014, https://fortune.com/2014/09/18/mary-barra-general-motors

20 Feloni, 'GM CEO Mary Barra said the recall crisis of 2014 forever changed her leadership style', Insider (website), 14 November 2018.

21 'Profile: Mary Barra', Forbes, https://www.forbes.com/profile/mary-barra

22 Audre Lorde, 'The Transformation of Silence into Language and Action', in Audre Lorde, Sister Outsider (London: Penguin Classics, 2019).

23 Ryan, Haslam et al., 'Getting on top of the glass cliff: Reviewing a decade of evidence, explanations, and impact', The Leadership Quarterly, 27(3), June 2016, pp. 446–55.

24 Ibid.

25 Ibid.

26 Kelly Oakes, 'The invisible danger of the "glass cliff"', BBC (website), 7 February 2022, https://www.bbc.com/future/article/20220204-the-danger-of-the-glass-cliff-for-women-and-people-of-colour; Emily Stewart, 'Why struggling companies promote women: the glass cliff, explained', Vox (website), 31 October 2018, https://www.vox.com/2018/10/31/17960156/what-is-the-glass-cliff-women-ceos

27 Robert Hof, 'Yahoo Fires CEO Carol Bartz – Here's Why', Forbes, 6 September 2011, https://www.forbes.com/sites/roberthof/2011/09/06/report-yahoo-cans-ceo-carol-bartz-heres-what-went-wrong

28 Kara Swisher, 'Exclusive: Carol Bartz Out at Yahoo; CFO Tim Morse Names Interim CEO', All Things D (website), 6 September 2011, https://allthingsd.com/20110906/exclusive-carol-bartz-out-at-yahoo-cfo-interim-ceo

29 Jena McGregor, 'Here's why women CEOs are more likely to get sacked from their jobs', *The Washington Post*, 2 May 2014, https://www.washingtonpost.com/news/on-leadership/wp/2014/05/02/heres-why-women-ceos-are-more-likely-to-get-sacked-from-their-jobs

30 Oakes, 'The invisible danger of the "glass cliff"', BBC (website), 7 February 2022.

31 Freakonomics podcast, episode 327, 25 March 2018, https://freakonomics.com/podcast/extra-carol-bartz-full-interview

32 Dominic Rushe, 'Carol Bartz blames Yahoo "doofuses" for firing her in foul-mouthed tirade', *The Guardian*, 8 September 2011, https://www.theguardian.com/business/2011/sep/08/carol-bartz-blast-yahoo-after-being-fired

33 Karin Hederos Eriksson and Anna Sandberg, 'Gender Differences in Initiation of Negotiation: Does the Gender of the Negotiation Counterpart Matter?', *Negotiation Journal*, 28(4), October 2012, pp. 407–28, https://onlinelibrary.wiley.com/doi/full/10.1111/j.1571-9979.2012.00349.x

34 Linda Babcock, Sara Laschever, Michele Gelfand and Deborah Small, 'Nice Girls Don't Ask', *Harvard Business Review*, October 2003, https://hbr.org/2003/10/nice-girls-dont-ask; Suzanne de Janasz and Beth Cabrera, 'How Women Can Get What They Want in a Negotiation', *Harvard Business Review*, 17 August 2018, https://hbr.org/2018/08/how-women-can-get-what-they-want-in-a-negotiation

35 'Negotiation Advice for Women', Lean In (website), https://leanin.org/negotiation

36 Emily T. Amanatullah and Michael W. Morris, 'Negotiating Gender Roles: Gender Differences in Assertive Negotiating Are Mediated by Women's Fear of Backlash and Attenuated When Negotiating on Behalf of Others', *Journal of Personality and Social Psychology*, 98(2), February 2010, pp. 256–67, https://www.researchgate.net/publication/41087504_Negotiating_Gender_Roles_Gender_Differences_in_Assertive_Negotiating_Are_

Mediated_by_Women%27s_Fear_of_Backlash_and_Attenuated_
When_Negotiating_on_Behalf_of_Others

37   Margaret A. Neale, 'Negotiation', Stanford University VMware
     Women's Leadership Innovation Lab, https://womensleadership.
     stanford.edu/resources/voice-influence/negotiation

38   Katie Shonk, 'Women and Negotiation: Narrowing the Gender Gap
     in Negotiation', Harvard Law School Program on Negotiation Daily
     Blog, 17 August 2023, https://www.pon.harvard.edu/daily/business-
     negotiations/women-and-negotiation-narrowing-the-gender-gap

39   Thomas F. Denson, Siobhan M. O'Dean et al., 'Aggression in
     Women: Behavior, Brain and Hormones', *Frontiers in Behavioral
     Neuroscience*, vol. 12, 2 May 2018, https://www.frontiersin.org/
     articles/10.3389/fnbeh.2018.00081/full

40   Laura J. Kray, Leigh Thompson and Adam Galinsky, 'Battle of the
     Sexes: Gender Stereotype Confirmation and Reactance in
     Negotiations', *Journal of Personality and Social Psychology*, 80(6),
     July 2001, pp. 942–58, https://www.researchgate.net/publication/
     11926564_Battle_of_the_Sexes_Gender_Stereotype_Confirmation_
     and_Reactance_in_Negotiations

41   Amanatullah and Morris, 'Negotiating Gender Roles: Gender
     Differences in Assertive Negotiating Are Mediated by Women's
     Fear of Backlash and Attenuated When Negotiating on Behalf of
     Others', *Journal of Personality and Social Psychology*, 98(2),
     February 2010, pp. 256–67.

42   Raina Brands, 'Negotiate "Like A Woman"', Care Equally (website),
     27 September 2022, https://www.careerequally.com/post/
     negotiate-like-a-woman

43   'Counteracting Negotiation Biases Like Race and Gender in the
     Workplace', Harvard Law School, Program on Negotiation, Daily
     Blog, 19 September 2023, https://www.pon.harvard.edu/daily/
     leadership-skills-daily/counteracting-racial-and-gender-bias-in-
     job-negotiations-nb

44   Laura J. Kray, Adam D. Galinsky and Leigh Thompson, 'Reversing
     the Gender Gap in Negotiations: An Exploration of Stereotype

Regeneration', *Organizational Behavior and Human Decision Processes*, 87(2), March 2002, https://web.mit.edu/curhan/www/docs/Articles/15341_Readings/Social_Cognition/Kray_et_al_2002_Reversing_the_gender_gap_in_negotiations.pdf

45 Toni Morrison, 'The Work You Do, The Person You Are', *The New Yorker*, 29 March 2017, https://www.newyorker.com/magazine/2017/06/05/toni-morrison-the-work-you-do-the-person-you-are

46 Mark Sweney, 'Netflix to lose 700,000 UK customers in two years, analysts predict', *The Guardian*, 1 January 2023, https://www.theguardian.com/media/2023/jan/01/netflix-to-lose-700000-uk-customers-in-two-years-analysts-predict

47 Kari Paul, 'Netflix lays off 300 employees in second round of job cuts', *The Guardian*, 23 June 2022, https://www.theguardian.com/media/2022/jun/23/netflix-layoff-300-employees-second-round-job-cut

48 'Why women leaders are switching jobs', Women in the Workplace 2022, Lean In and McKinsey & Company, https://leanin.org/women-in-the-workplace/2022/why-women-leaders-are-switching-jobs

Chapter 5

1 Virginia Woolf, from her anti-war essay 'Three Guineas', 1938.

2 Hilary Burns, 'Julia Pierson, first female Secret Service director, resigns', BizWomen, The Business Journals (website), 1 October 2014, https://www.bizjournals.com/bizwomen/news/latest-news/2014/10/secret-service-director-julia-pierson-has-resigned.html; Mary Johnson, 'Former State Dept. official: Pierson resignation is "the price of leadership in the most sensitive of jobs"', BizWomen, The Business Journals (website), https://www.bizjournals.com/bizwomen/news/latest-news/2014/10/former-state-dept-official-pierson-resignation-is.html

3 Ewen MacAskill, 'Julia Pierson: veteran agent becomes first woman to lead US secret service', *The Guardian*, 27 March 2013,

https://www.theguardian.com/world/2013/mar/26/julia-pierson-woman-secret-service

4 Burns, 'Julia Pierson, first female Secret Service director, resigns', BizWomen, The Business Journals (website), 1 October 2014.

5 Ibid.

6 Dan Roberts, 'Secret service director Julie Pierson resigns after series of security lapses', *The Guardian*, 1 October 2014, https://www.theguardian.com/world/2014/oct/01/secret-service-director-resigns-white-house-security-lapses

7 Ibid.

8 Hilary Burns, 'A case study on the hot seat: Why some execs stay cool while others get burned', BizWomen, Dayton Business Journal (website), 9 October 2014, https://www.bizjournals.com/dayton/bizwomen/news/profiles-strategies/2014/10/a-case-study-on-the-hot-seat-why-some-execs-stay.html?page=5

9 Bryce Covert, 'Secret Service Director Julia Pierson Was a Victim of the "Glass Cliff"', The New Republic (website), 2 October 2014, https://newrepublic.com/article/119675/julia-pierson-women-leaders-and-perils-glass-cliff; Karen McVeigh, 'Secret service scandal in Colombia has agency's culture under a microscope', *The Guardian*, 20 April 2012, https://www.theguardian.com/world/2012/apr/20/secret-service-scandal-columbia-agency

10 McVeigh, 'Secret service agents took 20 women to Colombian hotel, says senator', *The Guardian*, 17 April 2012, https://www.theguardian.com/world/2012/apr/17/secret-service-scandal-colombia-twenty-women

11 AP Washington, 'Secret service agents sent home over drunken incident in Amsterdam', *The Guardian*, 26 March 2014, https://www.theguardian.com/world/2014/mar/26/secret-service-agents-disciplined-drunken-amsterdam

12 McVeigh, 'Secret service scandal in Colombia has agency's culture under a microscope', *The Guardian*, 20 April 2012.

13 David Nakamura and Scott Wilson, 'More military personnel might have been involved in misconduct before Obama's trip', *The*

Washington Post, 17 April 2012, https://www.washingtonpost.
com/politics/more-military-personnel-might-have-been-involved-
in-misconduct-before-obamas-trip/2012/04/16/gIQAJ3bqLT_story.
html; Carol Leonnig and David Nakamura, 'Secret Service
scandal: Rising supervisor set uncovering of misconduct in
motion', *The Washington Post*, 21 April 2012, https://www.
washingtonpost.com/politics/secret-service-scandal-rising-
supervisor-at-heart-of-uncovering-misconduct/2012/04/21/
gIQApy37XT_story.html; Chris Cillizza, 'The Secret Service had
the "Worst Week in Washington"', *The Washington Post*, 22 April
2012, https://www.washingtonpost.com/blogs/the-fix/post/
the-secret-service-had-the-worst-week-in-washington/2012/04/22/
gIQAna6qZT_blog.html

14 McVeigh, 'Secret service scandal in Colombia has agency's culture
under a microscope', *The Guardian*, 20 April 2012.

15 Ibid.

16 Ibid.

17 Ibid.

18 Amy Argetsinger and Roxanne Roberts, 'Reliable Source: Tareq
and Michaele Salahi crash Obamas' state dinner for India', *The
Washington Post*, 26 November 2009, https://www.washingtonpost.
com/wp-dyn/content/article/2009/11/25/AR2009112504113.html

19 McVeigh, 'Secret service scandal in Colombia has agency's culture
under a microscope', *The Guardian*, 20 April 2012.

20 Carol D. Leonnig, Spencer Hsu and Annys Shin, 'Secret Service
reviews White House security after fence-jumper enters mansion',
The Washington Post, 20 September 2014, https://www.
washingtonpost.com/local/crime/secret-service-reviews-white-
house-security-after-fence-jumper-enters-mansion/2014/09/20/
23df4f6a-40e0-11e4-b03f-de718edeb92f_story.html

21 MacAskill, 'Julia Pierson: veteran agent becomes first woman to
lead US secret service', *The Guardian*, 27 March 2013.

22 Covert, 'Secret Service Director Julia Pierson Was a Victim of the
"Glass Cliff"', The New Republic (website), 2 October 2014.

23 Josh Hicks, 'Did sequestration cause the Secret Service's problems?', *The Washington Post*, 1 October 2014, https://www.washingtonpost.com/news/federal-eye/wp/2014/10/01/did-sequestration-cause-the-secret-services-problems

24 Leonnig, Hsu and Shin, 'Secret Service reviews White House security after fence-jumper enters mansion', *The Washington Post*, 20 September 2014.

25 Noor Nanji, 'Aviva chief responds to "sexist" shareholder jibes', BBC News (website), 11 May 2022, https://www.bbc.co.uk/news/business-61411229

26 Ibid.

27 Women in the Workplace 2022, Lean In and McKinsey & Company, https://leanin.org/women-in-the-workplace

28 Ibid.

29 Vishal K. Gupta, Sandra C. Mortal et al., 'You're Fired! Gender Disparities in CEO Dismissal', *Journal of Management*, 46(4), 2020, pp. 560–82, https://journals.sagepub.com/doi/10.1177/0149206318810415

30 Kirsten Bellstrom, 'Female CEOs Are More Likely to Be Fired Than Men – Even When Their Companies Are Thriving', *Fortune*, 30 November 2018, https://fortune.com/2018/11/30/female-ceo-fired-study

31 Alice G. Walton, 'Female CEOs Are More Likely To Be Fired Than Males, Study Finds', *Forbes*, 1 December 2018, https://www.forbes.com/sites/alicegwalton/2018/12/01/female-ceos-are-more-likely-to-be-fired-than-males-study-finds

32 Ibid.

33 Ibid.

34 Emily Stewart, 'Why struggling companies promote women: the glass cliff, explained', Vox (website), 31 October 2018, https://www.vox.com/2018/10/31/17960156/what-is-the-glass-cliff-women-ceos

35 Jeremy Schneider, 'Are female CEOs better than male CEOs?',

Personal Finance Club (website), 7 March 2023, https://www.
personalfinanceclub.com/are-female-ceos-better-than-male-ceos

36 Jack Zenger and Joseph Folkman, 'Research: Women Score Higher
    Than Men in Most Leadership Skills', *Harvard Business Review*, 25
    June 2019, https://hbr.org/2019/06/research-women-score-higher-
    than-men-in-most-leadership-skills

37 Research by Supriya Garikipati and Uma Kambhampati, 'Leading
    the Fight Against the Pandemic: Does Gender "Really" Matter?', 3
    June 2020, https://papers.ssrn.com/sol3/papers.cfm?abstract_
    id=3617953; also reported by Jon Henley, 'Female-led countries
    handled coronavirus better, study suggests', *The Guardian*, 18
    August 2020, https://www.theguardian.com/world/2020/aug/18/
    female-led-countries-handled-coronavirus-better-study-jacinda-
    ardern-angela-merkel

38 Ibid.

39 Future of Women in Tech, DisruptHers podcast, episode 1,
    'Leading in a Crisis: Women in Tech on 2020's Unique Challenges
    and Opportunities', https://www.futureofwomenintech.com/
    disrupthers

40 Zenger and Folkman, 'Research: Women Score Higher Than Men
    in Most Leadership Skills', *Harvard Business Review*, 25 June 2019.

41 Travis Bradberry, 'Emotional intelligence: What it is and why you
    need it', World Economic Forum (website), 13 February 2017,
    research carried out with partners TalentSmart, https://www.
    weforum.org/agenda/2017/02/why-you-need-emotional-intelligence

42 Ibid.

43 Sara Connell, 'Dr. Vanessa Akhtar Of Kotter On The Five Things
    You Need To Be A Highly Effective Leader During Turbulent
    Times', *Authority Magazine*, 29 May 2022, https://medium.com/
    authority-magazine/dr-vanessa-akhtar-of-kotter-on-the-five-
    things-you-need-to-be-a-highly-effective-leader-during-
    c45a587fee2a

44 Robert Logemann, 'How Strong Are Your Leadership Soft Skills?',
    Forbes, 10 January 2023, https://www.forbes.com/sites/

forbesbusinesscouncil/2023/01/10/how-strong-are-your-leadership-soft-skills

45 Tara Van Bommel, 'The Power of Empathy in Times of Crisis and Beyond', Catalyst (website), 2021, https://www.catalyst.org/reports/empathy-work-strategy-crisis

46 Belinda Parmar, 'Why empathy is a must-have business strategy', World Economic Forum (website), 18 October 2021, https://www.weforum.org/agenda/2021/10/empathy-business-future-of-work

47 'Make your workplace work for women: a conversation with Indeed CMO Jessica Jensen, Lena Waithe, Reshma Saujani and Jen Welter', Indeed (website), 3 January 2023, https://uk.indeed.com/lead/make-your-workplace-work-for-women-a-conversation-with-indeed-cmo-jessica-jensen

Chapter 6

1 Miriam Makeba, South African musician and anti-Apartheid campaigner, see video here: https://www.instagram.com/reel/Ct7V8zuLSqw/?igshid=MzRlODBiNWFlZA%3D%3

2 Rachel Sklar, '3 Undeniable Ways Ellen Pao Was Pushed Off a Glass Cliff at Reddit', *Elle*, 14 July 2015, https://www.elle.com/culture/tech/a29322/3-undeniable-ways-ellen-pao-was-pushed-off-a-glass-cliff-at-reddit

3 Anna Sillers, 'Reddit CEO Ellen Pao bans salary negotiations', PBS News Hour (website), 7 April 2015, https://www.pbs.org/newshour/economy/reddit-ceo-ellen-pao-bans-salary-negotiations; Biz Carson, 'Ellen Pao: Reddit doesn't negotiate salaries because that helps keep the playing field even for women', Insider (website), 12 June 2015, https://www.businessinsider.com/reddit-doesnt-negotiate-salaries-ellen-pao-2015-6?r=US&IR=T

4 Lindy West, 'How Reddit's Ellen Pao survived one of "the largest trolling attacks in history"', *The Guardian*, 22 December 2015, https://www.theguardian.com/lifeandstyle/2015/dec/22/reddit-ellen-pao-trolling-revenge-porn-ceo-internet-misogyny

5　Martin Pengelly and Kevin Rawlinson, 'Reddit chief Ellen Pao resigns after receiving "sickening" abuse from users', *The Guardian*, 11 July 2015, https://www.theguardian.com/technology/2015/jul/10/ellen-pao-reddit-interim-ceo-resigns

6　Andrew Griffin, 'Reddit bans "revenge porn", tries to stop future nude photo leaks', *Independent*, 25 February 2015, https://www.independent.co.uk/tech/reddit-bans-revenge-porn-tries-to-stop-future-nude-photo-leaks-10068563.html

7　Adi Robertson, 'Reddit bans "Fat People Hate" and other subreddits under new harassment rules', The Verge (website), 10 June 2015, https://www.theverge.com/2015/6/10/8761763/reddit-harassment-ban-fat-people-hate-subreddit

8　Pengelly and Rawlinson, 'Reddit chief Ellen Pao resigns after receiving "sickening" abuse from users', *The Guardian*, 11 July 2015.

9　Michael D. Nguyen, 'Reddit Users Turn on Interim CEO Ellen Pao', NBC News (website), 21 June 2015, https://www.nbcnews.com/news/asian-america/reddit-users-turn-interim-ceo-ellen-pao-n377226

10　Alex Abad-Santos, 'The Reddit revolt that led to CEO Ellen Pao's resignation, explained', Vox (website), 10 July 2015, https://www.vox.com/2015/7/8/8914661/reddit-victoria-protest

11　Jen Yamato, 'Reddit Fired the Woman Trying to Save It', Daily Beast (website), 14 April 2017, https://www.thedailybeast.com/reddit-fired-the-woman-trying-to-save-it

12　Abad-Santos, 'The Reddit revolt that led to CEO Ellen Pao's resignation, explained', Vox (website), 10 July 2015.

13　Andy Campbell, 'Reddit Community Revolts After "Ask Me Anything" Administrator Is Dismissed', Huffington Post (website), 3 July 2015, https://www.huffingtonpost.co.uk/entry/reddit-ama-administrator_n_7723618

14　Abad-Santos, 'The Reddit revolt that led to CEO Ellen Pao's resignation, explained', Vox (website), 10 July 2015.

15　Jana Kasperkevic, 'Reddit CEO sorry for "letting down" users after popular subforums shut down', *The Guardian*, 4 July 2015, https://

www.theguardian.com/technology/2015/jul/04/reddit-subforums-ellen-pao-explains; Matt Vella, 'Reddit's Ellen Pao and Alexis Ohanian Explain Site Shut Down', *Time*, 3 July 2015, https://time.com/3945718/reddit-moderator-shut-down

16 Mike Isaac, 'Reddit's Chief Apologizes After Employee's Dismissal', *The New York Times*, 6 July 2015, https://www.nytimes.com/2015/07/07/technology/reddits-chief-apologizes-after-employees-dismissal.html; Abad-Santos, 'The Reddit revolt that led to CEO Ellen Pao's resignation, explained', Vox (website), 10 July 2015.

17 West, 'How Reddit's Ellen Pao survived one of "the largest trolling attacks in history"', *The Guardian*, 22 December 2015; Pengelly and Rawlinson, 'Reddit chief Ellen Pao resigns after receiving "sickening" abuse from users', *The Guardian*, 11 July 2015.

18 Kasperkevic, 'Reddit CEO sorry for "letting down" users after popular subforums shut down', *The Guardian*, 4 July 2015.

19 Sam Altman, 'An old team at reddit', r/announcements, Reddit (website), 10 July 2015, https://www.reddit.com/r/announcements/comments/3cucye/an_old_team_at_reddit/?rdt=61399

20 Pengelly and Rawlinson, 'Reddit chief Ellen Pao resigns after receiving "sickening" abuse from users', *The Guardian*, 11 July 2015.

21 Yishan Wong, 'TheoryOfReddit', comment, Reddit (website), 12 July 2015, https://www.reddit.com/r/TheoryOfReddit/comments/3d2hv3/comment/ct1ecxv; Mike Isaac, 'Details Emerge About Victoria Taylor's Dismissal at Reddit', *The New York Times*, 13 July 2015, https://archive.nytimes.com/bits.blogs.nytimes.com/2015/07/13/details-emerge-about-victoria-taylors-dismissal-at-reddit

22 Ellen K. Pao, Twitter post, Twitter (website), 13 July 2015, https://twitter.com/ekp/status/620652654822191104

23 West, 'How Reddit's Ellen Pao survived one of "the largest trolling attacks in history"', *The Guardian*, 22 December 2015.

24 Alexis Krivkovich and Lareina Yee, 'Women in the workplace: Breaking up to break through', McKinsey & Company (website), 23 February 2023, https://www.mckinsey.com/featured-insights/

diversity-and-inclusion/women-in-the-workplace-breaking-up-to-break-through

25 Women in the Workplace 2022, Lean In and McKinsey & Company, https://leanin.org/women-in-the-workplace

26 Ibid.

27 Rachel Treisman, 'Women leaders switch jobs at record rates as they demand better from their workplaces', NPR (website), 28 October 2022, https://www.npr.org/2022/10/28/1132232414/women-workforce-switching-jobs; Courtney Vinopal, '"Quick Quitting" Among Female CEOs Highlights the Obstacles Facing Executive Women', Observer (website), 29 November 2022, https://observer.com/2022/11/quick-quitting-among-female-ceos-highlights-the-obstacles-facing-executive-women

28 Women in the Workplace 2022, Lean In and McKinsey & Company, https://leanin.org/women-in-the-workplace

29 Treisman, 'Women leaders switch jobs at record rates as they demand better from their workplaces', NPR (website), 28 October 2022; 'Companies are starting to lose the few female leaders they have', NPR *Morning Edition*, 31 October 2022, https://www.npr.org/2022/10/31/1132163742/companies-are-starting-to-lose-the-few-female-leaders-they-have

30 Jennifer Liu, '"It's a huge concern": Senior-level women are calling it quits after decades climbing the career ladder', CNBC (website), 21 February 2023, https://www.cnbc.com/2023/02/21/why-youtube-ceo-susan-wojcicki-and-other-powerful-women-keep-quitting.html; Susan Wojcicki, 'A personal update from Susan', YouTube Official Blog, 16 February 2023, https://blog.youtube/inside-youtube/a-personal-update-from-susan

31 Liu, '"It's a huge concern": Senior-level women are calling it quits after decades climbing the career ladder', CNBC (website), 21 February 2023.

32 Ibid.

33 Linda K. Stroh, Jeanne M. Brett and Anne H. Reilly, 'Family Structure, Glass Ceiling, and Traditional Explanations for the

Differential Rate of Turnover of Female and Male Managers',
Journal of Vocational Behavior, 49(1), August 1996, pp. 99–118,
https://www.sciencedirect.com/science/article/abs/pii/
S0001879196900366

34 S. Alexander Haslam and Michelle K. Ryan, 'The road to the glass
cliff: Differences in the perceived suitability of men and women
for leadership positions in succeeding and failing organizations',
The Leadership Quarterly, 19(5), October 2008, pp. 530–46,
https://www.sciencedirect.com/science/article/abs/pii/
S1048984308000957

35 Women in the Workplace 2017, Lean In and McKinsey &
Company, https://www.mckinsey.com/featured-insights/diversity-
and-inclusion/women-in-the-workplace#section-header-2017

36 Steve Hatfield, Jen Fisher and Paul H. Silverglate, 'The C-suite's
role in well-being', Deloitte (website), 22 June 2022, https://www2.
deloitte.com/us/en/insights/topics/leadership/employee-wellness-
in-the-corporate-workplace.html

37 Ibid.

38 Ibid.

39 Women in the Workplace 2022, Lean In and McKinsey &
Company, https://leanin.org/women-in-the-workplace

40 Krivkovich and Yee, 'Women in the workplace: Breaking up to
break through', McKinsey & Company (website), 23 February 2023

41 Women in the Workplace 2022, Lean In and McKinsey &
Company, https://leanin.org/women-in-the-workplace

42 2023 Gen Z and Millennial Survey, Deloitte (website), https://
www.deloitte.com/global/en/issues/work/content/
genzmillennialsurvey.html

43 Ibid.

44 For more information, see 'The state of diversity in global private
markets: 2022', McKinsey & Company (website), 1 November
2022, https://www.mckinsey.com/industries/private-equity-and-
principal-investors/our-insights/the-state-of-diversity-in-global-
private-markets-2022

45 Women in the Workplace 2022, Lean In and McKinsey & Company, https://leanin.org/women-in-the-workplace

46 Ibid.

47 Treisman, 'Women leaders switch jobs at record rates as they demand better from their workplaces', NPR (website), 28 October 2022.

48 Krivkovich and Yee, 'Women in the workplace: Breaking up to break through', McKinsey & Company (website), 23 February 2023.

49 Treisman, 'Women leaders switch jobs at record rates as they demand better from their workplaces', NPR (website), 28 October 2022.

50 Ibid.

51 Krivkovich and Yee, 'Women in the workplace: Breaking up to break through', McKinsey & Company (website), 23 February 2023.

52 'We Are in the Midst of a "Great Breakup": Women Leaders Are Demanding More and Leaving Their Companies in Unprecedented Numbers to Get It', Cision PR Newswire (website), 18 October 2022, https://www.prnewswire.com/news-releases/we-are-in-the-midst-of-a-great-breakup-women-leaders-are-demanding-more-and-leaving-their-companies-in-unprecedented-numbers-to-get-it-301651447.html

53 Alan Burkitt-Gray, 'Diverse companies are "more productive and make more money", says report', Capacity (website), 26 August 2022, https://www.capacitymedia.com/article/2ajigf91qpl5lz7fgcu80/news/diverse-companies-are-more-productive-and-make-more-money-says-report

54 The 'romance of leadership' phrase has been used previously by academics James R. Meindl, Sanford B. Ehrlich and Janet M. Dukerich.

55 James R. Meindl, 'The romance of leadership as a follower-centric theory: A social constructionist approach', *The Leadership Quarterly*, 6(3), Autumn 1995, pp. 329–41, https://www.sciencedirect.com/science/article/abs/pii/1048984395900128; James R. Meindl, Sanford B. Ehrlich and Janet M. Dukerich, 'The

romance of leadership', *Administrative Science Quarterly*, 30(1), 1985, pp. 78–102, https://psycnet.apa.org/record/1985-26805-001

56 Michelle K. Ryan, S. Alexander Haslam et al., 'Getting on top of the glass cliff: Reviewing a decade of evidence, explanations, and impact', *The Leadership Quarterly*, 27(3), June 2016, pp. 446–55, https://www.sciencedirect.com/science/article/abs/pii/S104898431500123X

57 Ibid.

58 Liu, '"It's a huge concern": Senior-level women are calling it quits after decades climbing the career ladder', CNBC (website), 21 February 2023.

59 Jena McGregor, 'Here's why women CEOs are more likely to get sacked from their jobs', *The Washington Post*, 2 May 2014, https://www.washingtonpost.com/news/on-leadership/wp/2014/05/02/heres-why-women-ceos-are-more-likely-to-get-sacked-from-their-jobs; 'AMC Networks CEO Chris Spade leaves', Exechange (website), 29 November 2022, https://exechange.com/22383/amc-networks-ceo-chris-spade-leaves

60 Eric Luis Uhlmann and Geoffrey L. Cohen, '"I think it, therefore it's true": Effects of self-perceived objectivity on hiring discrimination', *Organizational Behavior and Human Decision Processes*, 104(2), pp. 207–23, https://www.researchgate.net/publication/222686807_I_think_it_therefore_it's_true_Effects_of_self-perceived_objectivity_on_hiring_discrimination

61 Ibid.

62 Ibid.

63 Warren Tierney, Jay H. Hardy III et al., 'Creative destruction in science', *Organizational Behavior and Human Decision Processes*, vol. 161, 2020, pp. 291–309, https://eprints.keele.ac.uk/id/eprint/9989/1/1-s2.0-S0749597820303678-main.pdf

64 Michelle K. Ryan, S. Alexander Haslam et al., 'Reactions to the glass cliff: Gender differences in the explanations for the precariousness of women's leadership positions', *Journal of Organizational Change Management*, 22(2), 10 April 2007,

https://www.emerald.com/insight/content/doi/10.1108/
09534810710724748/full/html; Marianne Cooper, 'Why women
are often put in charge of failing companies', PBS News Hour
(website), 22 September 2015, https://www.pbs.org/newshour/
economy/women-often-put-charge-failing-companies

65 Ryan, Haslam et al., 'Reactions to the glass cliff: Gender
differences in the explanations for the precariousness of women's
leadership positions', *Journal of Organizational Change
Management*, 22(2), 10 April 2007.

66 Ibid.

Chapter 7

1 Quoted in a Facebook post by Gretchen Koch, reposted by Allies
Academy, 2 December 2019, https://www.facebook.com/
alliesacademy/photos/transcript-gretchen-kochadam-bates-said-a-
thing-that-applies-to-so-much-right-no/2148406805455223; also
posted on Twitter by Remy, 4 November 2019, https://twitter.
com/remygryph/status/1191399526269145088?lang=en

2 Emily Stewart, 'Why struggling companies promote women: the
glass cliff, explained', Vox (website), 31 October 2018, https://www.
vox.com/2018/10/31/17960156/what-is-the-glass-cliff-women-ceos

3 Anne M. Mulcahy profile, The Franklin Institute (website), 2018,
https://www.fi.edu/en/laureates/anne-m-mulcahy; 'Xerox Back
From The Brink', *Forbes*, 6 November 2002, https://www.forbes.
com/2002/11/06/1106soapbox.html

4 Lisa Vollmer, 'Anne Mulcahy: The Keys to Turnaround at Xerox',
Insights by Stanford Business (website), 1 December 2004, https://
www.gsb.stanford.edu/insights/anne-mulcahy-keys-turnaround-
xerox

5 'The Cow in the Ditch: How Anne Mulcahy Rescued Xerox',
Knowledge at Wharton (website), 16 November 2005, https://
knowledge.wharton.upenn.edu/article/the-cow-in-the-ditch-how-
anne-mulcahy-rescued-xerox

6 Vollmer, 'Anne Mulcahy: The Keys to Turnaround at Xerox', Insights by Stanford Business (website), 1 December 2004.

7 Ibid.

8 Anne M. Mulcahy profile, The Franklin Institute (website), 2018

9 Vollmer, 'Anne Mulcahy: The Keys to Turnaround at Xerox', Insights by Stanford Business (website), 1 December 2004.

10 'The Cow in the Ditch: How Anne Mulcahy Rescued Xerox', Knowledge at Wharton (website), 16 November 2005.

11 'Fortune 50 Most Powerful Women in Business 2005', CNN Money (website), https://money.cnn.com/magazines/fortune/mostpowerfulwomen/2005/full_list

12 Vollmer, 'Anne Mulcahy: The Keys to Turnaround at Xerox', Insights by Stanford Business (website), 1 December 2004.

13 Ibid.

14 Ibid.

15 Stewart, 'Why struggling companies promote women: the glass cliff, explained', Vox (website), 31 October 2018.

16 Ibid.

17 Nanette Byrnes and Roger O. Crockett, 'Ursula Burns: An Historic Succession at Xerox', *BusinessWeek*, 28 May 2009, https://web.archive.org/web/20090611155419/http://www.businessweek.com/magazine/content/09_23/b4134018712853.htm

18 Elizabeth Judge, 'Women on board: help or hindrance?', *The Times*, 11 November 2003, https://www.thetimes.co.uk/article/women-on-board-help-or-hindrance-2c6fnqf6fng

19 Edward Helmore, 'Why did the $212bn tech-lender Silicon Valley bank abruptly collapse?', *The Guardian*, 17 March 2023, https://www.theguardian.com/business/2023/mar/17/why-silicon-valley-bank-collapsed-svb-fail

20 'What really went wrong at Silicon Valley Bank', *The Economist*, 13 March 2023, https://www.economist.com/leaders/2023/03/13/what-really-went-wrong-at-silicon-valley-bank

21 Andy Kessler, 'Who Killed Silicon Valley Bank?', *The Wall Street Journal*, 12 March 2023, https://www.wsj.com/articles/who-killed-

silicon-valley-bank-interest-rates-treasury-federal-reserve-ipo-loan-long-term-bond-capital-securities-startup-jpmorgan-bear-stearns-lehman-brothers-b9ca2347

22 Ibid.

23 Bess Levin, 'The *Wall Street Journal* Goes Full White Supremacist, Blames Silicon Valley Bank Collapse on "1 Black" and "1 LGBTQ+"', *Vanity Fair*, 13 March 2023, https://www.vanityfair.com/news/2023/03/wall-street-journal-column-silicon-valley-bank

24 Justin Ray, 'No, "wokeness" isn't the reason Silicon Valley Bank collapsed', *San Francisco Chronicle*, 15 March 2023, https://www.sfchronicle.com/opinion/openforum/article/silicon-valley-bank-wokeness-17841353.php

25 AJ McDougall, 'WSJ Makes Ludicrous Suggestion "Diverse" Board May Have Doomed SVB', Daily Beast (website), 13 March 2023, https://www.thedailybeast.com/wall-street-journals-andy-kessler-suggests-diverse-board-doomed-silicon-valley-bank

26 Jason Koebler, 'WSJ Wonders: Did Silicon Valley Bank Die Because One Black Person Was on Its Board?', *Vice*, 13 March 2023, https://www.vice.com/en/article/xgwq9a/wsj-wonders-did-silicon-valley-bank-die-because-one-black-person-was-on-its-board

27 Ibid.

28 Helmore, 'Why did the $212bn tech-lender Silicon Valley bank abruptly collapse?', *The Guardian*, 17 March 2023.

29 James Comer on Fox News, clip posted on Twitter by Aaron Rupar, 12 Mar 2023, https://twitter.com/atrupar/status/1634932203741216775

30 Katherine Donlevy, 'While Silicon Valley Bank collapsed, top executive pushed "woke" programs', *New York Post*, 11 March 2023, https://nypost.com/2023/03/11/silicon-valley-bank-pushed-woke-programs-ahead-of-collapse

31 Helmore, 'Why did the $212bn tech-lender Silicon Valley bank abruptly collapse?', *The Guardian*, 17 March 2023.

32 Christine L. Williams, 'The Glass Escalator, Revisited: Gender

Inequality in Neoliberal Times, SWS Feminist Lecturer', *Gender and Society*, 27(5), October 2013, pp. 609–29, https://www.jstor.org/stable/43669820

33 Christine L. Williams, 'The Glass Escalator: Hidden Advantages for Men in the "Female" Professions', *Social Problems*, 39(3), August 1992, pp. 253–67, https://www.jstor.org/stable/3096961

34 Jenna Goudreau, 'A New Obstacle for Professional Women: The Glass Escalator', *Forbes*, 21 May 2012, https://www.forbes.com/sites/jennagoudreau/2012/05/21/a-new-obstacle-for-professional-women-the-glass-escalator

35 Ibid.

36 Arica Brandford and Angela Brandford-Stevenson, 'Going Up!: Exploring the Phenomenon of the Glass Escalator in Nursing', Nursing Administration Quarterly, 45(4), October–December 2021, pp. 295–301, https://pubmed.ncbi.nlm.nih.gov/34346908

37 'Gender in the NHS infographic', NHS Employers (website), 12 May 2019, https://www.nhsemployers.org/articles/gender-nhs-infographic

38 Brandford and Brandford-Stevenson, 'Going Up!: Exploring the Phenomenon of the Glass Escalator in Nursing', *Nursing Administration Quarterly*, 45(4), October–December 2021, pp. 295–301.

39 Dame Vivian Hunt, Lareina Yee, Sara Prince and Sundiatu Dixon-Fyle, 'Delivery through diversity', McKinsey & Company (website), 18 January 2018, https://www.mckinsey.com/capabilities/people-and-organizational-performance/our-insights/delivering-through-diversity

40 Sundiatu Dixon-Fyle, Kevin Dolan, Dame Vivian Hunt and Sara Prince, 'Diversity wins: How inclusion matters', McKinsey & Company (website), 19 May 2020, https://www.mckinsey.com/featured-insights/diversity-and-inclusion/diversity-wins-how-inclusion-matters

41 Arielle Duhaime-Ross, 'Apple promised an expansive health app, so why can't I track menstruation?', The Verge (website),

25 September 2014, https://www.theverge.com/2014/9/25/6844021/
apple-promised-an-expansive-health-app-so-why-cant-i-track

42 Amanda Taub, 'NASA thought Sally Ride needed 100 tampons
    for 1 week "just to be safe." From what?', Vox (website), 26 May
    2015, https://www.vox.com/2015/5/26/8661537/sally-ride-tampons

43 Taylor Synclair Goethe, 'Bigotry Encoded: Racial Bias in
    Technology', Reported (website), 2 March 2019, https://reporter.
    rit.edu/tech/bigotry-encoded-racial-bias-technology; Nick Schulz,
    'The Crappiest Invention of All Time', Slate (website), 7 March
    2006, https://slate.com/culture/2006/03/the-crappiest-invention-
    of-all-time.html

44 PA, 'H&M apologises over image of black child in "monkey"
    hoodie', The Guardian, 8 January 2018, https://www.theguardian.
    com/fashion/2018/jan/08/h-and-m-apologises-over-image-of-
    black-child-in-monkey-hoodie

45 Amy Held, 'Gucci Apologizes And Removes Sweater Following
    "Blackface" Backlash', NPR (website), 7 February 2019, https://
    www.npr.org/2019/02/07/692314950/gucci-apologizes-and-
    removes-sweater-following-blackface-backlash

46 Caroline Edwards, 'Creators slam brands for tokenism plus
    "insulting" lack of diversity and inclusivity at events and on press
    trips', CORQ. (website), July 2023, https://corq.studio/insights/
    creators-slam-brands-for-tokenism

47 Elise Roy, 'When we design for disability, we all benefit',
    TEDxMidAtlantic, September 2015, https://www.ted.com/talks/
    elise_roy_when_we_design_for_disability_we_all_benefit?
    language=en

48 'Why Designing for Accessibility Helps Everyone', AI Media
    (website), https://www.ai-media.tv/knowledge-hub/insights/
    why-designing-for-accessibility-helps-everyone

49 Ibid., and 'Provision of Access Services: Research Study
    Conducted for Ofcom', Ofcom, March 2006, https://www.ofcom.
    org.uk/__data/assets/pdf_file/0019/45343/provision.pdf

50 Arwa Mahdawi, 'I thought needing subtitles on TV just meant I

was getting old. Turns out it is all the rage among the kids', *The Guardian*, 3 August 2022, https://www.theguardian.com/ commentisfree/2022/aug/03/i-thought-needing-subtitles-on-tv-just-meant-i-was-getting-old-turns-out-it-is-all-the-rage-among-the-kids; Ian Youngs, 'Young viewers prefer TV subtitles, research suggests', BBC News (website), 15 November 2021, https://www. bbc.co.uk/news/entertainment-arts-59259964

51 Kevin Dolan, Dame Vivian Hunt, Sara Prince and Sandra Sancier-Sultan, 'Diversity still matters', McKinsey & Company (website), 19 May 2020, https://www.mckinsey.com/featured-insights/ diversity-and-inclusion/diversity-still-matters

52 Marcus Noland and Tyler Moran, 'Study: Firms with More Women in the C-Suite Are More Profitable', *Harvard Business Review*, 8 February 2016, https://hbr.org/2016/02/study-firms-with-more-women-in-the-c-suite-are-more-profitable

53 Rajalakshmi Subramanian, 'Lessons From The Pandemic: Board Diversity and Performance', BoardReady (website), 13 July 2021, https://www.boardready.io/report

54 Dixon-Fyle, Dolan, Hunt and Prince, 'Diversity wins: How inclusion matters', McKinsey & Company (website), 19 May 2020.

Chapter 8

1 A concept attributed to Anton Chekhov in a letter to his brother.

2 Jill Abramson, 'The Importance of a Truly Free Press', Wake Forest University graduation ceremony 2014, 19 May 2014, https:// commencement.news.wfu.edu/2010s/c2014/2014-speaker-jill-abramson

3 'In Jill Abramson's Firing, Was The "Glass Cliff" To Blame?', *All Things Considered*, NPR (website), 19 May 2014, https://www.npr. org/2014/05/19/313996720/in-jill-abramsons-firing-was-the-glass-cliff-to-blame; Danielle Kurtzleben, 'Everything you need to know about the Jill Abramson—New York Times split', Vox (website),

13 June 2014, https://www.vox.com/2014/6/13/17761106/jill-abramson-new-york-times-firing-explained

4   Alison Cook and Christy Glass, 'In Jill Abramson's Firing, Was the "Glass Cliff" to Blame?', Utah State University Jon M. Huntsman School of Business News Collection, 31, 19 May 2014, https://digitalcommons.usu.edu/cgi/viewcontent.cgi?article=1185&context=huntsman_news

5   Frank Ahrens, 'Mexican Billionaire to Lend $250 Million to New York Times Co.', *The Washington Post*, 21 January 2009, https://www.washingtonpost.com/wp-dyn/content/article/2009/01/20/AR2009012003988.html

6   Dan Barry, David Barstow, Jonathan D. Glator et al., 'CORRECTING THE RECORD; Times Reporter Who Resigned Leaves Long Trail of Deception', *The New York Times*, 11 May 2003, https://www.nytimes.com/2003/05/11/us/correcting-the-record-times-reporter-who-resigned-leaves-long-trail-of-deception.html

7   Cook and Glass, 'In Jill Abramson's Firing, Was the "Glass Cliff" to Blame?', Utah State University Jon M. Huntsman School of Business News Collection, 31, 19 May 2014.

8   Matthew Yglesias, 'The Jill Abramson-era New York Times was a business success', Vox (website), 14 May 2014, https://www.vox.com/2014/5/14/5717848/the-jill-abramson-era-new-york-times-was-a-business-success

9   Ibid., and Jordan Weissmann, 'The *New York Times* Just Fired One Successful Editor', Slate (website), 14 May 2014, https://slate.com/business/2014/05/the-times-fires-jill-abramson-bad-move-gray-lady.html

10   Danielle Kurtzleben, 'What happened to Jill Abramson shows everything that sucks about being a woman leader', Vox (website), 14 May 2014, https://www.vox.com/2014/5/14/5717926/the-jill-abramson-story-highlights-everything-thats-bad-about-being-a

11   Yglesias, 'The Jill Abramson-era New York Times was a business success', Vox (website), 14 May 2014.

12   Ken Doctor, 'New numbers from The New York Times: A gold

star for managing the digital transition', NiemanLab (website), 24 April 2014, https://www.niemanlab.org/2014/04/new-numbers-from-the-new-york-times-a-gold-star-for-managing-the-digital-transition

13 Weissmann, 'The *New York Times* Just Fired One Successful Editor', Slate (website), 14 May 2014; Kurtzleben, 'Everything you need to know about the Jill Abramson–New York Times split', Vox (website), 13 June 2014.

14 Lloyd Grove, 'Good Jill, Bad Jill', *Newsweek*, 31 July 2013, https://www.newsweek.com/2013/07/31/good-jill-bad-jill-executive-editor-jill-abramson-queen-new-york-times-237814.html

15 Kurtzleben, 'Everything you need to know about the Jill Abramson–New York Times split', Vox (website), 13 June 2014.

16 Weissmann, 'The *New York Times* Just Fired One Successful Editor', Slate (website), 14 May 2014.

17 Dylan Byers, 'Turbulence at The Times', *Politico* (website), 23 April 2013, https://www.politico.com/story/2013/04/new-york-times-turbulence-090544

18 Ibid.

19 Kurtzleben, 'What happened to Jill Abramson shows everything that sucks about being a woman leader', Vox (website), 14 May 2014.

20 Grove, 'Good Jill, Bad Jill', *Newsweek*, 31 July 2013.

21 Ibid.

22 Ken Auletta, 'Why Jill Abramson Was Fired', *The New Yorker*, 14 May 2014, https://www.newyorker.com/business/currency/why-jill-abramson-was-fired; see also Tom McCarthy, 'New York Times fights to limit criticism over apparent Abramson pay disparity', *The Guardian*, 16 May 2014, https://www.theguardian.com/media/2014/may/16/new-york-times-jill-abramson-pay-inequality; Connor Simpson and Sara Morrison, 'Pay Gap Dispute Cited in Jill Abramson's Split from The New York Times', *The Atlantic*, 14 May 2014, https://www.theatlantic.com/national/archive/2014/05/dispute-over-pay-cited-in-jill-abramsons-split-from-the-new-york-times/370909

23 Auletta, 'Why Jill Abramson Was Fired', *The New Yorker*, 14 May 2014.

24 Leslie Kaufman, 'Times Issues Response on Abramson Pay', *The New York Times*, 15 May 2014, https://www.nytimes.com/2014/05/16/business/media/times-issues-response-on-abramson-pay.html

25 Kurtzleben, 'What happened to Jill Abramson shows everything that sucks about being a woman leader', Vox (website), 14 May 2014; David Carr and Ravi Somaiya, 'Times Ousts Jill Abramson as Executive Editor, Elevating Dean Baquet', *The New York Times*, 14 May 2014, https://www.nytimes.com/2014/05/15/business/media/jill-abramson-being-replaced-as-top-editor-at-times.html

26 Auletta, 'Why Jill Abramson Was Fired', *The New Yorker*, 14 May 2014.

27 Ibid.

28 Cook and Glass, 'In Jill Abramson's Firing, Was the "Glass Cliff" to Blame?', Utah State University Jon M. Huntsman School of Business News Collection, 31, 19 May 2014.

29 Abramson, 'The Importance of a Truly Free Press', Wake Forest University graduation ceremony 2014, 19 May 2014.

30 Thekla Morgenroth, Teri A. Kirby et al., 'The who, when, and why of the glass cliff phenomenon: A meta-analysis of appointments to precarious leadership positions', *Psychological Bulletin*, 146(9), 2020, pp. 797–829, https://psycnet.apa.org/record/2020-53290-001

31 Kelly Oakes, 'The invisible danger of the "glass cliff"', BBC (website), 7 February 2022, https://www.bbc.com/future/article/20220204-the-danger-of-the-glass-cliff-for-women-and-people-of-colour

32 Sebahattin Yildiz and Mehmet Fatih Vural, 'A Cultural Perspective of The Glass Cliff Phenomenon', *Ege Akademik Bakis* (*Ege Academic Review*), 30 July 2019, pp. 309–21, https://dergipark.org.tr/en/pub/eab/article/451162

33 Department for Business, Energy & Industrial Strategy and Andrew Griffiths, 'Revealed: The worst explanations for not appointing women to FTSE company boards', gov.uk (UK

government website), 31 May 2018, https://www.gov.uk/government/news/revealed-the-worst-explanations-for-not-appointing-women-to-ftse-company-boards

34 Rob Davies, 'Male bosses' "pitiful excuses" for lack of women in boardroom criticised', *The Guardian*, 31 May 2018, https://www.theguardian.com/business/2018/may/31/pitiful-excuses-by-male-bosses-for-lack-of-women-in-boardroom-are-lambasted

35 Department for Business, Energy & Industrial Strategy and Andrew Griffiths, 'Revealed: The worst explanations for not appointing women to FTSE company boards', gov.uk (UK government website), 31 May 2018.

36 Ibid.

37 Rob Davies, 'Male bosses' "pitiful excuses" for lack of women in boardroom criticised', *The Guardian*, 31 May 2018.

38 Susanne Bruckmüller and Nyla R. Branscombe, 'How Women End Up on the "Glass Cliff"', *Harvard Business Review*, January–February 2011, https://hbr.org/2011/01/how-women-end-up-on-the-glass-cliff

39 Ibid.

40 Ibid.

41 Emily Stewart, 'Why struggling companies promote women: the glass cliff, explained', Vox (website), 31 October 2018, https://www.vox.com/2018/10/31/17960156/what-is-the-glass-cliff-women-ceos

42 Kara Arnold and Catherine Loughlin, 'Continuing the Conversation: Questioning the Who, What, and When of Leaning In', *Academy of Management Perspectives*, October 2017, https://www.researchgate.net/publication/320186899_Continuing_the_Conversation_Questioning_the_Who_What_and_When_of_Leaning_In

43 Katie Bohn, 'The way new women CEOs are announced may shorten their tenure', Penn State University (website), 16 June 2021, https://www.psu.edu/news/research/story/way-new-women-ceos-are-announced-may-shorten-their-tenure

44 The researcher was Vilmos Misangyi, professor of strategic management at Penn State, ibid.

45 Jena McGregor, 'Here's why women CEOs are more likely to get sacked from their jobs', *The Washington Post*, 2 May 2014, https://www.washingtonpost.com/news/on-leadership/wp/2014/05/02/heres-why-women-ceos-are-more-likely-to-get-sacked-from-their-jobs

46 Ibid.

47 'The cost of ambition: new research finds almost 90 per cent of women worldwide are penalized and undermined because of their achievements at work', Women of Influence (website), 1 March 2023, https://www.womenofinfluence.ca/2023/03/01/tps-press-release

48 Ibid.

49 Ibid.

50 Ibid.

51 Ibid.

52 Oakes, 'The invisible danger of the "glass cliff"', BBC (website), 7 February 2022.

53 Michelle K. Ryan, S. Alexander Haslam et al., 'Getting on top of the glass cliff: Reviewing a decade of evidence, explanations, and impact', *The Leadership Quarterly*, 27(3), June 2016, pp. 446–55, https://www.sciencedirect.com/science/article/abs/pii/S104898431500123X

54 Huw Jones, 'EU approves law to break "glass ceiling" for women on company boards', Reuters (website), 22 November 2022, https://www.reuters.com/business/sustainable-business/eu-approves-law-break-glass-ceiling-women-company-boards-2022-11-22

55 Ibid.

56 Ibid.

57 Joe Caccavale, 'Should You Use Diversity Quotas? A Look at the Evidence', Applied (website), 31 August 2021, https://www.beapplied.com/post/diversity-quotas

58 'In wider diversity push, Norway proposes 40% gender quota for large unlisted firms', Reuters (website), 12 December 2022, https://

www.reuters.com/business/wider-diversity-push-norway-proposes-40-gender-quota-large-unlisted-firms-2022-12-12

59 Ibid.

60 Audrey Latura and Ana Catalano Weeks, 'Corporate Board Quotas and Gender Equality Policies in the Workplace', *American Journal of Political Science*, 67(3), July 2023, pp. 606–22, https://onlinelibrary.wiley.com/doi/10.1111/ajps.12709; also cited in Liz Elting, 'Stop Saying Quotas "Don't Work" Because They Demonstrably Do', *Forbes*, 22 September 2022, https://www.forbes.com/sites/lizelting/2022/09/22/stop-saying-quotas-dont-work-because-they-demonstrably-do

61 Ibid.

62 Elting, 'Stop Saying Quotas "Don't Work" Because They Demonstrably Do', *Forbes*, 22 September 2022.

63 Anna Sillers, 'Reddit CEO Ellen Pao bans salary negotiations', PBS News Hour (website), 7 April 2015, https://www.pbs.org/newshour/economy/reddit-ceo-ellen-pao-bans-salary-negotiations

64 Ibid.

65 Steve Hatfield, Jen Fisher and Paul H. Silverglate, 'The C-suite's role in well-being', Deloitte Insights (website), 22 June 2022, https://www2.deloitte.com/us/en/insights/topics/leadership/employee-wellness-in-the-corporate-workplace.html

66 Shawn Achor, Andrew Reece, Gabriella Rosen Kellerman and Alexi Robichaux, '9 Out of 10 People Are Willing to Earn Less Money to Do More Meaningful Work', *Harvard Business Review*, 6 November 2018, https://hbr.org/2018/11/9-out-of-10-people-are-willing-to-earn-less-money-to-do-more-meaningful-work

67 Ibid.

68 Ibid.

69 'Workers Value Meaning at Work; New Research from BetterUp Shows Just How Much They're Willing to Pay for It', BetterUp (website), 7 November 2018, https://www.betterup.com/press/workers-value-meaning-at-work-new-research-from-betterup-shows-just-how-much-theyre-willing-to-pay-for-it

70 Ibid.

71 Diana O'Brien, Andy Main, Suzanne Kounkel and Anthony R. Stephan, 'Purpose is everything', Deloitte Insights (website), 15 October 2019, https://www2.deloitte.com/us/en/insights/topics/marketing-and-sales-operations/global-marketing-trends/2020/purpose-driven-companies.html

72 Ibid.

73 Ibid.

74 Rupert Jones, 'UK staff to have right to ask for flexible working from day one in job', *The Guardian*, 5 December 2022, https://www.theguardian.com/money/2022/dec/05/uk-staff-to-have-right-to-ask-for-flexible-working-from-day-one-in-job

75 Ashleigh Webber, 'Lack of flexibility pushes half of women to consider leaving job', Personnel Today (website), 16 May 2022, https://www.personneltoday.com/hr/women-flexibility-at-work-linkedin-research

76 Krivkovich and Yee, 'Women in the workplace: Breaking up to break through', McKinsey & Company, 23 February 2023, https://www.mckinsey.com/featured-insights/diversity-and-inclusion/women-in-the-workplace-breaking-up-to-break-through

77 'Increased flexible working could unlock £55bn for the UK economy', MotherPukka (website), https://www.motherpukka.co.uk/flexonomics

78 Rachel Pelta, 'Survey: Men & Women Experience Remote Work Differently', Flexjobs (website), https://www.flexjobs.com/blog/post/men-women-experience-remote-work-survey

79 Hannah Hickok, 'Are men-dominated offices the future of the workplace?' BBC (website), 6 May 2021, https://www.bbc.com/worklife/article/20210503-are-men-dominated-offices-the-future-of-the-workplace

80 Krivkovich and Yee, 'Women in the workplace: Breaking up to break through', McKinsey & Company, 23 February 2023.

81 Women in the Workplace 2022, Lean In and McKinsey & Company, https://leanin.org/women-in-the-workplace

82 Hickok, 'Are men-dominated offices the future of the workplace?' BBC (website), 6 May 2021.

83 Ibid.

84 Erica Pandey, 'The case for going back to the office', Axios (website), 17 March 2021, https://www.axios.com/2021/03/17/should-you-go-back-to-office

85 Krivkovich and Yee, 'Women in the workplace: Breaking up to break through', McKinsey & Company, 23 February 2023.

86 Ibid.

87 Elizabeth Faber (Deloitte's Global Chief People & Purpose Officer), 'Millennial and Gen Z employees are rejecting assignments, turning down offers, and seeking purpose. Here's what they expect of their employers, according to Deloitte's latest survey', *Fortune*, 6 July 2023, https://fortune.com/2023/07/06/millennial-gen-z-employees-are-rejecting-assignments-turning-down-offers-and-seeking-purpose-they-expect-of-employers-according-to-deloittes-latest-survey

88 2023 Gen Z and Millennial Survey, Deloitte (website), https://www.deloitte.com/global/en/issues/work/content/genzmillennial survey.html

89 Faber, 'Millennial and Gen Z employees are rejecting assignments, turning down offers, and seeking purpose. Here's what they expect of their employers, according to Deloitte's latest survey', *Fortune*, 6 July 2023.

90 Ibid.

91 Hatfield, Fisher and Silverglate, 'The C-suite's role in well-being', Deloitte Insights (website), 22 June 2022.

92 Orianna Rosa Royle, 'The Body Shop asked a group of Gen Zers to critique the company and it was a disaster, so it rolled to Plan B: Create a whole board of 20-somethings', *Fortune*, 5 July 2023, https://fortune.com/2023/07/05/the-body-shop-gen-z-board-youth-collective

93 Ibid.

94 Ibid.

Conclusion

1   Josh Taylor and Alex Hern, 'Elon Musk says he will resign as Twitter CEO when he finds a "foolish enough" replacement', *The Guardian*, 21 December 2022, https://www.theguardian.com/technology/2022/dec/20/elon-musk-resign-twitter-ceo-finding-replacement

2   Ryan Mac and Tiffany Hsu, 'Twitter's U.S. Ad Sales Plunge 59% as Woes Continue', *The New York Times*, 5 June 2023, https://www.nytimes.com/2023/06/05/technology/twitter-ad-sales-musk.html

3   Brian Fung, 'Twitter may be worth only a third of its pre-Musk value, Fidelity says', CNN (website), 31 May 2023, https://edition.cnn.com/2023/05/31/tech/twitter-value-fidelity-estimate/index.html

4   James Clayton, 'Elon Musk BBC interview: Twitter boss on layoffs, misinfo and sleeping in the office', BBC News (website), 12 April 2023, https://www.bbc.co.uk/news/business-65248196

5   Mac and Hsu, 'Twitter's U.S. Ad Sales Plunge 59% as Woes Continue', *The New York Times*, 5 June 2023.

6   Ashton Jackson, 'These are the 7 most hated brands in America – Elon Musk's Twitter is No. 4', CNBC (website), 1 June 2023, https://www.cnbc.com/2023/06/01/most-hated-brands-in-america-trump-organization-ftx-fox-corporation.html; 'The 2023 Axios Harris Poll 100 reputation rankings', Axios (website), 23 May 2023, https://www.axios.com/2023/05/23/corporate-brands-reputation-america

7   Saqib Shah, Mary-Ann Russon and Rachael Davies, 'Who is Linda Yaccarino? Twitter's new CEO takes charge', *Evening Standard*, 5 June 2023, https://www.standard.co.uk/tech/who-is-linda-yaccarino-twitter-new-ceo-elon-musk-b1080644.html

8   Kari Paul, 'Linda Yaccarino: does Twitter's CEO have the most difficult job in tech?', *The Guardian*, 27 July 2023, https://www.theguardian.com/technology/2023/jul/27/linda-yaccarino-twitter-x-ceo-elon-musk

9 Ibid.

10 Ibid.

11 'The Truest Eye', *O: The Oprah Magazine*, November 2003, https://www.oprah.com/omagazine/toni-morrison-talks-love/4

Acknowledgements

1 Shaun Usher, 'With my weak organs I am very fond of you', Letters of Note (website), 3 September 2021, https://news.lettersofnote.com/p/with-my-weak-organs-i-am-very-fond

2 '"Alex & Me": The Parrot Who Said "I Love You"', *Fresh Air*, NPR, 31 August 2009, https://www.npr.org/2009/08/31/112405883/alex-me-the-parrot-who-said-i-love-you